Stanley T. Gibson

Religion and Science

Their Relations to Each Other at the Present Day - three essays on the grounds of religious belief

Stanley T. Gibson

Religion and Science
Their Relations to Each Other at the Present Day - three essays on the grounds of religious belief

ISBN/EAN: 9783337191450

Printed in Europe, USA, Canada, Australia, Japan

Cover: Foto ©Lupo / pixelio.de

More available books at **www.hansebooks.com**

RELIGION AND SCIENCE

THEIR RELATIONS TO EACH OTHER
AT THE PRESENT DAY

THREE ESSAYS
ON THE GROUNDS OF RELIGIOUS BELIEF

BY

STANLEY T. GIBSON, B.D.

RECTOR OF SANDON, IN ESSEX; AND LATE FELLOW OF QUEEN'S COLLEGE, CAMBRIDGE

LONDON
LONGMANS, GREEN, AND CO.
1875

All rights reserved

PREFACE.

I PUBLISH the following Essays as an attempt to do something for an object which seems to me of the highest importance in these days, viz. the reconciliation of religion and science. When I do so, I feel strongly that they fall much short of accomplishing such a reconciliation. For even if their success in dealing with the questions of which they treat should be much greater than I have any right to believe that it is, still it would be true that they did nothing as to that class of difficulties which concerns the nature and extent of the inspiration of the Bible, and the alleged discrepancies between its statements and the results of modern science and criticism. But I still hope that what I now put forward may have some value. I have endeavoured fairly to take into account what I suppose to be the ultimate position of modern science; that position to which at all events men of science are tending, viz. the recognition of a universal reign of law both now and also at least for an immense period of past time, and the consequent belief that the universe has come into its present state by a very prolonged evolution of some kind. How far this view is well founded I have not undertaken to decide; but I have endeavoured to judge what are its bearings upon the fundamental doctrines of the Christian religion, and to establish the truth of those doctrines without any assertion necessarily inconsistent with this view. My object has been to show how men who hold the views of modern science may still accept the Christian religion.

As argument to be of any good effect must proceed upon common ground, I have wished upon all occasions to assume nothing which a moderate and candid opponent might not, I hoped, allow; and I have honestly tried to take into account any objection which seemed to me plausible. Thus I have not urged the authority of the Fourth Gospel as a work of the Apostle St. John, although it would much strengthen my case, because I thought that the sceptical party would generally refuse to allow that the Gospel was St. John's. And when I came to examine the critical point in the historical evidences of Christianity, viz. the proofs of the resurrection of Christ, I thought it right to mention and consider all the weak points in the evidence which are known to me. In writing thus I may at times have expressed myself in a way painful to some Christians, although it has been my endeavour not merely to observe the limitations imposed upon me by my position as a clergyman of the Church of England, but also to respect the feelings of my fellow-Christians. If I do give offence, I must plead in my defence the great need at the present day of answering sceptical arguments, and also the great need of manifest moderation and fairness, if our answers are to have a good effect.

My work, I allow, has a negative part. I have examined the arguments of a school of Christian apologists whose reasonings certainly cannot be reconciled with the scientific view mentioned above, but who have been much relied upon in this country as argumentative defenders of Christianity. I have taken Bishop Butler and Archdeacon Paley as representing this school probably to the best advantage, and I have felt obliged to conclude that their arguments have lost much of their value, though not all. But at the same time I have tried to show that there were other grounds, viz. the witness of the moral faculty, on which the authority of the moral teaching of our religion and the truth of its principal doctrines might be rested. One doctrine, indeed, of popular Christianity I have not felt able to defend in this way, that is, the everlasting misery of the wicked. Nor, again, can I support a certain view as to the atonement which is, I believe, popular, although it has not, I hold, any title to be thought orthodox. Whether my opinions on these points can be justified must be decided by argument, and for such arguments as I have to offer I must refer to my Essays.

But there is one consideration which I would at once bring forward to mitigate any prejudice which these admissions upon my part may produce. It cannot be denied that a large class of thoughtful and well-informed men in this country are dissatisfied with the popular religious opinions. They, at least think, that they see an opposition between our traditional Christianity and modern thought and science. This class is, I believe, still larger on the Continent. Its existence, all will allow, is a very grave fact, and I contend that it behoves religious men, in the presence of that fact, seriously to consider what it is which they put forward as religious truth, to insist upon nothing for which they cannot see a secure foundation, and not to suffer any mere prejudice, or sympathy, or habit of belief, to hinder them from modifying those statements, which especially give offence, if they can conscientiously do so.

As I have to deal with the relations of religion to science I have spoken only of those grounds of religious belief which are commonly thought to be rational and argumentative. No doubt as a matter of fact religious belief is brought about and modified by many other influences, and the study of such influences and their effects may be of high interest and have its place in the domain of science. But it is not contemplated here. I have treated only of the intellectual grounds of religious belief. They may not hitherto have been the common grounds of such belief, but it may, I think, be assumed that they will become so more and more. As knowledge and the diffusion of knowledge advance, men will be less and less ready to rest their convictions as to the most important of all subjects upon authority, tradition, mere feeling, or a supposed practical necessity. These last are the guides of the pupilage, not of the maturity of our race.

CONTENTS.

ESSAY I.

THE BELIEF IN GOD.

PART I.

	PAGE
The design argument	1
The objections to it	3
The Positivists	13
Past popularity of the argument	14
Influences of modern science	15
Review of past conclusions	30
Modification of the argument	31
General considerations as to the universe	32
Appearance of progress	34
Therefore of beneficent purpose	35
Appearance of waste	36
How explained	37
Influence of recognising general laws	38
The real schism between science and religion	42

PART II.

The *à priori* argument	50

PART III.

The old first cause argument	54
Dr. Samuel Clarke	57
Professor Birks	59

CONTENTS.

PART IV.

	PAGE
The theory of energy	61
Theological conclusion from it	69
Argument from the atomic theory	75
Weakness of such arguments	80
Their data with reference to the design argument	84
The book called 'The Unseen Universe'	86

PART V.

Arguments on moral grounds	92
Objections to moral argument	97

PART VI.

Combination of the arguments	102
The origin of evil	104
The effect of attributing infinity to God	110
Conclusion	120

ESSAY II.

THE MIRACULOUS EVIDENCE OF CHRISTIANITY.

PART I.

The argument from miracles	121
Hume's attack	124

PART II.

The *à priori* objections	126

PART III.

The argument from miracles	139
Paley's general proposition as to non-evangelical miracles	140
His particular exceptions	144
His special cases	152
Need to try all cases alike	153

PART IV.

	PAGE
St. Augustine of Hippo .	155
Bede	157
St. Francis of Assisi	158
Baxter . .	172
Bengel . . .	174
The tomb of the Abbé Paris	175
The Moravians . .	177
The early Methodists	180
Accounts of miracles common under certain circumstances .	182
Scientific incredulity sometimes mistaken	184
The cure of Pascal's niece . . .	186
The case of Miss Fancourt	190
Louise Lateau . . .	193
Similar cases .	195
The King's touch .	196
Dr. Carpenter's explanation . .	199
Other wonders in modern days . .	201
Spiritualism . . .	206
Conclusions .	208

PART V.

Paley's tests applied to the Gospels .	. 209
The authorship of the Gospels .	. 226
Further tests of history . .	. 236
Result of the examination	. 237

PART VI.

The resurrection of Christ	240

PART VII.

	PAGE
The evidential inference	272
Miracles possibly not divine	276
Conclusion as to the argument	281
Reflections on this conclusion	282

ESSAY III.

THE RELATION OF THE GOSPEL TO THE MORAL FACULTY IN MAN.

PART I.

The evidence of conscience	286

PART II.

Where to be found	288
What Christian morality is	289
Its permanent goodness	294

PART III.

Christian doctrines tried by the moral faculty	302
Doctrines of natural religion	306
Value of religion	307
Worship of Christ	311
Christian doctrine of grace	312
The atonement	315
The work of the Holy Ghost	323
Original sin	326
Predestination and future misery	327
Everlasting punishment	332

CONTENTS.

	PAGE
Mr. Maurice	335
Dr. J. H. Newman	336
Professor Birks	337
Dr. Bushnell	338
Everlasting punishment	339

PART IV.

Bishop Butler	346
Answer to his 'Analogy'	349
Particular cases of analogy	353
NOTE ON ESSAY II.	363

Errata.

Page 34, line 4 from the top, *for* I do *read* I do not
,, 54, *note*, also pages 57, 58, in the heading, also page 57, line 8 from the top, and page 58, lines 18, 23, *for* 'Clark' *read* 'Clarke'
,, 101, line 14 from the top, *for* national *read* natural
,, 115 ,, 3 from the top, *for* have *read* has
,, 158-171, in the heading, also page 158, line 14 from the top, and page 163, line 10, *for* Assissi *read* Assisi
,, 160, *note*, *for* con *read* confessore
,, 185, line 22 from the top, *for* Le tres *read* Lettres
,, 228, *note* ², *for* xxi., xxii., *read* xxv
,, 316, *note*, *for* Archbishop Magee *read* Archbishop Magee on the Atonement

ESSAY I.

THE BELIEF IN GOD.

PART I.

OF all the arguments for the existence of God, the argument from Design has been in past days by far the most popular. Philosophers, it is true, have pointed out flaws in the reasoning and defects in the conclusion, but mankind at large have certainly found it more clear, instructive, and convincing, than any other. But there has been a change. Its popularity has declined, at least with the educated classes. I purpose to begin this essay with a criticism of the argument, and an examination how far the change in its esteem is well founded.

Mr. Mill has described the argument as an induction by the method of agreement; and this, I suppose, would be its logical classification. But in popular language it may be spoken of as an argument by analogy. Our minds, acting under the control of our wills, and employing the physical powers at our command, produce certain works. We see that these works are adapted to certain ends, and we know that this adaptation arose from contrivance, and that contrivance from design upon our part, or upon that of our fellow men. We conclude that design precedes adaptation. We look upon nature, and we see the same appearance of adaptation. Often, indeed, we see adaptation much more striking, ingenious, and perfect, than any which we can produce. We conclude that nature is the work of some supreme mind and will, in which the design corresponding to this adaptation had its seat.

This argument has been popular, partly from its simplicity, and partly from the number and force of its concrete illustrations. It is not subtle, or refined, or abstruse. It deals with no difficult abstractions or generalisations. It is common sense, rather than metaphysics. And many of the instances in which the reasoning can be applied in the visible world are most striking. When we are contemplating one of the wonderful machines of nature, say the human eye, for example, we feel driven to believe that it had an intelligent maker. Yet the reasoning here gone through, when considered as a proof of the existence of God, has long been felt by thoughtful men to be open to several objections. The principal of these I will state.

We are seeking, it must be remembered, to prove

the existence of an Eternal and Omnipresent Being, of *infinite* power, wisdom, and goodness. Now it may easily be shown, in more than one way, that this argument can never prove the infinity of these attributes. It makes God known to us only as the Maker of the Universe; and, since the Universe known to us can never be more than finite, we cannot conclude that its maker is in any respect infinite. We must attribute to him that amount of wisdom and power needed to make the works which we know, and no more. For example, we must believe that he has the power and wisdom needed to make man, but we are not at liberty, without further evidence, to conclude that he has also the power and wisdom needed to raise man from the dead. Further, apart from this necessary limitation in our premisses, it is easily seen that our argument, from the very nature of its principle, could never prove the existence of an Eternal Being. For it is an argument whose principle is the law of causation, and, further, that law in a concrete form. Works of design have, we say, intelligent makers. That is a generalisation drawn from a series of phenomena appearing in time. One term of such a series requires its predecessor. To apply this principle to the case before us, we have to look upon the whole universe as such a phenomenon appearing bounded in time, and it follows that its Maker, as thus disclosed, would likewise appear bounded in time. There is no reason why a maker should not be logically required for him. His intelligence, as thus made known, is only a human intelligence, so stupendously magnified as to be thought equal to the task of making the universe; and if so, the mutual adaptation and co-ordination of its faculties is an evidence of design, and, according to our reasoning, a proof of a second intelligent cause. Atheistical writers have actually reasoned thus, and, though their adversaries exclaimed against the proceeding as monstrous, they did not show that it was illogical. The fact is that the law of causation, being essentially a law of succession in time, can never carry us beyond the limits of time. If, indeed, we suppose the universe to have been eternal, and the work of the Deity to have been fashioning and governing, but not creating, this objection would not apply. But, as I have pointed out, this supposition can never be more than a conjecture, and it certainly is not a conjecture generally made by divines.

A more recondite difficulty may be raised as follows, against our argument as a proof of the wisdom of God. When we speak of wisdom and goodness as shown in adapting means to ends, we argue from a proceeding which is common and intelligible enough in the case of finite beings, dealing with outward conditions, to which they must conform their doings. But the like cannot be so easily made out in the case of the Maker of all things. The evidence of wisdom is contrivance to accomplish the desired result, in spite of certain adverse conditions. To take the case of the eye, we have the production upon the retina of a well defined, properly shaped, and colored image, in spite of spherical and chromatic aberration, and this for objects varying in distance and direction. But in the case of the world-maker we have to bear in mind that he ordained the adverse conditions, as well as the contrivance by which they have been overcome. And hence, to form an estimate of the wisdom of the whole proceeding, we must be able to survey the ends answered by the conditions also. If they be not adequate, if, to take our illustration, seeing has been made needlessly difficult, then the ingenuity of the contrivance by which the difficulty has been overcome, however great, fails to prove wisdom on the part of him who appointed the obstacles as well as the escape. Now, if we should really attempt an investigation of the uses of these conditions, we might have further to enquire into the profitableness of some anterior conditions to which the former were related, and so we should embark on an enquiry to which there would be no end.

It will be seen that this objection goes only to show a practical difficulty in proving wise contrivance on the part of God. Mr. Mill, in his posthumous work, the 'Three Essays on Religion,' finds, in the nature of contrivance, a more fundamental objection to our argument, as a proof of God's power and wisdom. For contrivance, he contends, implies limitation, either in power or wisdom. A really Omnipotent Being would, he thinks, accomplish his ends by simple volition. He would not submit to the delay and the imperfect carrying out which arise from working by a scheme of general laws. It is not, I think, a sufficient answer to say that the means may themselves be ends. For that, after all, is only a conjecture, which at least, in the present state of our argument, has not appearances in its favour. But I will here state another consideration, which, to my mind, goes far to answer the objection of Mr. Mill, as well as the one which I have myself given before. With us it would no doubt be the reasonable and natural course to accomplish our ends by simple volition, if that would suffice. So far as we could do this, we should economise our time and means, and with us both time and means are limited. But the case is evidently different with a being of endless existence and unbounded resources. We must beware of transferring to him the feelings natural to us under the limitations of our life. He might ordain a scheme in which the results were tardy, or even some of the obstacles needless, without an impeachment of his wisdom, for the simple reason that with him delay or the waste of means would not be matter of objection. The one point for us to consider in ascribing design to him is whether the presumed end is really and adequately attained. If it be not, then I allow that there is a presumption of defect either in wisdom or power. For instance, if the apparent end was a happy life and the result a painful life, there is a difficulty. But if it be the bare use of contrivance, which is objected, or even the fact that the contriver may himself have placed in his own way obstructions with which he might have dispensed, there is nothing here which is strictly incompatible with infinite wisdom and power.

A more popular and a more serious objection arises thus. The Design argument proposes a belief in God as the explanation of the world. But the theory does not agree with all the facts. The hypothesis fails to explain many of the phenomena. There are multitudes of things in the world which do not appear to be the work of infinite wisdom and goodness, or indeed of wisdom and goodness at all. It has been customary to meet this objection by pointing out that the works of an infinite mind may have many purposes hidden from us, that our difficulties in this matter spring from misunderstanding, that if we were but wiser we should see wisdom everywhere. That this reply has a measure of truth few will deny. It is at all events a possible explanation where inanimate nature is concerned. We can, for example, reconcile ourselves to uninhabited worlds by calling to mind that God may have other purposes in creating suns and planets besides providing habitations for living beings. But it is not so easy to admit this explanation with regard to the sensitive and still more to the moral creation. Pain, and still more sin, seem absolute evils, and not mere contrivances, not yet understood. We shrink from accepting this last view. We cannot think of God as creating wicked creatures to the end that they might answer some good purpose. This looks too much like doing evil that good may come. It is a conduct plainly at variance with the rigid and imperative character of the moral law,[1] and least of all to be defended in an Omnipotent Being raised above the difficulties and impediments which beset human conduct. I know that this difficulty may be relieved by considerations drawn from the liberty of the creature. But in the present state of our knowledge it cannot, I think, be altogether taken away. It remains a perplexing question why God should have created beings who would he knew plunge into sin and misery. This perplexity has been felt from the very dawn of

---

[1] See Kant's 'Metaphysic of Ethics,' Semple's translation, edition by Calderwood, ch. ii.

religious thought, and it remains a difficulty to this day.

To conclude generally as to this defence from presumed partial understanding upon our part of the Divine plans, we may say that its satisfactoriness depends to some extent on the prevalence of the seeming exceptions to wisdom and goodness. If they were few, the explanation might be readily accepted. We should probably not be bold to press the logical conclusion. But as a matter of fact, they are many. There is, for example, the whole system of the maintenance of the carnivorous animals. How directly and unavoidably does it work wholesale suffering and slaughter. We have here, it is true, evidence of design in abundance, but it is of a design to destroy. We have a whole armoury of weapons to tear, to wound, to kill living beings innumerable. In the words of Tennyson, man has trusted that 'God was love,' and love creation's final law, but 'Nature red in tooth and claw with ravine shriek'd against his creed.' We are forced to conclude that the design argument by itself fails to establish the moral attributes of God.

There is yet another objection to our argument of which I must speak. I do not myself consider it so well founded as some of those which we have reviewed, but it has an interest, not only because it strikes at the very root of the argument, but also because it is kindred in principle to a philosophy which has had a good deal of acceptance in our day, that of the Positivists. Hume has objected that our argument employs the law of causation in an illicit manner. The inductive principle that like consequents have like antecedents, which is at the bottom of our reasoning, may hold throughout nature, but will it hold outside of nature? We have no right, he contends, to stretch the analogies of the Universe beyond its limits, and thus assert the existence of a supramundane Being. We reason, we say (in popular language), by analogy. But has the Universe, as a whole, any analogue? Works of design may have intelligent makers within the limits of our world, but we have no right to apply the law to the world as a whole, and so rise above it.

I have already fully admitted that this argument from design could never establish the existence of an Eternal Being of infinite wisdom and power. The Maker of the Universe, as thus made known to us, is after all only a finite Being. We need some other line of reasoning, pointing to the same Being, to convince us that he is in any respect truly infinite. If this shortcoming of our argument were all that Hume[1] meant to assert, his criticism might at once be admitted. But I understand him

---

[1] See Hume's Essay 'On a Particular Providence and a Future State;' and also on 'Necessary Connection.'

to mean something more, viz., that this reasoning cannot in reality disclose anything at all as to God. It becomes illicit as being carried beyond the limits of the Universe. Now, there seems to be here an arbitrary circumscribing of the space within which our generalisation will hold. We do but proceed by that principle of induction which, as I shall endeavour hereafter in another essay more fully to point out, is at the bottom of all our objective knowledge. Why must we stop at the limits of the visible creation? Let us review our proceeding. Like consequents, we say, have like antecedents. In the works of man we see that traces of design have arisen from an intelligent Maker. We examine a part of nature. We see traces of design. We say this part must have had an intelligent Maker. We examine more, we repeat the conclusion. We see a unity in nature which implies a common author. We accordingly extend our inference to the whole known Universe. Where does the reasoning become illicit? Certainly not because the Being whose existence is inferred is invisible, or, in more general language, is known only from the hypothesis of our argument. If so, we should have no right to attribute reasonable minds to one another. The natural philosopher has no such scruples. He freely imagines invisible agents to explain sensible phenomena on mechanical principles, as in the undulatory theory of light or the atomic theory of matter, and I think I may add the Newtonian theory of gravity. No doubt he is very careful to compare his hypothesis with facts, to test it by observation and experiment. But if it stands this test well and persistently, he will accept the hypothesis at last with confidence. And indeed in so doing he only carries further the conduct of everyday life. Much of sensation itself is subjective.[1] What we popularly call seeing, for instance, is an interpretation of certain physical effects on our frames, which we learn to make by comparison of other sensations and other mental work. Dr. Whewell was right when he contended that there was no stable distinction between facts and theories, paradoxical as the saying may seem. And it would be a just exhibition of the same truth to say that our notion of the external world is in reality a hypothesis which our minds have framed to explain certain sensations. If so, why should it be illicit to frame, according to principles drawn from mental experience, a further hypothesis of a God to explain this first hypothesis of a world?

I have dwelt a little longer on this objection of Hume because, as I have said, the principles involved seem to me to be the same as those at the

[1] See 'Popular Lectures on Scientific Subjects,' by H. Helmholtz, translated by E. Atkinson.

bottom of the controversy with the Positivists. So far as the teaching of M. Comte was a protest against purely *à priori* speculation, and an insisting upon the need of conforming our theories to the results of observation, it seems to me worthy of praise. The continued and wonderful success of the experimental philosophy must, I think, justify such teaching to everyone. The progress of that philosophy, indeed, gives hope that it will explain consistently those mental phenomena over which metaphysicians have wrangled in vain. But when M. Comte goes further, when he seems to restrict the sphere of knowledge to mere phenomena, and the work of science to their registering and arrangement, then he is to my thinking unphilosophical. As I have pointed out, we cannot observe without making hypotheses—without doing something of the very thing which M. Comte would forbid as characteristic of the metaphysical or theological stage of human thought. As is well known, he objected to the undulatory theory of light. His principles, thoroughly carried out, would leave us in universal ignorance or doubt, a self-destructive conclusion. One remark more before I leave this objection. I have said that we needed some other reasoning besides this causation argument to prove the eternity of God, or, indeed, his infinity in any respect. On that subject I will speak further by-and-by. But let me at once notice one point. It may be thought that if upon any grounds we pronounce the Deity to be an eternal, and therefore an uncaused, Being, we set aside the very principle of sequence upon which we have been reasoning. I should reply that we cannot upon any grounds assert that an eternal or uncaused being cannot be a cause to a finite being—the starting point of such a series as we see in nature. It is true that experience does not suggest the idea of such a being, but at the same time it cannot justify us in refusing to accept a reason that may come from any other quarter for believing that such a being exists.

The objections which I have now described were felt, and were more or less distinctly brought forward, in past days, but they did not prevent the Design argument from having the popularity of which I have spoken. So recently as forty years ago, in the days of the Bridgewater Treatises, it was generally relied upon in this country. As an instance of its influence at a still later time, I may, I think, quote the tenacity with which the habitation of other worlds was maintained. This persuasion arose in great part from an inverse application of the argument. If worlds were not inhabited, why had they been made? But there has been a change. Let us now go on to examine how.

There has been of late years a prodigious advance of knowledge, and especially of the physical sciences.

This has been the great cause of the change which we have to investigate. But its effects have not been all one way. Some have been favourable to the Design argument, and of these we will speak first.

In the first place, many new and brilliant examples of adaptation have been brought to light. The contrivances for the fertilisation of orchids, which Mr. Darwin has detailed, are not less striking than those which Sir Charles Bell found in the mechanism of the hand. Again, some broader considerations, due to this progress of science, have helped to strengthen our argument, and make it more adequate. Those grand views of the antiquity and extent of the creation, which geology and astronomy have opened out, have made our ideas of the Creator so stupendous that in some aspects they can scarcely be distinguished from the infinite. It still remains true that the ideas thus gained are not strictly infinite. But at the same time they have been enlarged so prodigiously that the mind is prepared to concede indefinite expansion as at least credible. Further, what is really important, though at first sight it may not appear so, modern science witnesses most strongly to the unity of God. That form of the Design argument which starts from apparent purpose in individual objects, is on this point weak. But the great doctrine of modern science, universal law, speaks conclusively. With

Gods many and Lords many, how could such uniformity be? The recognition of this truth makes polytheism impossible.[1] And, indeed, when I speak only of the universality of the same laws, I understate the unity which science has disclosed in the universe. Not only have we evidence that the same laws of gravitation, motion, heat, light, hold in the remote stars, and perhaps remoter nebulæ, as well as here, but further that those distant bodies, and indeed the whole universe, so far as we can judge, is composed of the same kinds of matter as those with which we are familiar. Further we have learned that several of the principal agents of nature, motion, heat, light, electricity, magnetism, are mutually convertible—to all appearance different modes of the same agent. And, lastly, it is worthy of note, in connection with this subject of cosmical unity, that the most active of all the forces of nature, gravitation, at least seems to bind together the Universe by a power instantaneous in its effect at all distances,[2] an image

[1] See 'Origin and Development of Religious Belief,' ch. xii. By S. Baring-Gould.

[2] I am not aware of any evidence that the transmission of gravitation is not instantaneous, however difficult that conception may be metaphysically. Mrs. Somerville, in her work 'The Connection of the Physical Sciences,' § 28, p. 431, mentions that the acceleration of the moon's mean motion was at one time thought to be due to the non-instantaneous transmission of gravitation. It was computed that the speed of transmission must be 50,000,000 times as great as the velocity of light. But this acceleration has since been otherwise explained, as by change in the eccentricity of the earth's orbit, and possible retardation of her diurnal rotation.

indeed of omnipresent action. All these things are evidence for a common character and a common rule for the whole material creation, as it now exists throughout space. And we have evidence too of the like unity throughout time. For there is a growing conviction that the present state of the universe is the result of an evolution, *i.e.* a long protracted working of the same forces on the same materials, according to the same laws as those which we now behold. This belief has gained a footing in astronomy, geology, natural history, and even anthropology.[1] Many philosophers now ask no longer for special interventions of God to explain the formation of the heavens, or of the crust of the earth, the development of life, or the origin of human speech and civilisation. There may be others, also men of eminence, who would not go so far. But the former must, I think, be allowed to be the rising school. And even their opponents, who would believe in special interference on the part of God, say in the origin of the particular species of living beings, would still allow that even here there has been an order, a system, an observation of type. On all hands it would be admitted that there has been a unity of character between the present and the past for an enormous period of time. And this unity speaks for

[1] See Address of Sir W. R. Grove to the British Association, Nottingham, 1866, 'On Continuity.'

a common author. There is evidence of one God throughout time, as well as throughout space.

This may suffice for the favourable effects. I turn now to the adverse results, which have, as I have said, been the greater of the two. They may I think be arranged under three heads.

1. Discovery of cases in which Design seems wanting. A wider acquaintance with the Universe has not strengthened the belief that the explanation of the several objects of Nature is to be found in some special design as to each of them. At no time was there thought to be universal evidence of such Design as I have said already; difficulties and exceptions were allowed. But the phenomena of organic life were thought to give great support. Here was the stronghold of the belief. Indeed, at one time,[1] this idea of beneficent Design was thought to be the true key to the understanding of organic structures, the clue to discovery as to their parts. But it is now I believe generally allowed, that often some of these parts do not serve any object useful to the organism as a whole. The idea of a necessary functional fitness is abandoned. Mr. Darwin indeed states[2] 'that it would be difficult to name one of the higher animals in which some part

---

[1] Dr. Carpenter's 'General Physiology,' art. 354.
[2] 'On the Origin of Species,' by C. Darwin, ch. xiii. p. 535, 5th edition.

is not in a rudimentary condition. In the mammalia, for instance, the males always possess rudimentary mammæ; in snakes one lobe of the lungs is rudimentary; in birds the "bastard wing" may safely be considered as a rudimentary digit, and in not a few species the wings cannot be used for flight, or are reduced to a rudiment.'

'What can be more curious,' he adds, 'than the presence of teeth in fœtal whales, which when grown up have not a tooth in their heads, or the teeth which never cut through the gums in the upper jaws of embryo calves?' And this assertion of the inadequacy of the notion of Design to explain fully organic structures is not at all peculiar to the writers who adopt Mr. Darwin's views. Long before the publication of the 'Origin of Species' it was recognised that some further idea besides adaptation was needed. It was thought that this idea might be found in the notion of a general plan, adhered to at times and in places where it had no functional fitness. Professor Owen, in his work on 'The Nature of Limbs,' recognises this absence of adaptation in some parts of various animals, and accounts for those parts as the carrying out of a general type. He instances the fin of a whale as needlessly complex in structure, as having in fact nearly every segment and bone which is found in the human hand, and again the cranium of the chicken as composed of a great number of bones, an arrangement not needed for its safety, as it is in the case of man at birth. Dr. Carpenter, in the eighth chapter of his work on the 'Principles of Physiology,' has developed the same view.

Some striking examples of this want of adaptation may be brought forward from embryology. The embryo is always in early stages very closely similar to that of other animals of lower organisation,[1] and it is found that it has often parts which serve no purpose either for its present or its future welfare. The quotation already given from Mr. Darwin's work on the 'Origin of Species' gives two examples. Others are alluded to in the same book, and this resemblance in the organs of the earliest forms of life is pointed to as supporting Mr. Darwin's views.[2]

Mr. G. H. Lewes[3] has stated this fact perhaps rather too strongly in opposition to the Design argument. Taking up the metaphor which speaks of the Deity as 'the great architect,' he asks what would be thought of an architect who, when he had a palace to build, began by setting up a hovel; then pulled it down, and built a cottage; then added story to story, and room to room, not with a view

[1] See 'Elements of Physiology,' by Dr. J. Müller, translated by Dr. W. Baly, book viii. p. 1591.
[2] 'Origin of Species,' by C. Darwin, p. 523, 5th edition.
[3] 'Fortnightly Review,' June 1, 1868.

to the final edifice, but with reference to the way in which houses were built in ancient times?

I may add that the whole system of the reproduction of plants and animals seems attended with an enormous waste—a waste which gives rise to great improvement according to Mr. Darwin's views, but which is not easily understood if we think of each species as a separate creation, the result of a wise and good design, and look for evidence of this wisdom and goodness in the adaptation of the species to the circumstances of its life.

Some of the evidence last given has been objected to as drawn too much from peculiar and exceptional facts. You look, it has been said, into 'the nooks and crannies' of creation. If we do, it is because those nooks and crannies lie in the quarter said to be peculiarly fruitful in evidence of Design. But here we have a great broad fact before us, one to be traced over almost the whole face of the animal and vegetable world. This truth as to organic life is very effectively brought out in a book which attracted much notice some years ago, the 'Plurality of Worlds,' attributed to the late Dr. Whewell. The writer makes use of it to refute by analogy the objection raised from final causes against his theory of the non-habitation of the heavenly bodies. Among several striking statements he mentions an old calculation, that a single female fish contains in her body two hundred millions of ova, and thus might by herself alone replenish the seas if all these were fostered into life, and he adds with truth that though this may excite wonder it cannot excite wonder as anything uncommon. It is only an example of what continually occurs with the lower forms of life.

I need not say upon how great a scale astronomy has disclosed the phenomena to which Dr. Whewell sought thus to reconcile our minds. Modern views as to the waste of energy in sun heat are a well-known and most impressive illustration. Nor yet need I point out what much more serious difficulties the Design argument encounters when it is applied to the history of man himself, regarded as it now is by many as a long ascent from savagery. Now the existence of these very numerous cases in which we seem to see the absence or the frustration rather than the carrying out of Design is a real and undeniable objection to our argument. I pointed out before that the force of this objection would depend a good deal on the number of these apparent exceptions, and I now call attention to the increase of that number, as an active cause of the decline of our argument in popularity. The principle of these remarks is not, however, always admitted. In an article in the 'Quarterly Review' for July 1869, I find it contended that if Design is once clearly recognised in any

INFLUENCES OF MODERN SCIENCE.

phenomenon, it can never be separated from that phenomenon. It remains a fact, a witness to an intelligent creator, whatever may be discovered elsewhere.

In reply we may argue thus. Nothing is clearer, in the present state of knowledge, than that the universe is under one government. We cannot isolate a part, and infer the Maker's character only from that. We must take account of the whole, so far at least as it is known to us. If in many cases, perhaps even in the greater number, we cannot trace beneficent design, we must hesitate to declare God's wisdom and goodness established in this way. To take the well-known illustration of the watch: if we knew that a certain man had made many watches, some good ones, several indifferent ones, many scarcely worthy of the name, we should conclude either that he cared little about making good watches, or that he was an indifferent workman. To some extent this reply may be put aside by a remark already made, viz. that a being of infinite resources would have no motive for being sparing in their use. He might reasonably adopt a mode of proceeding by which a great deal would be to our thinking thrown away. This consideration might avail in the astronomical case, but as I have said before, I do not think that it would be a satisfactory explanation where life and happiness and right and wrong are concerned.

2. Increase of the recognition of general laws.

The feeling of Design at all in Nature has been weakened by the recognition of universal laws. The two ideas, special purpose and general law, are not, in the actual case of the universe, logically incompatible. Yet the one does tend to thrust out the other. The reconciliation, by pre-arrangement of the laws for individual ends, or in any other way, is not an easy idea. And the whole of the vast progress of modern science has been a bringing of the phenomena of the universe more and more under this conception of law. Furthermore, the Design argument found its strongest support in what was looked upon as distinctly interruption of law, miracle as distinguished from providence. Its best foundation was thought to be seen in the acts of creation, by which each separate species of the animal and vegetable world had been originally placed upon our planet. Now a belief in the reign of law here also has gained ground, even with some who do not hold Mr. Darwin's views, as, for example, the Duke of Argyll.[1] And, wherever that belief does gain ground, the sense of special contrivance will diminish. Creation by law, like anything else which is done by law, does not suggest special appointment. The adaptation of

---

[1] See the 'Reign of Law,' by the Duke of Argyll, ch. v., 5th edition.

the species to its environment is seen as part only of a general plan, with a wider scope, in which the real design is to be looked for. Generally, science is offering a new interpretation of Nature, in place of the old theological view; that is, the reign of law in the place of special appointment. She might allow that her view was less fertile in immediate moral results, but she urges that it is true. Every year the difficulties of the theological scheme increase, whilst fresh evidence is found for the universality of law.

3. Explanations of adaptation without the notion of special Design.

Some modern writers have denied that the so-called appearances of Design in Nature were really what these words imply.[1] Dr. Strauss, for instance, following Schopenhauer, asserts that the proper analogy for explaining these appearances is to be found in the workings of animal instinct. It may, however, be contended that instinct is, after all, not essentially distinct from intelligence—it is only a very low form of intelligence, dominated by habit, personal and inherited. Neither of these last could be ascribed to God. If we explain instincts as supernaturally implanted at creation, we give the Theist a new argument. If, with Mr. Darwin, we suppose them to survive from utility, we introduce an idea inapplicable to the maker of the world. If it be the uniformity of

[1] See 'The Old Faith and the New,' by D. F. Strauss, translation by M. Blind, p. 134, 2nd edition.

the Divine proceedings, which is held to have more in common with the uniformity of the action of instinct than with the variability of conscious voluntary action, then we have only a re-statement of the incompatibility of action by general law and special purpose. If the work of the Divine mind be the co-ordination of a system of permanent and universal laws, then nothing could be more remote from the mechanical action of instinct under special circumstances. There is the antithesis of mentally grasping all things and looking only at one.

I do not, however, suppose that this objection has had much influence. I go on to speak of another, which certainly has had—which, indeed,[1] Professor Huxley regards as the deathblow of our argument. We have noticed more than once that our reasoning had its best foundation in the adaptation of living creatures to their circumstances. Inanimate Nature might show signs of power and arrangement. We might see there order, arrangement, beauty, which suggested mind. But we do not find those wonderful pieces of mechanism which we do see in organic life, and which certainly suggest an intelligent Maker more strongly; and, further, when we come to sensitive life, we have indications of a moral kind, in the contrivances for comfort or pleasure, and these,

---

[1] Professor Huxley's 'Lay Sermons, Addresses, and Reviews,' ch. xiii. p. 330.

I need not say, have been thought a very valuable branch of the argument. It is here, as to these contrivances of organic life, the very stronghold of natural theology, that the new views of Mr. Darwin have made a difference. They have very plausibly suggested a new explanation. With Mr. Darwin the adaptation of the organism to its surroundings is only a gradual accumulation of small improvements, selected and perpetuated out of miscellaneous changes by the simple cause that those individuals who had any of these improvements were thereby placed at an advantage in the struggle for life. The process by which the wonderful results were at last brought about is resolved into three simple elements.

1. A general resemblance between parent and child, with slight deviations of uncertain character.

2. A multiplication greatly in excess of the means of subsistence.

3. A consequent struggle for existence, in which those who have any advantage of organisation survive.

Certainly this view of the origin of adaptation suggests design far less forcibly than the theory of different species, each permanently reproduced, and having its origin in a special creation, at which its character was, by immediate Divine appointment, fitted to its circumstances. We might, perhaps, describe the contrast by comparing it to that which

Paley has drawn between real and tentative miracles. If the perfection of the organism be supposed to be Nature's object, Mr. Darwin makes her to attain it only after many trials. Dr. Whewell, in his Bridgewater Treatise, enumerates nineteen circumstances in the character of our globe to which man's physical frame is so adapted that, if any of them were materially changed, the whole race would perish. Now, if we think of man as specially made for his dwelling-place, we have here a striking evidence of Design. But if we adopt Mr. Darwin's views, and see in the human frame the final result, so to speak, of an immensely protracted series of experiments upon the part of Nature, by far the greater part of which were failures, then the peculiar cogency of our evidence is gone. But I do not think that the traces of a Divine mind are altogether lost. We must remember that there are laws of the variation between parent and child, at present little known, and that these co-operate with the influences of inanimate Nature in the process of Mr. Darwin's theory. There is no chance; there is Divine supervision, if not immediate Divine appointment. So much we may still assert, but I allow that, so far as natural selection does explain animal mechanism, it obscures the view of purpose; and that it is, to some extent at least, the true explanation must be admitted. For variability and the struggle for life are facts abundantly attested, apart from Mr. Darwin's theory. They are veræ causæ, no mere creations of his hypothesis, and, to some extent at all events, they must perform the work which he assigns to them. And further it has now been shown, in the case of one at least of the most convincing of the grounds of the Design argument, the construction of the eye, that the adaptation is rather of the character which natural selection would bring about, than the perfect workmanship which we might look for from an infinite and all-powerful mind. The eye has a wonderful practical fitness for its work, such as the constant selection of the best instrument by practical trial would bring about, but still theoretically it is very far from perfection. It has somewhat of every defect which such an optical instrument could have.[1]

I have now examined the argument from Design, and the influences which, in recent times, have diminished its popularity. We are next to enter on the second topic of my essay, the modification which may be given to this argument to meet the requirements of the present state of the human mind. We will subsequently endeavour to estimate its value in these days, and then take account of any additional considerations which can be brought forward on behalf of Theism, so as to form a complete idea of the

[1] See 'Popular Lectures on Scientific Subjects,' by H. Helmholtz, translated by E. Atkinson.

intellectual grounds of this belief at the present day.

First let me recall the principal points in our conclusions so far. Our argument could never claim to prove the existence of a God of infinite attributes. But it did go far to convince men that the universe was the work of a Being of inconceivable power and intelligence. A doubt hung over the evidence of his goodness. Many obvious facts could be quoted against it. But it was thought that peculiar evidence of Design upon his part was to be found in animal mechanism, and that this evidence made generally for benevolent purpose. A great deal of this supposed evidence has been explained away, and further a conviction is growing up in the cultivated mind, that all phenomena are the fruit of general law and not of special appointment. It is in deference to this last assertion that I would frame my modification. No doctrine, it appears to me, is so clearly taught by modern science as this, that God works by general laws. His appointments are at least *primâ facie* general, not special, though it may be that every special case has been considered in making them. I do not mean here to prejudge the question, whether exceptions to such law have ever taken place, say in original creation or subsequent miracle. But I wish to detach the argument from Design altogether from these difficult questions.

MODIFICATION OF THE ARGUMENT.

Looking upon Nature in the light of modern science in quest of evidence for an originating mind, what we see is the co-operation of a number of general laws; and the question for our consideration is, does this co-operation indicate an intelligent and moral author? Such an origin does not imply a definite beginning in time, at which the Divine Being impressed the laws upon the Universe. That is only an anthropomorphic idea of the Divine action, to which our fancy may incline. This action of God may as well or more properly be thought to be the now-acting power of Nature following the laws as its method. To continue our search for Design; we are not to argue from isolated facts. We cannot, like Paley,[1] infer the Divine benevolence from the gambols of shrimps. We must take account at least of all that we know, and endeavour to grasp the character of the Universe as a whole. On the one hand, we are not to expect discernible traces of Design everywhere, nor yet, on the other hand, are we to disregard such traces if they appear too often to be accounted chances, *i.e.* effects for which we cannot venture to assign a cause. When we make this bold attempt we are met by a great difficulty—the smallness of our insight into the working of Nature's laws, compared with what we may justly conjecture their scope to be. It is but a little corner of the universe

---

[1] Paley's 'Natural Theology,' ch. xxvi.

which we can explore. We see unnumbered worlds in the sky, but we know nothing of the economy of Nature there, nothing at least which would justify any conclusion as to the moral or intellectual character of her author. Our grasp is a little but not much greater in respect of time than of space. For, indeed, according to the well-known saying of Sir Charles Lyell, men are apt, from certain prepossessions,[1] to be parsimonious in their estimates of time past. This is true even of men with ideas enlarged as to this point. They talk sometimes of tracing things back to the nebulæ as though they were thus obtaining a comprehensive view of the entire history of creation. But supposing that the solar system did originate from a nebula, have they a right to assume this development to be coeval with the Universe? We have good reason to think that stars are by no means of equal antiquity, and that our own sun is not one of the oldest. Further that nebula out of which it sprang need not be thought the primitive state of matter. It might have been the result of some previous condition of things, say a collision of two great cosmical bodies and the vaporising of their masses. We have evidence for such catastrophes.[2] May not such episodes repeat them-

[1] Sir Charles Lyell's Address to the British Association.
[2] See 'Appearances of Temporary Stars,' in Sir J. Herschel's Astronomy, and in Helmholtz's lectures on the Conservation of Energy, 'Medical Times,' April 23, 1864.

selves in the long history of the Universe? The beginning of one order of things may be only the extinction of another. We can never feel sure that we have reached an absolute beginning. Able writers, speaking of the present working of the Universe, have distinguished between physical laws and collocations of matter; for example, the law of gravitation and the masses of the planets. In the latter they have seen something arbitrary which might be attributed to the immediate appointment of the Deity. But was not this a contracted view, an unstable distinction? May not these collocations be quite as much as present physical effects the result of physical laws working at an earlier period? In short, we cannot frame, from purely scientific sources, anything which could be reasonably taken for a general history or scheme of things. But still we may survey a part of creation, and our wisdom seems to be to form the best judgment which we can from that. The course of events on the surface of our planet is at all events known to us in its general outlines for an enormous period of time. Perhaps we may go further, and say that we can trace a vast plan for the formation of our own planet, and further of the particular system to which she belongs, carried out over an immense stretch of past time. This would be true either on the nebular or the meteor hypothesis of the origin of the solar system. But be this last point as it may, we are certain that for many millions of years a development of life has taken place upon our planet, and that this development has undeniable marks of progress. I do mean to say that there has been steady uniform improvement. Some types of life, reptile life for instance, may have flourished more in times past than they do now.[1] But allowing for irregularities and fluctuations, on the whole higher and higher forms of life have appeared. There has been unquestionably an enormous advance between the times of the Eozoon Canadense and our own. And further we have to notice that a new kind of progress of far greater intrinsic importance than mere physical improvement has of late appeared. I mean intellectual and moral progress, as it is seen in man. Here, too, I allow that progress is not uniform or universal. But, on the whole, and in the long run it is manifest.[2] It is indisputable that the earlier races of men were both intellectually and morally below the present, and there is great reason to hope that progress has finally established itself and is advancing with accelerated rapidity. And this progress, I would say, is most important in our argument as to the character of God, for it is full of promise of far better things than this sad world has ever seen. It points most decidedly to a supre-

[1] Sir C. Lyell's 'Principles of Geology,' chap. ix.
[2] Sir John Lubbock's 'Origin of Civilisation,' Appendix, Part II. Tylor's 'Primitive Culture,' chap. ii. Sir C. Lyell's 'Antiquity of Man.'

macy of the power for good, and a great hope of final happiness for our race. It speaks for our Maker's goodness not only far more strongly, but also more unequivocally, than the mere physical progress which had gone before. For not only are the fruits of happiness which it bears much greater in amount and higher in character, but the way of its advance is more in harmony with beneficence—peaceful and happy, not winning good through pain and death, like that physical progress which brought in higher forms at the cost of exterminating lower.

Now here is a great fact, a great fact for good, to set against that widely spread appearance of evil in creation which has so embarrassed theologians. The code of Nature's laws has so co-operated as to work a long and wonderful progress towards good. Does not this fact indicate controlling mind and beneficent purpose? I may be reminded that, to a great extent, this progress has been a mere result of the conditions of existence. Those conditions eliminate the inferior forms of life. But is there anything here to oppose the idea of design? Are not those conditions of existence a fruit of the co-operation of natural laws? I may also be reminded that if we could survey the Universe we might see spectacles of different meaning. We might find the co-operation of Nature's laws not issuing in this progress elsewhere. In fact, we might find that this progress, as matters now stand with the Universe, was only one of those occasional results from which, as I have said, it seems unsafe to infer the character of Him who made the whole.

We have, of course, here before us the much-debated question of the plurality of worlds. If, indeed, our own little world could be shown to be the only scene of life and of the progress of organisation and mind in the whole Universe, then, indeed, the attributing of that exceptional fact to chance, or, to speak more properly, the denial, that in this single fact we had evidence of a design in the maker of the whole, might seem credible, though by no means certain. But surely we cannot assume so much. I allow that what we know of a vast number of the heavenly bodies, as the suns, comets, meteors, nebulæ (and among this number are not only a great majority but the largest also), leads us to believe that they are not inhabited. But surely it may be otherwise with some of the innumerable planets and satellites which may exist in the Universe. The Darwinian hypothesis does, it is true, impair the argument for habitable globes from final causes. It exhibits life as developed upon our globe upon a plan not so immediately capable of adaptation to any conditions as we must suppose that the direct working of the Almighty is. But, on the other hand, it does I think give us more solid grounds for expecting such habitation than can be found in conjectures as to the purposes of God—conjectures, I ought to add, which could not be admitted in our present argument. For the process to which it attributes the development of life is plainly one not merely capable in the long run of a wonderful adaptation to outward variations, but one which does in fact so adapt itself.

The mere relative paucity of inhabited worlds, what has been said of the appearance of waste in creation, may explain. And that there is more than this comparative paucity is only conjecture, and a conjecture not favoured by the modern view of the development of life. Such a conjecture, should not be pressed. We might fairly meet it by another conjecture in itself as likely, since we cannot by the nature of the case know the fact. It would be equally legitimate to suppose that in many parts at least where chaos reigns now a world of order and beauty and happiness will one day have been developed.[1] At the most we have only that imputation of apparent waste which, as I have said, cannot strictly be urged against the wisdom and goodness of God. He is patient, it has been said, because he is eternal. He is prodigal, it might be said, because he is infinitely rich. And indeed we should be careful how we call him prodigal. What seems to us waste

[1] See an article, 'Life Past and Future in other Worlds,' 'Cornhill Magazine,' June 1875.

may spring out of parts of the plan which have purposes the most important. It is mostly the observance of law which seems to make progress so slow and halting and devious. But that reign of law may serve the highest and most precious purposes. We have reason to believe that it has been the instrument of developing man's intellect, and his moral nature too.

I have spoken of the bearing of the recognition of law in Nature upon the argument from Design as applied to particular cases. I would now say something as to its influence, when that argument is applied to the general aspect of creation. There is a difference. I have remarked that the force of a particular instance of Design, as proof of the Divine intelligence, is diminished when the alleged contrivance is looked at as the result of the combination of a number of general laws. But this diminution does not arise from the individual appearance of contrivance becoming less striking. In and by itself it suggests the idea of contrivance as strongly as ever, or even more so. But now it reminds us of a number of other things. We are reminded that it is not a special appointment by itself with a discernible purpose, but a part of a set of general appointments, whose general working has not this appearance of purpose. Consequently, our particular case assumes more the appearance of a chance or coincidence, and so the idea of purpose recedes and disappears. To give an illustration.[1] So long as we look only at the revolution of our earth upon its axis by itself, we may see an appointment admirably adapted to animal life, but as soon as we consider this rotation as one example of a phenomenon to be seen throughout the universe, so soon as we contemplate every cosmical body from the giant Sirius down even to the tiny meteor as rotating in like manner, then the idea of special adaptation becomes lost. Such I conceive is the effect of recognising the character of generality in the Divine appointments upon our argument in its old form. But if we can grasp any general design to be traced in the whole aspect of Nature, or at least over so considerable a part as to seem not unworthy to be the purpose of the whole, this making void no longer takes place. If it be true, for example, that within the whole range of our observation, so far as that observation can be thought competent for the purpose, we do seem to trace a great scheme of evolution, bringing about more and more of organisation, intelligence, moral order, and happiness, then we have an evidence for an intelligent and beneficent Deity, which the reign of law does nothing to invalidate. Neither does the

[1] This idea is taken from an article in the 'Cornhill Magazine' for March 1872.

reduction of the laws at present known to higher and simpler laws have any such effect. If all were reduced to one simple but vast generalisation, a result which, as Mr. Mill[1] has argued, is perhaps impossible, our argument would still be unimpaired. It would remain a mark of design that this one law was exactly what was needed for such an amazing result. It would perhaps be a more convincing proof of an intelligent creator that so wonderful a development had been achieved by the working of such a single principle, just as it is a masterpiece of human genius to accomplish great and varied ends by simple means.

But though the reign of law does not impair any evidence of Divine supervision, which the general aspect of Nature may suggest, yet by itself it does not to my mind suggest the idea of God; at all events, it does not suggest that idea as God is generally thought of. Mere order and arrangement, apart from discernible purpose, does not I think give proof of a conscious intelligent moral author. The contrary has been asserted by an eminent writer, Dr. Newman.[2] But I venture to think that there is here on his part an incautious application of the analogies of human life. When we see arrangement we are accustomed to find that

---

[1] See Mill's 'Logic,' Book III. chap. xiv.
[2] 'Grammar of Assent,' p. 70.

it is the work of men, whom we know from other facts to be intelligent and moral agents. If we landed on an unknown island, and found rows of stones regularly arranged, our first inference would probably be that they had been so placed by men whom we should think of as more or less like ourselves. But if we knew nothing of a certain being but that he made such arrangements, if he were to us only a source of bare order apart from all trace of further purpose, we could not I think infer that he had a moral and intellectual character. And it is this last conclusion at which we wish to arrive in natural theology. I would repeat this last remark in answer to another way of putting the argument for a God which we sometimes see adopted. The alternative is stated to be between attributing the world to chance or to God. Now, chance would not be recognised I think by anyone who had at all studied what has been written upon it, as any agent or cause whatever.[1] The word has merely a subjective meaning. In common language it expresses ignorance of any cause. In mathematical language it expresses the degree of expectation which we should have from an imperfect knowledge of causes or conditions. To attribute the world to

[1] See Mill's 'Logic,' Book III. chap. xviii. I believe that the view taken by Mr. Venn, in his 'Logic of Chance,' differs from that given below, but not so as to affect the point before us, viz., the unintelligibility of attributing the world to chance.

chance would therefore be absurd. We believe that everything in the system of the world has its cause— that is, antecedents which it follows according to law. If my reasoning has been just, we may seek to explain the whole character of that system in the like way. And the real question between the Theist and the Atheist is what sort of being we are thus led to think of. Is it a moral and intelligent agent? If we get no further than the bare notion of law-making, of something, which leads to uniformity, without our getting any view of further purpose, much less of benevolent purpose, then I think that Pantheism and not Theism would be our conclusion. But if there be really a grand co-operation of Nature's laws for a beneficent end then we have an argument for an intelligent and moral Deity distinct from the world. That hypothesis explains the great fact.

But I must allow that any conclusions at which we can arrive as to the character of God from a general survey of his works fall short of what religion requires. We are led to think of God as one who cares for the race rather than the individual. The scheme of creation has brought about great progress for good upon the whole, and it may promise more. But it has not taken thought of the happiness of each sensitive creature. The most thoughtful poem of our day has bidden us trust.

> That nothing walks with aimless feet,
> That not one life shall be destroyed,
> Or cast as rubbish to the void,
> When God hath made the pile complete.
> That not a worm is cloven in vain,
> That not a moth with vain desire
> Is shrivel'd in a fruitless fire,
> Or but subserves another's gain.[1]

These are beautiful words. They express the yearning of a sympathetic heart. But they do not find any countenance from science. On the contrary, if Mr. Darwin's view be true, the individual has been freely and systematically sacrificed for the improvement of the race. I have said that the higher progress, moral and intellectual, of which we now see evidence in man, is not attended with this cost of individual suffering and sacrifice. And so we hope in the main that it is now, and will be for the future. But the same cannot be said of the past. Those who have done most either for the moral or intellectual improvement of their fellowmen have often been, in one way or other, victims of their own efforts. The world has seen many sad examples of injustice to the man before his age. And even apart from this, I think there is truth in what Mr. Lecky[2] has said that moral or intellectual superiority has often been unfavourable to the worldly comfort or welfare of its possessor.

[1] Tennyson's 'In Memoriam,' stanza 53.
[2] 'History of European Morals,' vol. i. pp. 60-70.

We have here brought before us what I take to be the real schism between science and religion. Some writers have contrasted these two great elements of our nature in this way. Religion, said they, brings out a personal, but science a pantheistic view of God. But if I am right, science is not here quite rightly described. She does point out traces of purpose in the world, and it is such purpose which suggests the idea of a personal God, independent of the Universe, its maker, or at least ruler, as opposed to the pantheistic view, which confounds the divine energy with the power of Nature, and does not make it independent and controlling. The idea of personality in God, when cleared, as far as we can clear it, of that anthropomorphism which so naturally adheres to it from our human experience and associations, implies no more than faculties acting under the direction of a will, itself determined by moral qualities. And so much the purpose in the world revealed by science seems to imply. But then this purpose is general in its scope. It is not directed towards individual creatures. And here I repeat is a deep division between science and religion. For religion is a direct transaction between God and man, and it needs a God who can be to man a father, a friend, a judge. It requires that God should be interested in us individually, and that the character and welfare of each of us should have a distinct place amidst the purposes of his infinite administration. Else how should we fear him, or trust him, or love him ? We might admire, and wonder, and reverence, but there could not be the deeper personal feelings that come of direct dealing with ourselves. If God cares for the race, but often neglects, or even sacrifices the individual, then each man can feel no certainty of moral government for himself. The hero who lays down his life for his country, or the martyr who dies for the cause of truth, may only be the victim of a sublime delusion. That conciliation between the moral and the self-caring instincts of mankind, which it is one great work of religion to accomplish, is lost.

It may perhaps be thought by some that I have been too sparing in my inferences from the data given by science. You admit, it may be said, that there are distinct traces of beneficent design in the universe. God does care for the happiness of his creatures, upon the whole and in the long run. But if there be this disposition in him, may we not feel assured that any seeming exceptions to his goodness are only seeming—that when we see the whole of his dealings with any of his creatures we shall find them redeemed from the appearance of harshness or neglect, that the apparent carelessness as to the individual arises only from the limitation of our own knowledge? In human government such neglect of the individual may sometimes be unavoidable. The utmost which man's power and intelligence can accomplish is to make laws which, on the whole and in a general way, shall work good. Cases of hardship will occur. But we would have this otherwise if we could; we do correct it as far as we can. We feel that it is imperfect work, and we cannot attribute such imperfection to our Maker. Infinite goodness, and wisdom, and power, cannot overlook anything, nor yet find the minutest supervision a task too great.

I am far from believing or saying that all this is not true. But I do not see how it is to be got out of the argument from Design. That argument reasons from the aspect of Nature, and the aspect of Nature shows general, not special, purpose. That the Divine goodness is such as to lead to the latter, or that, even if it did, the Divine wisdom and power are such as could carry out that purpose, is clearly more than our argument can prove. It will be noticed that the above remarks assume the infinity of the Divine attributes, and that in fact any argumentative force which they have arises from that assumption. But I have pointed out already that the Design argument by itself cannot prove this infinity. When we thought of the marvellous greatness of creation, this objection may have seemed a piece of logical captiousness. But here we see that it has a real and important bearing.

This radical difference between religion and science has been widely and strongly felt in some of its special forms, as in the case of prayer, of special providences, of miracles. And the questions which have thus arisen have often, I think, not been treated by divines in a satisfactory way. They have been too ready to content themselves with pointing out how their view of God led to such things, or at the most how the scientific view of God could be made to agree with such things. They have not been sufficiently careful to make it clear upon what grounds, independent of science, their view of God can be rested. Yet plainly this must be done, if we are to have the matter satisfactorily cleared up. Thus Paley sums up the controversy as to the credibility of miracles with these words :—' Once believe that there is a God, and miracles are not incredible.'[1] It has been pertinently asked, What kind of God? Certainly if, like Paley, we form all our ideas of God, antecedent to revelation, by arguing from the works of Nature, we shall not have a miracle-working God. For all that Nature strictly interpreted by science teaches to us, makes for law and against miracle. So again Dr. Mansel[2] asserts that the mere attributing

[1] 'Preparatory Considerations to Paley's Evidences.'
[2] 'Aids to Faith,' p. 26.

of design to God implies freedom on his part, and so involves the possibility of miracles. The present Bishop of Gloucester has repeated this assertion in his introduction to the first volume of the recent lectures of the Christian Evidence Society. It should, I think, be borne in mind that, in the case with which we have to deal, the case of Nature, Design appears only in subordination to law. Law is universal. Design has many apparent exceptions. Now a miracle is, so to speak, Design triumphing over law. Such an event, therefore, is not in harmony with what Nature teaches, when we apply the Design argument to her phenomena. Other writers, as the Duke of Argyll[1] and Dr. McCosh,[2] have, it is true, brought forward considerations more to the point. They have pointed out that each of the events of the world results, not from a single law of Nature, but from the co-operation or concurrent action of many. The like view of causation is recognised by a writer of a different class, Mr. J. S. Mill.[3] He justly tells us that the causal connection 'is seldom if ever between a consequent and a single antecedent.' 'It is usually between a consequent and the sum of several antecedents, the concurrence of all of them being requisite to produce, that is to be certain of being followed by, the consequent. According to these

[1] 'The Reign of Law,' chap. ii.
[2] 'The Method of the Divine Government.' Dr. M'Cosh, Book II., chap. i.
[3] Mill's 'Logic,' Book III. chap. v. art. 3.

views, we see that even under the strictest reign of natural law each particular event would be the final result of trains of antecedents of indefinite length and varied direction, and that herein lies a power of adaptation to special ends, a flexibility, so to speak, in the great machine of Nature, which may fit it to carry out in every special case the purpose of a moral ruler. These views no doubt are just, and they avail to show how the scientific view of God's government may be made to agree with the religious. But I must observe that it still remains to find an argumentative foundation for this last view. The Design argument has not supplied it. All that we have made out is that the view may be true.

I have now stated the modification which should, I think, be given in these days to the argument from Design, and also examined its effect, if it be so modified. A few words will point out our present position. The argument could never claim to prove the existence of a God of infinite attributes. But this perhaps may be neither possible nor needful. The limitation of our faculties may prevent it, and the wants of our moral being may not require it. It may suffice, if we can find reason to believe in a God whose power and wisdom and goodness suffice for the moral government of man. No doubt our argument did a great deal towards this end. But it was always beset with one great difficulty, the existence of extensive evil. We found that the views of modern science disclosed a progress towards good, which went a long way to counteract the ill inference which the existence of evil suggests. But, upon the other hand, the recognition of general in the place of special purpose, which those views require, gives an idea of God essentially different, though not of necessity incompatible, with that which religion requires. The result is, that we do need some other independent source of information. I will now enter on the next topic of my essay—the consideration of other arguments which have been thought to indicate the existence or the attributes of God.

PART II.

First I will speak of the *à priori* argument, the ontological argument, as it is sometimes called. It is an argument which has, I should think, little or no influence at the present day. But as it has been put forward by eminent men in past times, as Anselm and Descartes, I wish to say a few words concerning it.

The argument has been presented in two forms.

1. Man, it is said, has in his mind the idea of a

THE À PRIORI ARGUMENT.

perfect being. This idea includes the notion of necessary existence, and consequently the idea must have an objective counterpart, *i. e.* there must be a God.

2. The like inference is drawn from the alleged existence of this idea, by the simpler reasoning that such an idea could never have arisen except from the actual existence of its counterpart.

I would, in the first place, remark that it is very doubtful whether we have this alleged idea of a perfect being at all, if by those words is meant the idea of a being of infinite attributes, such as God is generally thought to be. And further, what is very important to our present inquiry, so far as we have any such idea, it is pretty clear that it did not come to us from without through sensation, or inference therefrom, but that we made it for ourselves by putting together certain abstract ideas.

The mere presence of an idea in our minds does not prove the existence of a corresponding reality outside our minds. We have an abundance of ideas, which, as we know, give no such warrant of an objective counterpart. An attempt, indeed, is made to get over this difficulty in the first form of our argument. We are told that necessary existence is a part of the idea in question, and therefore there must be something existing, which corresponds to this idea. But the presence of an idea of necessary existence in the mind can by itself no more prove that it has an objective counterpart—that is to say, that something necessarily exists, than the presence of any other idea. If, indeed, this idea of the perfect being had come to us from without, then we should have warrant for the external existence of all the predicates which we by analysing that idea could find out. But, as I have pointed out, such is not the case. The idea is a creation, or composition of the mind itself, and consequently its components exist only in the mind. All that we really can show is that the notion of necessary existence is part of the meaning which we give to the words Perfect Being.

I do not think it needful to dwell longer upon this argument, for, as I have said, the day of its influence is past. But I must allow that eminent writers, as Professor Max Müller for instance, do still use language in which its principles seem to me to lurk. They speak of man as having a direct intuition of the Infinite Being. The alleged universality of the idea of such a being has been brought forward as proof of this intuition. But with our present knowledge of the various races of men, past and present, we must I think admit that the idea of God, at least as we think of Him, has been far from universal.[1] A sense of some superior being, or the pre-

---

[1] Sir J. Lubbock's 'Origin of Civilisation,' chap. iv.

sence in the heart of feelings readily attributed to such a being, may be conceded as very widely prevalent. Perhaps this may be all that Professor Max Müller would contend for. An actual intuition of God, revealing his nature, is a notion beset with the greatest metaphysical difficulties, as was conclusively shown by Sir W. Hamilton in his criticism of Schelling, and it is a notion which certainly has no support from the actual history of religion.

PART III.

I will now speak of several arguments in succession, which may I think be classed together under the general name of first cause arguments. They all have this in common, that they seek to show that the series of phenomena which we see going on around us cannot have been going on for ever. The present laws of succession must at some period have had a start, or in other words the Universe an absolute beginning, and here, they say, is evidence of an uncaused cause or creator. God, it will be seen, is thus brought before us as the origin rather than the designer of the Universe. Accordingly, we have from these arguments confessedly less evidence for his moral or intellectual attributes than from the Design argument. But it has been thought that some at least of these arguments did more to show his eternity, omnipotence, omnipresence, in short, the infinity of his nature; that side of his character as to which the Design argument was obviously defective. If this view be sound we shall clearly have a valuable supplement to our former reasoning.

I will speak first of what may be called the old form of the argument; what has been called the cosmological argument.

Something, it is said, exists.[1] That something must have had a cause; that cause again a cause; and so on. But we cannot believe in an infinite series of dependent causes. We must stop at last at an uncaused cause or a first cause. This first cause must plainly be self-existent and eternal. By some questionable reasoning it is further sought to be shown that there can be but one such first cause, and that therefore all things depend upon that first cause, and by a little further exercise of ingenuity we are carried on from this point to the complete conclusion that the first cause must be independent, necessary, eternal, almighty, omnipresent. But into these details I do not mean to enter. My criticism will be directed to the earlier stages of the argument.

---

[1] See Dr. Samuel Clark's 'Demonstration of the Being and Attributes of God,' Sect. III., for an account of this argument.

On the first view of this argument we observe at once that it begins its reasoning by asserting the law of causation, and then attains its conclusion by setting that law aside. We refuse to continue inferring one finite cause from another for ever. Surely this step is a little arbitrary and inconsistent. At the best it can rest only on some evidence drawn from the mind itself—some intuition found there, and taken to be of objective truth. Nature gives abundant examples to support the law of causation, the law that every effect must have a cause. In physical nature, at all events, we have no exception; no uncaused cause to bring forward as an analogy for our first cause, or, to speak more correctly perhaps, as an instance of his appearance on the face of Nature. At all events, no such case can be brought forward as observable in the judgment of men of science, for miracles I do not contemplate now. Indeed, the only plausible analogy in the whole range of our knowledge is the human will, when taken to be self-determining. That view of the will is of course not universally allowed. It is not a settled truth. And even if it were, we should still have to bear in mind that the will of man can act on the physical world only under prior conditions of physical causation. The great chain of natural causes must have supplied it with means to direct. We have not then even here an analogue to our first cause—that is, to something acting altogether independently of that chain, being in fact its author. The assertion, too, that there cannot be an infinite series of finite causes, seems at first sight, at all events, discountenanced by the modern doctrines of the indestructibility of matter and energy.[1] With these ideas in view it seems more easy to conceive the eternal continuance than the beginning of the order of Nature. But still I do allow that to some minds it may seem more easy and natural to adopt the idea of a first cause. Such a preference would have its weight, upon the assumption, for which we have found grounds elsewhere, that the human mind had a moral and intelligent maker, if indeed it could be shown to be innate and universal. It might then be looked upon as an indication from him. But I, for one, do not think that any such character can be established on its behalf.

Attempts have been made to defend the argument from such criticisms as the above by auxiliary considerations. For instance, it has been said that the whole series of finite causes must have had a cause, or otherwise it might have been different

---

[1] Of the argument from the dissipation of energy I shall speak hereafter. That does not affect the mere continuance of the Universe in some shape or other, perhaps one of universal death. Nor yet again does it prove that the Universe cannot have been in existence for ever, unless we make the assumption that its matter can never have been diffused beyond a certain extent.

from what it is. There is a fallacy here, that of treating a possibly infinite series as a terminated whole. Each of the finite causes, which make up the series, is sufficiently determined in character by the cause which goes immediately before it. If there be no end, there is no need of some cause outside the series to make it what it is.

Dr. Samuel Clark, in the work to which I have referred, brought forward some ingenious considerations, with the end which I have just named, in support of the cosmological argument. They make use, indeed, of a different relation, that of substance and accident, not of cause and effect, but the end is plainly auxiliary to our argument to support the belief in an eternal Being. And I may remark that though his arguments may not be much to the taste of these days, they were adopted by Bishop Butler.[1] Briefly they stand thus. We cannot, he remarks, get rid of certain ideas, as of 'immensity and eternity.' We must, he argues, assume the existence of some being, in whom this immensity and eternity inhere as attributes; *i. e.* of an omnipresent and eternal Being. Now I do not deny that we have ideas of space and time as unbounded, and further as being in some way independent of our minds. That seems to me the natural interpretation of con-

---

[1] Bishop Butler's 'Analogy,' Part I., chap. vi.

sciousness. If we, with Kant, make them purely subjective, we shall, I think, sooner or later be landed in a complete idealism, as was indeed actually the case with some of his successors. If space and time be wholly subjective, what is motion? If motion be wholly ideal, simply a change in our subjective perception of matter, what, according to modern science, is energy? what are heat, light, electricity? We are driven forwards toward complete idealism, and such idealism puts what we feel to be an incongruous and inconsistent interpretation upon consciousness. Nay, further, if time be purely subjective, consciousness itself becomes of difficult understanding. For consciousness in us at least is essentially connected with the succession of thoughts in time. We become, indeed, perplexed as to the very basis of knowledge. But if we do grant that space and time are to some extent objective, I do not know that Dr. Clark's conclusion will follow. It is not clear that space and time are objective in the same way as material phenomena, *i. e.* in a way which requires, according to our common thinking, a substance in which they may inhere, as accidents. And this Dr. Clark's argument requires.

Professor Birks,[1] in a recent work on the Scripture doctrine of creation, has also put forward some considerations founded on the nature of time,

---

[1] 'The Scripture Doctrine of Creation,' by the Rev. T. R. Birks, chap. iv. London, 1872.

which he seems to regard as a proof of a beginning of the universe, and therefore of a creator. As the argument belongs to the class which I am discussing, I will briefly state and examine it here. If, says Professor Birks, there never was a beginning of time, the present moment could never have arrived. He has an illustration. In like manner no future point of time could ever be reached unless the interval between that point and the present were finite. Now I think that we have here an example how an acute man may be misled by the ambiguities which beset arguments as to the infinite. The original position is not sound, nor is the illustration trustworthy. To begin with the latter, we have plainly there two limits. There is the present point of time on the one hand, and the future epoch to be reached on the other. Hence the included time must of necessity be finite. But the contention as to the eternity of past time is, that there never was any such limit in the past. There was no beginning. Unless this contention be disproved, Mr. Birks' illustration does not apply. Plainly it does not help to disprove the position which he attacks, for it assumes a state of things which the position denies, and is of no force without this assumption. To turn now to the argument, we are told, indeed, that if this position were true, the present moment could never have arrived. Certainly not till after an infinite progress. But is this impossible? I allow that we cannot in imagination represent it to our minds. Infinity told out, so to speak, is inconceivable. But is not a beginning of time equally inconceivable? A mind so metaphysical as that of Sir W. Hamilton thought an absolute beginning inconceivable.[1] The infinite passing of time up to this present moment is, in fact, an infinite bounded on one side. The idea here meant to be conveyed may not perhaps be properly spoken of as that of an infinite. But still it is intelligible, and I ask is it impossible in fact? Let us take another illustration. Imagine a straight line indefinitely prolonged in both directions. Suppose a point moving uniformly along it in one direction always. This point may, I think, fairly represent the present moment, passing on out of the past into the future. Is it inconceivable that this point should have been so moving for ever? If it be not, why must there be a beginning in the analogue time? We can at least conceive the course of our point reversed, going back for ever.

I will not dwell longer on these arguments, drawn from highly abstract considerations. There may be others, but I think that we have considered enough as specimens, and I do not suppose that any others which might be produced would differ much in principle, or be found more satisfactory. Such

[1] 'Discussions on Philosophy and Literature,' Appendix I.

reasoning is not I believe popular now. It is not by such logical handling of abstract ideas that the popular philosophy seeks results. But there are, I must allow, certain arguments for the existence of God, founded on the most recent results of modern science, which are really kindred in principle. They seek to prove a creation, and therefore a creator, by showing, from the facts of the present universe, that it must have had a beginning. They fall, therefore, under the class of reasonings of which I am speaking, and I will accordingly notice them next.

PART IV.

The argument of which I shall speak first has its foundation in modern views as to force, or rather energy. The following account of it will, I fear, be tedious to anyone acquainted with those views; but my wish is to introduce such explanations as shall make the argument intelligible to those to whom the subject may be new.

I would begin by saying a few words as to the meaning of terms. Force is thought of by mathematicians as that which produces or changes motion in a body. They estimate force in two ways. First, they speak of accelerating force, which they measure simply by the change which is made in a body's velocity. Second, they speak of moving force, a term which they use when the mass of the body acted upon is taken into account. Moving force they measure by the mass of the body multiplied into the change in its velocity or, what is the same thing, the accelerating force. It is further a convention that work done should be measured by the moving force, multiplied into the distance through which it acts. And it is proved, by the aid of the infinitesimal calculus, that this work done, thus measured, is equal to half the mass into the change in the square of the velocity. The product of the mass into the square of the velocity, is called in mathematical books *vis viva*, and, what concerns us more at present, half of it is the measure, as I have just said, of the power to do work, what is called kinetic energy. I would call attention to the designation kinetic, because we shall have presently to speak of another kind of energy, called potential. The kinetic energy, then, of a body is measured by one half of the product mass multiplied into velocity squared, and whatever it be, it is the power that does work, say, carries up a heavy body from the earth against gravitation, or forces a bullet into a block of wood. Now it is a great discovery of modern times that this kinetic energy is convertible,

THE THEORY OF ENERGY.

according to fixed rules of equivalence, into things which at first sight seem to have nothing to do with motion, into heat, light, electricity, magnetism, chemical combination. Thus we have motion transformed into heat, according to the following rule. Take the quantity of water which weighs one pound avoirdupois in vacuo, at a temperature between $55°$ and $60°$ Fahrenheit. The amount of heat needed to raise the temperature of this water through $1°$ Fahrenheit is equivalent to the kinetic energy needed to raise 772 lbs. avoirdupois through 1 foot in our latitude, or, what would be the same, 1 lb. through 772 feet. We find that when motion is stopped, as by collision or friction, and when, therefore, kinetic energy at first sight seems to be destroyed, it is not really lost, but passes into some of these other forms, most commonly heat. Hence kinetic energy, once called into existence, is never destroyed. It may, however, be stored up in some latent form, as, for instance, when the energy in the sun's rays is used in the leaves of plants to chemically separate the carbon in the carbonic acid gas of the atmosphere from the oxygen, so as to supply material for the vegetable world. The energy thus used is, so to speak, stored up in the vegetables. And in this case it may be liberated again at a distant time by combustion of the vegetable matter. Kinetic energy, I repeat, is never destroyed; it passes into various forms, and sometimes it is laid by, so to speak, in forms in which it may again cause motion, and so appear as kinetic energy. These changes in the forms of energy, and this preservation of its amount, are called respectively the transformation and conservation of energy. Kinetic energy may be in many ways produced. Whenever, in fact, the forces of the universe are producing motion, they are calling this energy into existence. Gravitation is constantly doing so on a stupendous scale. But for gravitation, or indeed any of these forces, to do this, there must be a distribution of matter in space. It must not be all accumulated in a mass. Gravitation, for instance, cannot produce kinetic energy in a stone lying on the earth's surface. The stone must be in a position to fall freely. Here we obtain the idea of potential energy—of that energy which the forces of the universe have not yet called forth into kinetic energy, but which the arrangements and collocations of the universe give them the opportunity of calling forth. If we call this energy just described potential energy, we see that the action of force is to add to the stock of kinetic what it takes from the stock of potential energy. And we see also in some cases, as in that mentioned of the vegetable world, or in the case of vapours raised by the sun's rays from the surface of the water to the sky, that kinetic energy is withdrawn back into potential, so as partially to recruit the latter. We arrive at the conclusion that the sum of the two, the potential and the kinetic, throughout the Universe must always be the same. The changes of nature do but pass energy from one form to another. And hence arises at first sight the idea that the Universe may be eternal. Matter, its substance, is indestructible. Energy, its great agent of change, is indestructible. Can, then, its events be a perpetually recurring cycle? Here come in the considerations which constitute the theological argument, for whose examination I have been endeavouring to prepare my reader. It is maintained that, upon a comprehensive review of the changes going on in the Universe, it is clearly seen that those changes on the whole constantly pass its energy into forms less and less fitted to carry on the work of such a world as ours; that the general progress is to mutual rest, coldness, death; and that consequently the great machine cannot have been going for ever, or this state of mutual rest, coldness, and death would have supervened. This tendency of things is called the dissipation of energy. How it is thought to be shown I will try to explain more particularly.

The matter of the Universe known to us may be divided into an ether of extreme tenuity pervading all space, and the matter which composes the sun, stars, planets, satellites, meteors, comets, nebulæ, generally the heavenly bodies, including our earth.

No doubt there is in many of these latter matter of extreme rarity, as in the comets and the nebulæ. But it is to be distinguished from the ether. We will here speak of it under the general name 'cosmical bodies.' The main peculiarity which tends to destroy the present state of things is this, that the energy, either potential or kinetic, in the cosmical bodies, constantly tends to diffuse itself, either as light or heat, or in some kindred form, through the great ocean of ether; and when it is so diffused, there does not seem, so far as we can see, to be any adequate agency for again collecting it in the cosmical bodies, and so carrying on the work of a world like ours.

For simplicity's sake we will consider the solar system first. If we observe the radiation of heat from its members, we see at once one great cause of the change in question. So long as a cosmical body is hot enough to be fluid, this radiation goes on at a tremendous pace. The sun, for instance,[1] it has been computed, radiates every year a sufficient quantity of heat to boil sixty thousand billions of billions of pounds of ice-cold water. Professor Tyndall, in his work 'Heat a Mode of Motion,' has given some illustrations to help us to form some idea of this inconceivable radiation. It would in one hour melt a coat of ice all over the sun

---

[1] Sir W. Thomson's article on the 'Age of the Sun's Heat,' Macmillan's Magazine, March 1862.

2,400 feet thick. It would boil in the same time 700,000 million cubic miles of ice-cold water. It would equal the heat given out by burning in one hour a layer of coal over the sun's surface 10 feet thick. When the body is so far cooled that its surface becomes solid, the radiation is very greatly reduced, but not altogether destroyed. Again we observe another source of dissipation. The ether resists the motion of all the planetary bodies, and this resistance tends to abstract a portion of their motion, and convert it into diffused heat. It also tends ultimately to make the planets, the satellites, and the minor bodies, all fall into the sun. Of the retardation it is true that we can at present discern only the faintest traces—an effect upon a single comet. But the cooling has evidently made great progress. The form of the earth, for instance, shows that she was once a fluid mass. Our most probable conjecture as to the origin of the solar system is that its larger members have been formed either by the condensation of a nebulous vapour, or by the falling together of smaller bodies, even as meteors still fall on the surface of the earth. The consequent destruction of motion accounts for the originally heated state of the bodies of our system. But so great is the expenditure of heat from the sun, that Sir W. Thomson[1] has calculated

[1] See article just named.

that the above theory will not account, at the very most, for an amount of solar heat able to support that expenditure for more than 100 millions of years, probably very much less. We conclude, then, that there is a constant tendency in our system to burn out, so to speak. The falling in of the planets and satellites might keep up the sun's heat for a time, but only for a time.

We see, then, the prospect before our system. At some distant time—a time enormously distant, I allow, as we reckon duration—the sun and the planets, and all his other dependents, will have become a vast agglomeration of cold dark lifeless matter. It may be said that the falling in of the small bodies called meteors gathered in from the space through which the system is passing may retard the approach of this consummation. No doubt it will, but only for a time. Still further, a possible collision between our sun and some other great cosmical body may reverse the process altogether. In such a case a prodigious amount of heat might be evolved. The sun, even if grown partially solid, might be vaporised. Again, condensation might set in, and new planets might be formed. In fact, we might have the genesis and history of a new system. All this is conceivable, nay actually probable. But it would only lead to a repetition of the same process of cooling and accumulation. It is clear that the same agencies which we expect to destroy the solar system in the long lapse of time, would also in a much greater lapse of time destroy that more stupendous system of which it is a part. Our argument requires that we should extend this view to the entire physical Universe. It pronounces that the Universe tends ultimately to lose its available energies, to arrive at a condition in which the cosmical matter is accumulated in one unchanging mass, and it argues accordingly that the Universe cannot have existed from eternity under its present code of laws, or the catastrophe just described would have supervened already. In other words, the existing state of things cannot have been derived from other pre-existing states, through an infinite period of past time, according to existing laws. Hence we must assume an epoch at which these laws had a beginning. Metaphysically speaking, such a beginning is not identical with a creation, because this latter word is generally understood to mean the calling into existence of the substance of matter. But still such a beginning of the present order of nature does suggest origination in a divine will.

In this sketch of the argument from the dissipation of energy, I have endeavoured to describe the actual process by which that principle mainly takes effect upon the Universe at large. It seemed to me better to do this than to argue merely from the general truth, which may be proved,[1] that transformations of heat into motion are always attended with dissipation of energy, whilst those of motion into heat are often complete. This truth, however general, concerns after all only part of the transformations of energy. Nor have I dwelt on the dissipation taking place on our own planet, because after all it is not this which decides the general issue. No doubt here impact, friction, combustion, conduction, radiation, are continually converting energy into the form of diffused and unavailable heat to an extent which processes of an antagonist effect, such as the growth of vegetation or evaporation from the sun's heat, most inadequately counteract. But it is not the waste of a little world like ours which endangers the activity of the Universe. So long as the sun can supply us with his copious radiation, the earth may continue a scene of movement and perhaps of life. Even his exhaustion, as we have seen, need by no means be the final end of activity. There exist incalculable stores of energy, potential or kinetic, in the attractions and movements of the heavenly bodies. Yet if we steadily pursue our reasoning, we seem brought to the conclusion that the Universe, in spite of this

---

[1] See 'The Unseen Universe,' chap. iii. Tait's 'Thermodynamics,' Art. 66

vast recuperative power, does tend at last to be a scene of relative rest, coldness, darkness, and death. Is this reasoning, I ask, open to any objection; and if not, does it bear out the theological conclusion here sought to be rested upon it?

In attempting to pass a verdict upon the question here raised, we cannot but feel, not only the grandeur of the subject before us, but also the imminent risk of its being affected by considerations unknown to us. We certainly need to judge with diffidence. Perhaps the first question which arises is, are we to take the material Universe to be infinite? If it be, and if its stores of energy, potential and kinetic, have no limit, then it is no longer clear that the final stage of accumulation need have been reached, however long its past history may have been; nor yet, I may add, that it would ever be reached in the future. I may be reminded[1] that at present at all events only finite accumulations have arisen, and that this is not consistent with an accumulation through a past eternity. But this objection assumes that there never could have been more than some assignable degree of diffusion of matter. Why should this be? If at any past period there was a certain degree of diffusion, why may not there have been a greater degree at an earlier period? And if so, why may not this in-

[1] See 'Unseen Universe,' Art. 163.

tegrating, as I should propose to call it, have been going on for ever ? There seems to me to be here a fallacy similar to that of Professor Birks' Argument.

If on the other hand the Universe be finite, then, according to the principle of the conservation of energy, reflection of heat must take place from its boundaries,[1] and there may be re-concentration of energy on certain points, according to the form of the bounding surface.

A second inquiry arises thus. If it be impossible to imagine the present history of the Universe continued backward indefinitely under its present code of laws, are we therefore obliged to assume some anomalous interference ? We speak of course of these laws as they are known to us. Might there not be others, yet unknown, that would solve the difficulty ?

The history of the Universe, as immediately known to us, offers as its leading feature the falling together of small discrete bodies in enormous numbers and with great velocities, or the condensation of very rare and diffused gases. Hence the formation of bodies, some of vast size, others smaller, but all originally greatly heated. This process seems to point to an earlier state of things, in which such accumulations of matter, though sparse even

---

[1] See a paper in the 'Philosophical Magazine,' by Mr. W. T. M. Rankine, vol. iv. 4th series.

now, were far less common — a state in which, to use the expression which I have proposed, matter was far less integrated. It is quite true that the great change of which we thus obtain a glimpse is not a recurring process. It is not therefore fitted for eternal repetition and continuance. But it is a bold thing to say that this earlier state of things may not have followed from one still older by a natural process, and this again from one before, and so on through an indefinite regression. We have seen what an important part the ether plays in the present process of the dissipation of energy. The existence of that ether, the separation of matter into two main forms, may have sprung out of some previous condition of things wholly unknown to us. And so also there may be forms and stores of energy as yet unknown.

Mr. Proctor,[1] in his work on the sun, has cautioned us how we speculate on the physical constitution of that body, whilst we must feel uncertain how far the physical laws, which we observe here, will hold under the vastly different conditions obtaining there. He supports his caution by referring to cases in which what had been confidently thought by many to be safe generalisations have been shown to fail in novel circumstances. Thus

[1] 'The Sun : the ruler, fire, light, and life of the Planetary System,' by R. A. Proctor, chap. vii.

it was thought that the passage of a gas from the gaseous into the liquid form was always an abrupt change. But it has been found that carbonic acid gas can be made to pass into the liquid state by insensible gradations. Again, it had been thought that gas, when incandescent, always gave light whose spectrum was broken into thin lines; but it has been shown that hydrogen, under high pressure, may be made to give forth light with a continuous spectrum. Now surely this caution, which Mr. Proctor enters in the case of which he speaks, might still more wisely be entered when we come to consider a state of things so novel, so remote from our experience, as that which attended the origin of the Universe, or rather of that state of the Universe with which we are acquainted. We certainly must not be in haste to conclude that because the laws of nature, as they are known to us, will not explain what must have taken place at some very remote period, therefore those events must have been altogether anomalous. I will go on to speak of another argument recently put forward, kindred in principle, and the criticisms upon it which I shall have occasion to make will illustrate further the objections which I have just made.

The following passage is taken from a report in the 'Bradford Observer' of Tuesday, September 23, 1873, of an evening lecture delivered by Professor Clerk Maxwell at the Bradford meeting of the British Association in 1873 :—

'No theory of evolution can be formed to account for the similarity of molecules, for evolution necessarily implies continuous change, and the molecule is incapable of growth or decay, of generation or destruction. None of the processes of nature, since the time when nature began, have produced the slightest difference in the properties of any molecule. We are therefore unable to ascribe either the existence of the molecules, or the identity of their properties, to the operation of any of the causes which we call natural. On the other hand the exact equality of each molecule to all others of the same kind, gives it, as Sir John Herschel has well said, the essential character of a manufactured article, and precludes the idea of its being eternal and self-existent. Thus we have been led along a strictly scientific path very near to the point at which science must stop. Not that science is debarred from studying the internal mechanism of a molecule which she cannot take to pieces, any more than investigating an organism which she cannot put together. But in tracing back the history of matter science is arrested when she assures herself on the one hand that the molecule has been made, and on the other that it has not been made by any of the processes which we call natural.

Science is incompetent to reason upon the creation of matter itself out of nothing. We have reached the utmost limit of our thinking faculties when we have admitted that, because matter cannot be eternal and self-existent, it must have been created. It is only when we contemplate not matter in itself, but the form in which it actually exists, that our mind finds something on which it can lay hold. That matter as such should have any fundamental properties, that it should exist in space and be capable of motion, that its motion should be persistent, and so on, are truths which may, for anything that we know, be of the kind which metaphysicians call necessary. We may use our knowledge of such truths for purposes of deduction, but we have no data for speculating as to their origin. But that there should be exactly so much matter, and no more, in every molecule of hydrogen, is a fact of a very different order. We have here a particular distribution of matter, a collocation—to use the expression of Dr. Chalmers—of things which we have no difficulty in imagining to have been arranged otherwise. The form and dimensions of the orbits of the planets, for instance, are not determined by any law of nature, but depend upon a particular collocation of matter. The same is the case with respect to the size of the earth, from which the standard of what is called the metrical system has been derived. But these astronomical and terrestrial magnitudes are far inferior in scientific importance to that most fundamental of all standards, which forms the base of the molecular system. Natural causes, as we know, are at work which tend to modify, if they do not destroy, all the arrangements and the dimensions of the earth, and the whole solar system. But though in the course of ages catastrophes have occurred, and may yet occur, in the heavens, though ancient systems may be destroyed, and new systems evolved out of their ruins, the molecules out of which these systems are built, the foundation-stones of the material Universe, remain unbroken and unworn. They continue this day as they were created, perfect in number and measure and weight, and from the ineffaceable character impressed on them we may learn that those aspirations after accuracy in measurement, truth in statement, and justice in action, which we reckon amongst our noblest attributes as men, are ours because they are essential constituents of the image of Him who in the beginning created not only the heaven and the earth, but also the materials of which heaven and earth consist.'

Here we have an argument for an intelligent and moral first cause which may, if I understand it rightly, be stated thus. The atoms of the primary substances of matter have a character which suggests the work of a designing will. They are like 'manufactured articles.' This character, I presume, is seen in the similarity of the atoms of the same primary substance to one another, and in the affinities of the atoms of different substances for one another. Hence ultimately their capacity to build up the Universe.

This special character of theirs was essential at least to much of the order, arrangement, adaptation, and mechanism which we see in the natural world. And indeed, apart from its potentially involving much of the present character of the Universe, we are also to see in it, considered by itself, an evidence that there is in the Divine mind something corresponding to our desire of 'accuracy in measurement, truth in statement, and justice in action.' But it is not a character which they could have acquired by any evolution, for they are primitive and unchangeable. Natural selection, which may have done much to accomplish the wonders of animal mechanism, has no place here, for the things concerned have always been the same, so far as we can tell, through all the revolutions of nature. Hence it is reasonable to attribute that special character to the immediate appointment of a Creator who foresaw its results.

The following question arises. If it be granted that with our present knowledge we can point to no natural agency that would modify or produce the character of an atom, are we therefore justified in saying that no such agency ever existed ? Because we do not know the natural cause of any phenomenon—nay, if you will, cannot conjecture how it could have had a natural cause at all—is it safe at once to pronounce it supernatural ?

The atoms of the primary substances cannot, it is true, at present be resolved by chemists. But it has been at least plausibly conjectured that they might be composed of still more elementary atoms.[1] Dr. Prout put forth such a conjecture. His particular theory that they were composed of atoms in different combinations, each the half in weight of a hydrogen atom, has not perhaps been sufficiently verified so far. But there are resemblances among the atoms of certain of the primary substances which give encouragement to the idea of a common origin or composition. And of late Mr. Lockyer, arguing from Father Secchi's observations on the spectra of different stars, has given support to the idea, that what are in our experience atoms of different elementary substances, may be resolved, under intense heat, into some more elementary form of matter.[2] These facts of course make for the idea that the chemically indissoluble atom, as we know it, is not a primitive form of matter, but a result of some process.

[1] See 'The Unseen Universe,' chap. v.
[2] Address of M. Wurtz, No. of 'Nature' for August 27, 1874.

I do not insist upon the truth of these views. All I would urge is, that they have at least a better right to acceptance than the theory of immediate divine action. I would urge that this referring of inexplicable facts to such action has been shown to be mistaken innumerable times. The progress of physical science has been continually exposing such errors. There was a time when men saw in the motions of the sun and moon, in the winds, lightnings, pestilence, eclipse—nay, almost every phenomenon of nature—the working not of law but of some personal agent.[1] Even so great a natural philosopher as Sir Isaac Newton gave a striking example of this propensity.

By his theory of gravitation he explained generally the motions of the heavenly bodies; but he perceived that there would be upon his principles certain small disturbances and irregularities,[2] arising from the fact that the planets would attract one another even as the sun attracted them, though in far less degree. He thought that these disturbances would accumulate, and in time destroy our system. He did not fall back on the idea that there might be

[1] Tylor's 'Primitive Culture,' chaps. xv., xvi., xvii.
[2] Sir Isaac Newton's works edited by Dr. Horsley, London, 1782, vol. iv. p. 262, 3rd book of 'Optics.' Newton's words are: 'For while comets move in very excentric orbits in all manner of positions, blind fate could never make all the planets move in one and the same way in orbits concentric, some considerable irregularities excepted, which may have arisen from the mutual actions of the comets and planets upon one another, and which will be apt to increase till the system wants a reform.'

some provision in nature against this result, which his investigations had not been minute enough to detect, but he conjectured that the Almighty would, when the necessity arose, personally interfere and rectify the disorder. But the more complete and profound investigations of later astronomers, who have adopted his theory and worked it out, have shown that his apprehensions were groundless. Our solar system is so constructed that the disturbances, whose existence Newton rightly conjectured, do not tend permanently to accumulate. They only grow to a certain extent, then wane, and so run through successive cycles.[1] There is no need, at all events, from this cause, of miraculous intervention to preserve the system. Still, this last idea keeps its ground. Even till our own day it was very generally thought that the origin of the different species of plants and animals could be explained only in this way. The great geologist[2] who has just been taken from amongst us gave a fine example of scientific candour when he recanted that opinion. We have witnessed also a similar change of opinion as to the origin of human speech and civilisation.[3] Surely, with all these examples before us, we should not be

[1] See Pratt's 'Mechanical Philosophy,' Art. 379-383.
[2] Sir C. Lyell.
[3] See Prof. Max Müller's 'Lectures on the Science of Language.' Sir J. Lubbock's 'Origin of Civilisation.'

in haste to affirm the impossibility of natural explanation or the need of personal divine intervention.

These remarks apply to every case in which, because our natural philosophy is at fault, we fall back upon the *Deus ex machinâ*. The controversy as to the first origin of life affords another instance. Here, too, a theological conclusion has been drawn. If life, we are told, can in a natural way only originate from life, then, since we know that it did not exist on our planet at a remote period of her history, we have proof, even accepting the theory of development, that it must originally have been introduced here in some supernatural way. In the first place, I would refer to the explanation proposed by Thomson and Helmholtz, viz. the possible introduction of life upon our globe by the presence of a germ of life in one of the innumerable meteors which fall upon it. I allow the difficulty attending this theory, on account of the extremes of temperature to which such a body must have been exposed. But I do not see that it is absolutely incredible, and, if admitted, it may put back the origin of life indefinitely. In any case, I would again recur to the idea sanctioned by Prof. Huxley,[1] if I understand him rightly, that though within our present observation life does never originate with inanimate matter, we are not

---

[1] Address to the British Association for the Advancement of Science at Liverpool, 1870.

therefore positively to conclude that it never has done so in any state of our planet, or still more of the universe at large.

Before leaving this part of my subject, I would observe that my objections are directed against these scientific arguments as first-cause arguments. I do not see that they prove a beginning, and so establish the doctrine of a Creator. I may be reminded that I have been in reality opposing a conjecture to a fact. We cannot at present, I allow, produce with confidence any natural explanation of the primitive character of atoms, or of the origin of life. I meet that fact by the conjecture that we may discover some such explanation hereafter. It is too soon yet to say that there cannot be any such explanation. Now thus to rely on conjecture it may be said is contrary to my own views elsewhere expressed. I reply that the conjecture in question, that of future explanation by law, unlike the conjecture that no world but our own is inhabited, has much to say on its own behalf. It is, indeed, suggested by the whole of the past history of science. I would also observe that these arguments, even if allowed, do never attain the full force of a proof for a first cause. They come short in this respect of what the old cosmological argument professes at least to prove. They only show anomalous causation. Something must have acted not in accordance with known laws. But that something may have been the end of a series of finite causes. It is not necessarily self-existent. I know that the idea of a will readily arises, but this is really due to another view of the facts that have been before us, that which sees in them ground for the Design argument. Or more probably this idea arises from our thinking of a will as a first cause, a belief which is at least open to question.

To pursue my distinction as to the force of these objections I would further point out that they do not apply to the features in the character or history of the universe that have been under consideration, looked at as evidence of a God, because they show design. If the present order of nature, or, in other words, the code of her laws, has marks of design, as indeed I believe that it has, it does not lose the significance which it has so acquired by being thought of as resulting naturally from some previous order. The difference thus made is only a distinction on which I shall often have occasion to dwell, between purpose accomplished by a plan and by immediate intervention. Nor yet, if the fact that all atoms of hydrogen are alike carries to any mind the conviction of Divine appointment, should it cease to do so if it be shown that this fact also has its place in the orderly scheme of nature. But I must add that the grounds of the Design argument do not seem to me to be strengthened by thus looking back to the properties of elementary matter. This bare making of all hydrogen atoms alike does not, I think, do much to establish the existence of a wise and good creator, as I have elsewhere pointed out. That conclusion is in reality suggested by some remote consequences, as I have said, in animal mechanism. We have no right to look upon all the wonders of such mechanism as specially contemplated and provided for in the original properties of matter. We must bear in mind how much the process of their actual production, upon Mr. Darwin's hypothesis, takes away from this idea, viz. that matter was originally created and endowed with a special view to bringing them about. I have asserted that, with all abatements, the facts of animal and human life do seem to me to indicate at least an intelligent Creator. But I do not think that this present way of looking at the matter heightens their effect for that end, nor yet that we shall find much, apart from the phenomena of life, which will help us to such theological conclusions. If the nature and properties of atoms had done nothing more than produce a chaos of fire like the sun, or a barren rock like the moon, would they have suggested the thought of a wise and good Creator?

I will not say more on the various forms of the first cause argument, but, before going on to another class of arguments, I would say something as to a work which has just appeared—' The Unseen

Universe.' It is a book remarkable for the acquaintance shown with the present progress of physical science, and for the boldness and originality of some of its speculations. The writers assume a position precisely opposed to that of the first-cause arguments. They persistently assert the doctrine of continuity, sketched by Sir W. R. Grove in his well-known address to the British Association at Nottingham. This doctrine is what I have already spoken of as the growing belief of scientific men, viz. that the present state of the universe has grown out of past states, by the steady and uninterrupted action of general laws. There have been no breaks, no incoming of anomalous powers unrelated to this scheme of things. The authors of 'The Unseen Universe'[1] do, indeed, assert the existence of a God. They regard that assertion as in fact self-evident. But they hold that the Divine Being cannot have acted on the universe at any time in a direct, anomalous way, or we should have had breach of continuity. Yet they hold strongly that the present visible universe cannot have been eternal. They explain very clearly the tendency, of which I have spoken, to an ultimate dissipation of energy, a condition of things in which those transformations of energy, which are in fact the source of all the events of our universe, would come to an end. They think,

[1] 'The Unseen Universe,' Art. 54.

indeed, that not only does the visible universe clearly tend thus to a final state of rest, coldness, death, but that possibly its very matter, commonly thought of as indestructible, may come to an end. This last conjecture is founded upon Sir W. Thomson's theory, that an atom is a vortex ring in some invisible perfect fluid, that is, a filament of rotating fluid in the form of some closed or re-entering curve, something to which a twisting smoke wreath would have a rough resemblance. If the fluid were really perfect and frictionless, such a ring vortex would last for ever. This was the character which Sir W. Thomson gave it, but the book in question conjectures that this fluid, the basis of matter, may not be perfect. If, then, our visible universe be finite in duration, certainly as regards its activities, possibly as regards its material, how are we to avoid the idea of creation, how are we to hold to that of continuity? Here comes in the characteristic idea of the book.[1] The present visible universe is supposed to have been produced out of an invisible universe. The connection is not thought of as strictly that of antecedent and consequent. Rather the invisible universe is the contemporary as well as parent of the visible. The latter is, as it were, an island in the former as a sea. Or, to use perhaps a better analogy, even as some phenomenon that we behold,

[1] 'The Unseen Universe,' Art. 216.

say a smoke wreath, is a phenomenon in this visible universe, even so is that stupendous whole but a phenomenon in the yet older and greater unseen universe. And the idea is thrown out that this unseen universe, with which our material universe is immediately connected, may be again only a product of another universe still further removed from us, and so on *ad infinitum*. But a natural connection between these universes is supposed. None of these states of things is a creation in the common sense of that word. Energy, it is thought, may be transferred to our material universe from the unseen universe with which it is immediately connected, or *vice versâ*. The supernatural events alleged in connection with the origin of Christianity are accounted for by the coming in of the powers of this invisible universe. The hope of immortality is held out from the possibility of our personally obtaining a place in that unseen system, but this, it is allowed, cannot be thought of as indicated by science, apart from the resurrection of Christ. The entire stock of energy, whose transformations make up the development of the successive universes, is supposed to be infinite. The intelligent power which directs all these transformations is identified with the Second Person of the Christian Trinity; the source of life with the Third Person.

The fundamental idea of upholding the doctrine of continuity would, I suppose, be approved by many men of science. As I have said, it is not my wish here to attempt a decision as to its truth. It seems to me, indeed, one of those fundamental principles which are not proper subjects for argument, but must be intuitively accepted or modified by every individual mind. But if we accept this principle, there is still a good deal in the scheme which I have briefly and imperfectly sketched that is open to question. To begin with what is said as to God, it may be true that our minds do instinctively think of some mysterious infinite being, as the ground of this visible universe. But the idea to which we are thus led is not that definite conception of God which religious men cherish; it is not that of a being perfect in wisdom and goodness, as well as self-existent or all-powerful. The existence of a being corresponding to this last idea I cannot allow to be 'absolutely self-evident.' And next, to come to the characteristic idea of the book, it may be the most reasonable view to think of this present visible universe as evolved out of one unseen. If, as I have pointed out before, we consider the nature of human knowledge and the general drift of modern discovery, we may conclude that this idea of eternal development is to be preferred to that of absolute creation. But when we consider next the allegation that the present visible universe, as known to us, cannot have existed from eternity, or exist to eternity, by reason of the dissipation of energy, we see the objections which I have pointed out when considering that physical truth in connection with the arguments for a God. The conclusion does not follow without assumptions as to the limits in the diffusion of matter in past times, its finite amount, the unreasonableness of looking forward to a final state of coldness, darkness, and death. And if all these assumptions be made, they only lead us to the idea of some universe or state of the universe antecedent to that which now is, and differing as to its laws from it, and also of something so differing hereafter. They do not establish that this unseen universe is still in existence. On the contrary, the idea of causation, which makes it consist in the transformation of energy, clearly implies that the parent universe must have given place to the present. At least we have no evidence of the existence of any surviving part. Nor, indeed, do I see that we can have such evidence, unless we admit the accounts of the Spiritualists, or some other accounts of what are thought to be supernatural events, say the Christian miracles. For my own part, I am quite ready to believe in such an unseen universe, to look upon it as it is here put forward as the probable ground of what is seen, and to welcome it as the possible explanation of much which we wish to believe, but feel to be open to the objection of being supernatural. But I cannot say that I think that the authors of 'The Unseen Universe' have shown a scientific foundation for this faith. They bring forward a supposed absorption of light, as it is being transmitted through the luminiferous ether.[1] Their evidence for this supposition is a speculation of Struve, in which such an absorption is inferred from the observed brightness of the fixed stars, as compared with their supposed distribution in space. But this speculation rests, as our authors themselves tell us, upon much that is doubtful. They mention that it was not accepted by Sir John Herschel. And even if it be true, it would not follow that the energy which thus disappeared in the absorption of light must pass into some other unseen universe. It might be diffused over the ether in some other form than light. Nor yet is it clearly made out that the universe out of which our visible universe has proceeded contains life and intelligence. As to the first point, the only real reason given is the impossibility of abiogenesis; that is to say, life must have sprung from life. Therefore, it must have come into our universe from its predecessor. I have already explained the reservations under which I think that we should admit this allegation. As to the second point, reliance is placed upon the uniformity of atoms, of which also I have spoken already.

[1] 'The Unseen Universe,' Arts. 147 and 208.

PART V.

I will now speak of a fresh class of arguments, founded on a basis altogether distinct.

No one can doubt that our moral feelings have done much to suggest, to define, and to strengthen our ideas of God. Further, many thinkers have believed that they could find in those feelings an independent proof of the existence of God. Thus Kant argued that the existence of God was needed to harmonise the authority of the moral law with our instinctive desire of happiness. Conscience often dictates a course which, so far as we can see, is at variance with our natural care for self. A God is needed to bear the good man out in his course, to make the way of right ultimately the way of happiness as well. If there be no such power our nature is divided into contradictory and hostile principles. This argument has been disallowed by writers as widely apart as Dean Mansel and Dr. Strauss. It has been condemned as inconsistent with the Christian doctrine of man's unworthiness in the sight of God, and again as opposed to enlightened views of human happiness, views which make virtue by itself apart from any outward reward the greatest source of happiness. I do not think much of these objections. God's government does make a difference between the good man and the bad, however imperfect and blended the character of either may be, or else there is an end of all religion. And, again, man's happiness is undoubtedly affected from many outward sources. He 'has too much weakness for the Stoic's part.' There are many trials for the good man; yea, often for the best of men. The alleged basis of our argument is true as regards the account which it gives of human nature, but at the same time I do not think that it is an adequate foundation for what that argument builds upon it. For it is obviously open to this criticism. The indications of conscience and of self-love may be really opposed —one or the other may be misleading—it is a mere assumption to say that there must be some unknown fact to reconcile the two. Still more would a similar criticism apply to another simpler form of the moral argument. It has been said that the bare existence in the mind of that law of right and wrong pointed to a lawgiver, that is to God. Here, as Mr. Mill has pointed out, there seems to be some confusion as to the meaning of the word law. The law of conscience is self-asserting. Its authority is intuitively felt. It is not dependent, like that of human law, upon the sanction of some external lawgiver. In both these arguments no safe objective basis for a belief in God is established. And we cannot accordingly regard them as adequate independent arguments for his existence. But if his existence as a conscious and intelligent Being can be otherwise shown, then I think that the facts of conscience do throw a very valuable light upon his character. Let us recall the conclusions of the argument from Design. That argument may have failed to prove the existence of God according to the full conception of his attributes, eternal, omnipresent, infinite in power, wisdom, and goodness. But it did give us reason to believe that the universe was fashioned and ruled by a Being in whose general appointments we could trace purposes wise and good. I say in his general appointments. For it must, I think, be allowed that we often fail to do so in the particular appointments of his Providence. Nor is there anything in this latter fact inconsistent with the hypothesis of a wise and good God. For in attempting to trace the purposes of such a Being, in any of his appointments, we are plainly open to this great source of error, that we may but imperfectly know the bearings and connections of the appointment according to the scheme of things which he has ordained. Now this obvious source of error is much less likely to mislead us in the case of some broad general appointment, whose results we can trace in a great variety of cases, as in the fact that a sense of obligation attends the dictates of conscience, than in the case of some special individual appointment, say the death of a good and truly useful man, where we can see only one immediate effect, and are possibly ignorant of other connections. The risk of our being misled from ignorance of such other results is as a mere matter of probability less when we see the appointment as in the general case cited occurring in a great variety of circumstances. It may perhaps be said that there are such general appointments, and some even in which from analogy we should most expect to see traceable Design, in which we fail to do so. Our remarks upon the appearance of waste in nature may perhaps explain the common cases of this kind, but of those special cases just alluded to I will say a word or two more, as they may seem to have a resemblance to this case of the moral faculty. The atrophied or aborted organs in man or animals are a good example. Some, indeed, are parts of the same organism as the faculty in question. I would remark, however, that probably they have had a use at some former period of the animal's development. They are remains, or survivals, so to speak, of what had once an important function. If, then, we take a wide view, we cannot confidently say that they have been introduced without a purpose. And certainly they are no fit analogues for the moral faculty. For the latter is certainly not a dying out or a functionless part of human nature. Rather, we hope that it has a growing power, and certainly it is very closely connected with the best interests of our race. There is no other part of that nature of like importance in which we do not trace Design. Indeed, if Divine purpose can be read anywhere, surely it must be here in something so important. And if we do accept this view, if we do venture to attribute to God that purpose which the nature of the fact before us suggests, then we have a strong intimation of his character. He has placed within us a faculty dictating right, forbidding wrong. It speaks with authority. We feel that it is the proper law of our nature. We conclude, accordingly, that it was meant by our Maker to be the rule of our conduct. And we say also that it bears witness to the goodness of God himself. For we cannot believe that an evil being would implant in his creatures a law of righteousness. There is something in the nature of right which makes us think that, if any conscious being should prescribe it to another as obligatory, he must recognise that obligation himself. He who ordained truth, justice, and charity to be the rule of conduct for man, must himself be true, and just, and good.

There are one or two objections that may be taken to this reasoning which I would notice. Some may say, you speak of conscience as teaching us about God. But what do you mean by this abstract conscience? As a matter of fact, we know only the conscience of each individual man.[1] And we find that these individual consciences speak very differently. They differ even amongst us. They differ still more widely and decidedly if we extend our view to other ages and countries. It has been said that there is hardly anything in human conduct, not even what we count the grossest immoralities, as prostitution, robbery, parricide, which some nation or other may not be found to have approved.[2] Which, then, is the true and authoritative conscience —the standard conscience, so to speak? When individual consciences contradict one another so decidedly, is not the testimony of any of them made questionable?

This difficulty may look formidable at first sight. And of course it does show that any knowledge of God, which we may derive from conscience, must be subject to correction. It cannot be looked upon as certain and infallible. But this is not the same thing as being wholly uncertain and worthless. It is only an admission, which we have to make as to much the greater part of all our knowledge, and what is especially to be noticed, as to that part

---

[1] See 'Maurice on the Conscience,' Lect. II.; and Bain on the 'Emotions and Will.'

[2] For evidence, see Sir J. Lubbock's 'Origin of Civilization,' chaps. iii. and vii.

of our knowledge which is most practically important. Those things which concern us most, as the conditions of health or prosperity, are often matters of uncertainty. The lesser differences in moral judgment among contemporaries at the same stage of civilization may fairly be paralleled by differences of opinion among them upon many other subjects, and so also may those greater differences between men of different times. Man's knowledge is essentially progressive. To say this, indeed, is only to assert the truism that his intellect is finite. As a matter of fact, the views of civilized man have changed less upon moral subjects than upon many others. Moral science has altered less in the last two thousand years than astronomy, geography, geology, natural history, or indeed perhaps any science except the geometrical. As a basis of inference with regard to God it would certainly be found less shifting than the knowledge of creation, upon which the argument from Design is built. Nor does it want signs of assuming, like other knowledge, a more fixed and certain character as time goes on. We see that certain moral truths receive a wider and wider assent. It has often been observed, and indeed it is clear beyond contradiction, that the feeling of sympathy, so fundamental in morals, has very visibly strengthened in these latter days. Perhaps the most striking feature in the vivid picture which Macaulay has drawn of our forefathers two hundred years ago, is the absence of that 'sensitive humanity' which certainly may often be seen in our days. Even at one of the most dark and discouraging epochs of modern history, amidst all the material evils and moral perversion which sprang out of the convulsions and wars of the first French revolution and empire, Mackintosh was still able to point out that certain crimes, as political assassinations, which disgraced such struggles at no distant time before, had then disappeared. There is growing up, in fact, a consensus on moral subjects throughout the civilised world which may not unreasonably claim to be a beginning of that universal conscience which is asked for. And we see also that the conviction of moral truth deepens as well as widens, inasmuch as its power becomes greater to mould public opinion, to correct public evils, and to withstand hostile influences, as those of a superstitious religious belief.

A second objection may be raised by a certain class of thinkers. I allude to the believers in evolution, whose opinions I have particularly in view in these essays. The idea that the moral faculty may not be a primary part of our nature but a result of the action of others as the mind develops, like the love of money, did not by any means originate with them. It may be found, for instance, in the writings of Adam Smith. But it is of course a necessary part of their system. Man's brute progenitors were unquestionably devoid of such a faculty. And the hypothesis has undoubtedly gained credibility in their hands by the bringing in of the notion of inherited tendencies of feeling and thought. Herein the theories of Mr. Spencer and Mr. Darwin have an advantage over older views. It is to the latter writer[1] that we owe the most complete and definite theory of the kind. He has explained the rise of moral sentiments in man, at least plausibly, from social influences, from sympathy with our fellow men, and sensibility to their praise and blame, and furthermore the rise of a sense of obligation to a given course, and of repentance, when it has been departed from, by the greater persistence of the sympathetic than of the selfish feelings. Now I do not wish to discuss the truth of this particular theory, or of any other. I desire only to point out that such a theory does not affect the force of our reasoning. That peculiar significance of the moral sense upon which I have relied arises from its dictates being attended by this feeling of obligation. Hence the alleged indication of the Divine will and character. Now we must look upon this feeling as implanted by God, as much, if we adopt the supposition which makes human nature to have been gradually

[1] See Mr. Darwin's 'Descent of Man,' Part I. ch. iii.

evolved by the action of natural laws and circumstances, as if we held the older view of special creation. In either case it is a work of God. The difference is only in our idea of the Divine action. We have the older conception in one case, the more modern in the other. Certainly the latter is more in harmony with that unquestionable progress in the moral faculty which we have recognised; nor can I see that either the authority or the dignity of this faculty is lowered by such a theory as Mr. Darwin's, although I find that an opposite view is expressed by an able writer of our day, Miss Cobbe.[1]

PART VI.

I have now reviewed as many of the arguments of National Theology as it seems to me needful to notice. There may be others, but I do not think that the consideration of them would bring before us anything further of real weight in this inquiry. It is not, for example, pertinent to consider the value of a belief in God, however great that value may be. For now our question is simply as to the truth, and

[1] See 'Darwinism in Morals,' the first of a series of essays by Miss F. P. Cobbe.

not the usefulness of the belief. I will endeavour then, as a conclusion to my essay, to show how this great and solemn question of the existence and attributes of God should in my opinion be dealt with. My remarks upon the moral argument will perhaps have indicated already the course which is I think to be taken. Singly, none of our arguments suffice, but combined they give an evidence which is sufficient for the practical purposes of religion, if not for proving all the definitions of theology. In the first place, the Design argument does give evidence for one intelligent ruler of the world whose general purposes, at all events, we can apprehend and approve; next the moral argument on the assumption of this result bears witness to the perfect goodness of this Being. That goodness again assures us that his power must be at least equal to all that a perfect moral government requires at his hands. The Design argument by itself leaves us in doubt as to this last point. It may show that his wisdom and power are inconceivably great, but yet not infinite. But if he is perfectly good we may be sure that he has not ordained righteousness for the law of his creatures, without being able to bear them out in obedience. Our faith in him is raised above that sphere of strict inference from facts within which the causation argument must leave us. Even the first cause argument may acquire some force when thus taken in combination. If there be an instinct in our minds to believe in a first cause as the ultimate ground of phenomena, an instinct certainly not universal, but which tends to become so with the progress of the human mind, then, as in the case of the moral sense, this mental instinct acquires a value as evidence on the supposition of an intelligent and righteous maker of the world. I feel bound, however, to say that this tendency seems to me very doubtful. I am disposed to think that the tendency is really the other way. And unless that tendency were made out, I for one should not much rely on the alleged instinct. Mr. Mill's [1] cautions against trusting to supposed intuitions, as evidence of external fact, are certainly not without some reasonable grounds. We see, as a matter of fact, how able men, under different circumstances of knowledge and habits of mind, assert opposite dicta, as intuitions. Compare, for instance, Dr. Samuel Clark or Mr. Birks with the authors of the 'Unseen Universe.' The former see intuitively that there must have been a creation, the latter cannot admit a breach of continuity. On the other hand, I may add that when we reason as we have done, the mere fact that man's nature possesses faculties for worship which are never more conspicuous than in some of the best and wisest of men, that it has

[1] Mill's 'Autobiography,' p. 226.

sentiments of wonder, awe, trust, hope, love, which seem to find their only adequate object in a God of infinite perfection, may also be looked upon as an indication worthy of attention. This is plainly one of those general appointments in the interpretation of which we may have greater confidence than in that of particular events.

Such is the conclusion which I would propose to our inquiry. But I must allow that it is open to an objection which I am bound to consider. Are, it may be asked, all these arguments, whose results you assert, and which you make to help out one another, consistent? Is there anything in the method or in the results of one which does not agree with those of another? Now there are two cases of such alleged opposition. We will examine them both.

The first is between the Design argument and the moral argument. It is, indeed, the ancient and inveterate difficulty of theology, the existence of evil. In the Design argument we infer God's attributes from his works. Now we cannot shut our eyes to the fact that there is in the creation not only pain but also sin to a most serious extent. How are we to reconcile this fact with that perfect goodness which the moral argument attributes to God?

I have spoken of this subject already, when

criticising the argument from Design, and I then came to the conclusion that the Design argument could not establish the perfect goodness of God. The question now before us is different. We have to ask not does the argument from Design suffice to prove God's goodness, but does it disprove the conclusion to that effect suggested by the moral argument? If we take the teaching of our conscience as indicative of the character of God, is this evidence irreconcilable with the evidence from God's works?

Mr. Mill[1] has thought this difficulty so insuperable that he could not hold, in the face of it, the belief in an omnipotent God. He had, indeed, less right than we to insist upon the goodness of God, because he did not hold the authoritative and therefore significant character of the moral faculty. It was not to him a revelation of God's character. And consequently he had not this independent evidence of the goodness of God. When he sought to prove that goodness he could only point to a sort of balance of pleasure-giving over pain-giving contrivances in nature, and accordingly his conclusion did not go further than this, that the happiness of God's creatures was one, not the chief object of his government.[2] God might be all that

[1] Essay, 'Nature,' p. 39. Longmans & Co., London, 1874.
[2] Essay, 'Theism,' p. 192.

the most pious mind had ever thought him to be, but this was all for which we had evidence, and even this qualified estimate of the Divine goodness we cannot, Mr. Mill holds, accept unless we allow either that the power or the wisdom of God is limited. Now according to the views of this essay, we have an evidence on moral grounds for that higher notion of God's goodness, which pious men cherish. And it is therefore still more needful for me than it was with Mr. Mill to show how God's goodness can be reconciled with the existence of evil, to show in fact that our arguments do not contradict one another. We might do this of course by accepting Mr. Mill's view of a limitation either in the power or wisdom of God. There is nothing in any of the arguments upon which I have really relied to forbid this. As I have repeatedly pointed out, the Design argument never proves, nor indeed ever could prove, the infinity of any of the attributes of God; and upon the arguments which aspire to do so, as the *a priori* argument and the cosmological argument, I have not laid stress. There may be a limitation in the power or even in the wisdom of God for anything which we can learn from nature as distinct from revelation. It may be that he could not on this account accomplish a better result than this, that perfect happiness, or at least a great excess of happiness, should be brought about in the long run. That result would justify his creation of the universe. And this admission would suffice to defend the arguments relied upon in this essay; whilst, on the other hand, they could not be reconciled with the idea of imperfect goodness in God. For that would be opposed to the moral argument. I may also say what I think everyone will feel, that the idea of imperfection in power or wisdom on the part of God is vastly to be preferred to that of any imperfection in goodness. This last seems indeed to me the saddest thought in the world. But at the same time this notion of limitation is not the explanation of our great difficulty which I should myself put forward. We are not, I think, rigorously compelled to choose between imperfect goodness on the one hand, or imperfect power or wisdom upon the other. Our views of the relation of God to his creation and our own capacity for judging in the matter are not such as absolutely to shut us up to this dilemma. And I for one should prefer to think that the restraints, if I may so speak, which have led the Divine Being to admit into his works so large an alloy of evil, were restraints arising from his own perfect moral nature and not from physical or intellectual inability, if indeed that former explanation can be made credible. That would of course be a view more compatible with the ideas which good men have generally cherished. I will quote here a few words from Bishop Butler's 'Analogy,' which seem to me possibly to give a hint of such an explanation. 'Perhaps,' says the Bishop, 'Divine goodness with which, if I mistake not, we make very free in our speculations, may not be a bare single disposition to produce happiness, but a disposition to make the good, the faithful, the honest man happy. Perhaps an infinitely perfect mind may be pleased with seeing his creatures behave suitably to the nature which he has given them, to the relations which he has placed them in to each other, and to that which they stand in to himself.'[1] The point in this passage, to which I would call attention, is the suggestion that possibly the disposition of a perfect Being may not be simply to confer happiness in a promiscuous way, but to confer it according to character. The discrimination contemplated by the Bishop refers, it is true, only to man. But I am not sure that something of the same kind may not apply even to the lower animals, wherever indeed there is will or choice even in its lowest forms. Modern Science recognises more community between man and the inferior creation than was recognised formerly.[2] It may of course be asked, if God willed the happiness of his creatures, and if a certain character upon their part

---

[1] 'Analogy,' Part I., chap. ii., p. 35.
[2] See Darwin's 'Descent of Man.'

was needed for him to confer this happiness, consistently with his own nature, why did he not originally bestow this character upon them? They are his works. It may be, I reply, that this character is by its very nature inconsistent with being so bestowed. Moral character may lose its intrinsic worth, if immediately produced by the fiat of God. To say so much as this, I may be told is in effect to recognise some other origin of things than the will of the Creator, to make the course of events depend on something besides his appointment. That independence of him, I would reply, may be. For aught we certainly know it may be consistent with his character that it should be. And certainly to deny this, to take away the liberty of the creature altogether, and resolve everything into the appointment of God, would obliterate moral distinctions in the creature, would subvert the grounds of moral judgment between man and man, and by thus destroying the trustworthiness of our moral faculty, take away the grounds of the very difficulty in question, viz. a judgment of that faculty, and, I need not add, be altogether contrary to the principles of this essay. This disposition, I repeat, upon the part of God to bestow happiness only upon some conditions may be the impossibility in the nature of things which has led the Almighty to adopt the actual scheme of creation, tardy progress beset with long-enduring evils. Still, if the end be a great good, creation is justified, and if the obstacle spoken of existed the drawbacks were unavoidable. I may be told that there should be this excess of happiness for each individual sentient being, or that being at least should not have been created, and this remark would I think be just on the hypothesis of religion which supposes God to contemplate each individual creature. My reply is that there may be, for anything which we know, such a preponderance. Animal happiness we cannot well estimate. I am aware that in the case which we know best, that of man, there is often an appearance of the reverse. But it must be remembered that man may have another life in store, perhaps even animals too. This is at least a credible hypothesis, and it is such an explanation only that we need at present.

The second opposition which we have to consider lies between those arguments which lead up to an idea of God in which nothing is strictly speaking infinite, and those arguments, on the other hand, which profess, as the ontological and the cosmological, to establish the infinity of his attributes. Now I have not at all relied on these latter reasonings, nor am I sure that their professed conclusions are needed for practical religion. But those conclusions are dear to many religious minds; I have myself no idea of denying them. Let us examine, then, how far they are compatible with our other and more trusted arguments.

I would first remark that in the present essay infinity has been ascribed to God only in respect of certain attributes, as with regard to time, space, power, knowledge, goodness. The question is whether our doing this was inconsistent with the conclusions as to God's intelligence and goodness drawn from the Design and from the moral argument. Of the fact that to attribute eternity to God is to set aside, so far as he is concerned, that very law of causation, by which the Design argument attained to a conception of his character, I have spoken already. I have said that the bare idea of an uncaused cause could not be pronounced self-contradictory or absurd. We have now to examine a little more closely how far these unlimited attributes of God consist with the notion of Him as a wise and good intelligence. Of course we cannot represent a Being with such attributes to ourselves by any effort of the imagination. In that sense God's nature is inconceivable. We see at once that his intelligence must be vastly different from our own, the only intelligence from which we can gather an idea of what mind is. We see, for instance, that the Divine mind cannot be closely connected with a complex physical apparatus, as our minds are. Again, we say that there is no limitation in the Divine knowledge. That excludes a number of our most familiar mental acts, as learning, remembering, fixing the attention, inventing. All these things seem out of place with a Being who eternally knows all things. Nay, we cannot understand how, in the case of the Deity, there can be that succession of thoughts, or in other words of states of consciousness which plays so important a part in our own mental history. A consciousness always the same, philosophers have told us, would be no consciousness at all. And yet we cannot see how these mental changes are to be brought about with an eternal and omniscient Being. Perhaps other differences may be pointed out, and no doubt a difficulty arises as to what the nature of the Divine mind can be. Yet upon consideration I believe that none of these differences will hinder us from thinking of God as a supreme mind. They do not, after all, touch the idea of mind so fundamentally as to have that effect. It is at least conceivable that thought should take place independently of brain. If we see traces of mind in the order of the Universe, we are not bound to think ourselves mistaken merely because we cannot imagine that there is a brain in which this mind may reside, or through which it may act. That objection, raised I believe, by Shelley, plainly is not valid.[1] So again the absence in the

---

[1] See 'Christian Theism,' by Thompson, First Burnett Prize, 1855, vol. i. pp. 315-321.

case of God of those limitations which give a character to the mind of man does not after all prevent us from thinking of God as an intelligence. It may be true that it is the succession of thoughts or states of consciousness which leads us to that comparison, classification, perception of relation, and so forth, which does so much to make our minds what they are, and also true that no such succession is conceivable in the case of God. But still the important point for the mental result is the discernment of the differences and the succeeding changes in the Universe itself. With us of course the perception, of the latter at least, necessarily arises from changes in the state of consciousness itself. But for anything which we know, this perception might equally well exist in an eternal and omniscient mind. There might be a simultaneous and everlasting knowledge of all things, and all their relations. Perhaps some one might doubt whether such a manifold consciousness could consist with personal unity. It seems, however, that even in the case of man, the phenomena of unconscious cerebration show that there may be different simultaneous actions of the same mind. Thought, I allow, as it exists in God, must be very different from thought in us; but not so different as to lose its character as thought altogether. We must bear in mind that everything is known to us but in a partial and a relative way.

In that respect Theology only resembles every other science. We know things only as they are manifested in relation to us. We anticipate another like manifestation from our experience of a former. We say that the hypothesis of a world-maker of transcendent intelligence explains the phenomena within our experience. We adopt that hypothesis as a guide for our expectations of the future. This is exactly the process which we follow in all our dealings with outward phenomena. To enter upon the question how far the extension of the method to the Universe at large is just, would of course be re-opening an inquiry of which I have spoken already. We are concerned now with the question how far other considerations, especially the absence of certain limitations, show that God cannot be the being whom this hypothesis requires. And I repeat that whatever difficulty may attend conceiving his character, still so long as infinity is attributed to him only as it has been in the arguments of this essay, no case is established for rejecting the conclusion of the Design, or of the Moral argument. For anything that we certainly know, the material Universe may be infinite in time and space. Yet we can obtain some very useful information concerning it. I fully go with Mr. Matthew Arnold in his protests against the anthropomorphism of the 'magnified non-natural man,' but still I think that we may cherish some more definite idea of God than that of 'a tendency which maketh for righteousness.' But the question of the existence and character of God have been approached in a different way and certainly with different results. In the first place, God was identified with certain metaphysical conceptions, the Infinite, the Absolute, the First Cause. It was then sought to deduce his attributes logically from these conceptions, and no doubt contradictions did arise. In our own country two eminent writers, with very different purposes, have followed out this line of argument; Dean Mansel[1] and Mr. Herbert Spencer.[2] The conclusion to which they came was that our minds cannot form rational and consistent notions of God, at least as he is in himself. I will endeavour briefly to explain their position, and for this end I must say something first as to the meaning of the terms quoted above, again I fear at the risk of being tedious to those acquainted with philosophical language. The words Infinite and First Cause are soon explained. The first is taken absolutely, as that which is wholly unlimited, that from which nothing is excluded, the total of all things actual and possible. First Cause has that meaning which I have put upon it in the cosmological argument. It is the initial link

---

[1] 'Limits of Religious Thought,' Bampton Lectures by Dean Mansel, Lect. II.
[2] 'First Principles,' by Herbert Spencer, chap. iv. See also 'Mill's Examination of Sir W. Hamilton's Philosophy,' chap. vii.

in the great chain of phenomena or perhaps more correctly the underived origin of all things. But about the word Absolute I must speak at some greater length. To begin, I would remark that we know things only in relation to our own faculties for knowing them physical and mental. Mr. Mill[1] has defined matter to be 'a permanent possibility of sensation,' and however harsh and repugnant to our common ideas such a definition may sound, it is really a true account of what mere experience teaches to us. That is all which mere sensation makes known. But philosophers as well as the vulgar believe that there is a something which causes our sensations—a something which they call a noumenon, and which would probably in popular language be best expressed as the thing in itself. Now noumena, or things in themselves, it is acknowledged that we cannot know. We know only their relations to us. So far therefore all the world of our knowledge is relative. But this relativity strikes deeper. For we have reason to believe that the very noumena, or things in themselves, exist in constant relation to one another, and furthermore acquire those very properties which we apprehend in relation to our faculties, only from those relations to one another. Whatever it may be which is at the bottom of what we call their position, size, colour, weight, hardness,

[1] 'Examination of Sir W. Hamilton's Philosophy,' p. 198.

temperature, and the like, it can always be shown that some relation to something else, as for instance the relation of cause and effect, is always concerned therein. Hence we see that an absolute, a thing in itself out of relation to anything else, is removed altogether out of our knowledge. Yet we do mentally conceive that there is such a thing. We do so if it be only by contrast. Hence comes the idea of the Absolute, an idea, be it observed, which is only a creation of the mind, and that of a negative and undefined sort, not a mental creation like the hypotheses of natural philosophy, which are framed to explain facts of observation and in accordance with laws or analogies of nature. Before leaving this part of my subject I ought perhaps to add that some variation or ambiguity seems to have attended the use of this word Absolute. Sometimes it seems to have stood for that which *may* exist out of relation, as explained above; sometimes for that which must do so. But I do not think that we shall find this distinction important in our argument. In the views which we have now to consider it is, as I have said, taken for granted that the three terms which I have now endeavoured to explain express the nature of God.[1] Upon that assumption it is certainly easy to show that our ideas of God lead to contradictions. For example, it may be remarked that the idea of First

---

[1] See Mansel's Bampton Lectures, Lect. II.

Cause is inconsistent with that of the Absolute, because cause is a relation. Now if to avoid this objection we adopt the meaning of the word Absolute given first, and say that though God did at first exist as a pure absolute out of relation to anything, yet by an act of his will, what is commonly called creation, he passed into relation to his creatures, then we are met by the objection that an act of will implies consciousness, and consciousness implies a subject and an object. But this notion of God as a subject distinct from something else as an object is inconsistent not only with our ideas of him as Absolute but also as Infinite. For what is this which is not included in him, if he be the Infinite as it was defined a little while ago? And further does not this creation seem to make him different from what he was before, which is contrary to the full idea of the Infinite? Does it not add something to the sum total of things?

Without pursuing such reasonings any further, I would at once challenge their foundation. Can we justify the preliminary assumption? Have we a right thus to form abstract notions of the Infinite, Absolute, First Cause, and then say that they represent God? What objective foundation have we here, any more than in the *à priori* or ontological arguments? Is it not safer far to reason from some data of experience, according to rules which have guided us safely in other investigations? Of course this last process could never reveal, or profess to reveal, what God is in himself. It can only teach us of God in relation to ourselves and our own faculties. But what other knowledge do we want, or indeed what other knowledge are we capable of?

I have now finished my discussion of the subject of this essay, and have but a few more words to say. I would again acknowledge that my arguments do not pretend to prove the infinity of the attributes of God. From the very nature of the case such proof cannot be given, or pretended to be given, unless more stress be laid upon our mental intuitions, or what are taken to be such, than I have ventured to lay. Such proofs lie out of the range of that experimental philosophy which I regard as the rising system of thinking at the present day, and to which I have endeavoured to conform my reasoning. But at the same time I have aimed and hoped to show that this philosophy did not disclaim all knowledge of God—that even its most advanced forms, which account for our most axiomatic convictions and most imperative moral feelings by habit and inheritance, still leave a stable foundation upon which we may build a belief in a Divine Ruler of the world, one whose perfections, if not proved to be infinite, are still shown to be all that a perfect moral government for ourselves requires. For that end I have assumed only that inductive principle which is at the foundation of all our knowledge, and which the experimental philosophy at all events will not challenge. I have tried to keep clear of all doubtful philosophical questions—to make my arguments equally valid for the materialist, the idealist, or the dualist; for him who holds the atomic or the dynamic theory, or any other theory, of matter; for the disciple of Locke or of Kant, or of the modern physiological philosophy. My principal point has been the combination of the Design and the Moral arguments, and my principal weakness, so far as I myself can judge, will be found in the significance given to the moral faculty. I acknowledge that point to be vital, and I would wish accordingly as I conclude to say one word more in its defence. It is simply this, that the significance upon which I have relied is based upon a mental fact of world-wide experience, the sense of obligation attending the dictates of conscience.

ESSAY II.

THE MIRACULOUS EVIDENCE OF CHRISTIANITY.

PART I.

IN a former essay I have examined the evidence which we possess as to the existence and attributes of God in the appearance of nature, and in our own moral and intellectual faculties. The question which is now to come before us, if stated in its most general form, would stand thus: Has God made known to us anything concerning himself or our relations to him otherwise than by the evidence just named? Has he, for example, marked out in any way any human teachers as authorised by him to instruct us on those subjects? This I say would be the general question. But practically a narrower inquiry will suffice. It is the Christian revelation only which we need to consider, and further in this essay I mean to speak only of the evidence from the Gospel miracles, and shall not examine the argument from prophecy, from place in the apparent plan of the world's history, or from moral characteristics.

The argument from miracles was founded upon that view of God which represents him as conducting the affairs of the world partly by a system of general laws, partly by occasional interferences. The order of nature was the rule, but there were exceptions. Creation was such an exception, and it was an exception which had been often repeated. Not only was the Almighty thought to have originally called the universe into existence out of nothing, but he was also thought to have planted man, and indeed every distinct species of animals and plants, upon the earth, by a special creative act. In like manner, he had broken in upon the course of nature to make a change in man's spiritual state. The bare facts which had thus arisen, when looked at only in the light of natural science, were anomalies. A man had prophesied the future, cured the sick, stilled the tempest, raised the dead. But when all the circumstances of the case were taken into account, and interpreted by the light of God's moral attributes according to the doctrine of final causes, then these anomalies became signs, attestations direct from God. Such was the evidential argument from miracles, upon which so much stress was laid by Christian writers of the last century in this country. At an earlier period, in superstitious times, an abundance of miracles, which had no connection with Christian evidences, had been believed. But the evidential argument rejected these. Plainly it behoved that argument to show not only that its own miracles were true, but that others were false. At all events, it was essential to disprove miracles that were wild, arbitrary, or mischievous. Otherwise the notion that miracles arise from the interference of other beings than God, perhaps even evil beings, would have support. It is clear that the growth of a belief in the prevalence of law in nature must have greatly affected the reception of this argument. In one respect it favoured the argument. It strengthened our feeling that a miracle was an exception. The force of such an event, as a proof of Divine interference and attestation, arose from the conviction that it was an infraction upon natural law, and that no one but God the law-giver could effect such an interruption. Hence, as the reign of law seemed to extend and cover the face of nature, any seeming exception which remained appeared more and more as an occasion upon which the Almighty had departed from his usual course of proceeding; had, so to speak, come forth in person upon the stage of the world's history, and had dealt with man directly. There was less thought of any other supernatural explanation—less thought, for instance, of magic or of diabolic interference. But at the same time, if the belief in law sharpened the significance of miracles, it tended also to undermine all belief that they had ever occurred. And this latter effect was the more conspicuous of the two. It may be said that this last influence was at the bottom of all the most celebrated sceptical works of modern times.

About the middle of last century Hume[1] put forth his well-known position : it is contrary to experience that a miracle should be true, but not contrary to experience that testimony should be false. Considered as an objection to accounts of miracles, this argument is not very precisely stated, and certainly it is not so summarily conclusive as its author seems to have thought. For to say absolutely that miracles are contrary to experience, *i.e.* have never occurred, is to beg the question, and was not indeed Hume's meaning. And again, if we say only that from experience we have an induction against the occurrence of miracles, whilst we have no such induction against the falsehood of testimony, we may be met by the following answer. Testimony is not all alike. On the contrary, it is of the most varied strength. And there is some testimony so strong that the experimental induction, in its favour, may be as strong as the induction against a miracle. Such testimony was never known to be false.[2] Indeed,

---

[1] Hume's ' Essay on Miracles.'
[2] See Hume's ' Essay on Miracles.' The case which he supposes

Hume himself allowed the existence of such testimony, and specified an instance of what he would regard as such irresistible evidence. There was then ground for inquiry as to the case of Christianity. It would be reasonable to examine whether the testimony for its miracles was such testimony.

In the controversy which arose out of what Hume put forward, the writers who argued for the truth of Christianity from the fact of the Christian miracles gained the victory. It must I think be allowed that, for a time at least, the verdict of the public was for the cause defended by such writers as Douglas, Campbell, and Paley. But it must also I think be allowed that this victory has not been permanent. The argument from miracles was indeed suited to men in the stage of mental progress of our forefathers of last century; that is, men with a belief in a general, not a universal, reign of law. Since their day great progress has been made towards a still more complete establishment of the reign of law, and hence incredulity as to miracles has so strengthened that not only are particular narratives discredited, but general propositions not less exclusive of the miraculous than that of Hume are put forward by writers who are widely read and have had much

---

is that of a darkness for eight days over the whole earth from January 1, 1600. The tradition is supposed to be fresh and universal throughout the world.

influence. I may instance Strauss, Rénan, and, in our country, Baden Powell. Let us then, in the first place, consider the *à priori* objections. We will do so, upon the supposition of an intelligent and righteous God, the maker and ruler of the universe. When our inquiry touches upon his particular attributes, I shall assume the conclusions of my former essay.

PART II.

The *à priori* objections.

These objections are effectually two—one against the fact itself, the other against its evidence—one, that is to say, against the possibility of a miracle, and the other against the possibility of our knowing it as such. The first declares a miracle to be contrary to the analogy of the whole course of nature considered as the course of the Divine government, and consequently impossible. Such is not the way in which the Deity acts, so far as we have trustworthy knowledge concerning him. It is important here to notice, on the one hand, that we have to judge, not simply of the course of nature as commonly understood, but of that course as subject to any variation which we might reasonably expect to arise from its being the action of the Divine Will; and, on the other hand, that we are to think of this so-called will strictly as we have in a former essay found reason to do. Hume taking his notion of the Divine procedure solely from the course of nature, excluded miracles even on the supposition of an Almighty God. Dean Mansel and other Christian advocates, taking the human will as a strict analogue for the Divine, have brought forward the supposed anomalous interference of the former in the world's affairs to justify by analogy a belief in miracles.[1] Might not God's will much more interfere with natural law? Now, first as to human will, it cannot act on the outward world except under conditions of physical causation. It cannot create energy. But it can direct or distribute energy, and hence it is a source of events which would not have arisen from the mere laws of inanimate matter. But even if we regard this action as an interruption to the regular course of nature, we are not entitled to say that the Divine will may or will cause breaks in the same way. That will acts through the course of nature. Before we say that it will ever do otherwise we must find in our former conclusions concerning it some reason to expect this. That inquiry we will in due course make. For the present it is needful to remark that the mere analogy of the human will

[1] 'Aids to Faith,' 'Essay on Miracles,' Art. 16.

does not justify the expectation. That is assuming a resemblance more close than has been shown. After these cautions I will state the objection. Briefly it is this. The better the operations of the Almighty are known, the more perfectly according to law do they appear to be. If we except the sphere of human and possibly that of animal will, the course of nature presents an absolute uniformity. She does not swerve from her path at the most imperative calls of mercy or justice. If we take our notions of the Divine action from science, nothing is more impressed upon us than this observance of law. The Almighty works upon a fixed plan, and a departure from it seems altogether contrary to his government.

If we had no source of information as to God except the study of nature, if we thought of him solely and simply as natural science teaches us to do, this argument would I think have very great weight. But we have, as I have maintained, at least one more source of information in our own moral nature. If the evidence thence obtained can be received, then God is a moral Being. The ultimate source of events must be in his will, determined upon moral considerations. He is free. Law is the servant, not the ruler of God. Might he not then have ordained an exception to law? I cannot confidently say that this reasoning entitles us to say so much. In answer it might be said, if the course of nature be the appointment of a perfect moral Being, why may it not be adequate to carry out all his good purposes? Surely God is righteous in providence as much as in miracle. Indeed, this idea of perfect pre-arrangement seems to many a more elevated view of God's government, one more worthy of his wisdom and power, than that of occasional interference. The argument as to God's character from our moral instincts does seem to make out a case for special providence, and for answers to prayer. Without these God's government would not be moral. There must be some correspondence between his appointments, and the moral states and wants of his creatures. If, for instance, prayer alters their moral condition in his sight, then it must have an efficacy, even in the material world. But to establish a case for miracles we need something more. Our argument raises God above material fatalism, but it does not give a presumption for his departing from the course of nature. For this end, we need an actual precedent of his having done so.

We have still the first-cause arguments. If we adopt these we have of course the precedent for which we seek. In creation, at all events, God acts without law. Obviously if we think of him as then ordaining law, we may also think of him as afterwards suspending it. Thus the credibility of miracles, when looked at from this point of view, is made to depend on our acceptance of the first-cause arguments—a conclusion to which I take the late Mr. Warington to have come in his work, 'Can we Believe in Miracles?' I do not press these first-cause arguments, but yet they are worthy of consideration. It may also be remarked that if in obedience to them, or to any other considerations, we affirm the infinity of God, we weaken the argument from the analogy of his known works. Vast as the range of that known analogy may be, it cannot be comprehensive of all the doings of an infinite Being. On the strength of these reasonings we may, I think, refuse to allow this *à priori* objection to be conclusive. But when we do so we should bear in mind that only a defence, a negative conclusion, has been sustained against it. At the most, all that we have established is this. Our knowledge of the Almighty does not forbid us to believe in miracles. It is another thing to say that they are probable in any given case, say that of Christianity. All *à priori* speculations as to what God will do are precarious, as indeed daily experience teaches. Some evidential writers of last century may have ventured upon this, but those of our day are more cautious, as may be seen by comparing Dean Mansel[1] with Archdeacon Paley.

[1] 'Aids to Faith,' Mansel's 'Essay,' Sect. XXIV., p. 30; Paley's 'Preliminary Considerations.'

I now go on to the argument against the possibility of our knowing of a miracle. It is founded upon the nature of human knowledge, and may be thus explained.

The whole action of the human mind as to outward things proceeds upon the assumption of the uniformity of the order of nature. Professor Mozley [1] has spoken of this principle as man's guide in practical life. No doubt it is. If we did not believe that the future would obey the same laws as the past, the unknown as the known, we should be at a standstill in the commonest affairs of life. But the principle underlies our mental life even more completely than this account implies. Without it, there would be no evidence of the senses. This evidence assumes the observance of many laws. In the case of sight,[2] for instance, we assume laws as to light, as to our own organs of vision, as to our habits of mental interpretation. So again there can be no evidence from testimony without this assumption. Indeed, here we assume the constancy of nature where it is most questionable in the case of human action. The very rules on which evidential writers rely for proving the superlative strength of the evidence for the Gospel miracles are generalizations from experience. It is well known that scientific

---

[1] Prof. Mozley's ' Bampton Lectures on Miracles,' Lect. II.
[2] See H. Helmholtz's ' Lectures on Scientific Subjects,' translated by E. Atkinson.

induction rests wholly upon this principle; and not indeed scientific induction only, but any inference whatever which we draw in any case of cause and effect. In short, every means of knowledge which we have as to the outward world, observation and inference alike, make the fundamental assumption in question. A world in which like consequents do not follow like antecedents may be ontologically possible, but it would be a world unknowable to us. If we had been born in such a world our faculties must have remained undeveloped, our consciousness a chaos. Professor Mozley has disparaged this principle.[1] He speaks of it as not a principle of reason, but an irrational part of our nature—a mere effect of custom, of no philosophical authority. He means, I presume, that we must not rank it among axiomatic convictions. This may be true. I will not here raise the question as to the origin of such convictions—how far custom in us, or in our ancestors, may enter here as well. But I do venture to say that a principle which lies at the foundation of all our knowledge of the outward world, is entitled to respect. The writer to whom I have alluded has gone further. By one of those refinements of negative criticism which are not after all sound philosophy, he seeks to put aside this principle altogether, so far as the proof of miracles is

---

[1] 'Bampton Lectures,' by Prof. Mozley, Lect. II.

concerned. He denies that the so-called order of nature is any reason for disbelieving them. Strictly speaking, it is, he tells us, only a summary or generalization of our experience, and is of no force beyond the limits of what has been actually observed and known; consequently, no objection in a case where the facts are said to have differed from it. On this view, as the author of 'Supernatural Religion' has well observed, miracles lose their peculiar character. If there be no order of nature, there is no special interference of God. The evidential argument collapses. But this surely is not a view which sound philosophy can accept. Mr. Mill[1] speaks of the principle as being itself established by an induction *per enumerationem simplicem*, but as being the strongest possible case of such induction. It is very possible that the conviction of its truth may practically have sprung up in the mind through such a process, but, unless I am mistaken, when we come, as a matter of reflection, to give this principle full generality, to extend it in fact beyond the limits which Professor Mozley would impose, then if we treat it as a result of induction we are logically guilty of *petitio principii*, for it is the assumption of this principle itself which gives any induction its power to establish such a general result. I should prefer to look upon it as a preliminary postulate,

---

[1] Mill's 'Logic,' Book III., chap. iii.

without which all knowledge of the external world is an impossibility. We must make some assumptions, if human knowledge is to be made into a rational system, worked up into a logically coherent whole. We may argue for the assumption in question thus— You may deny it if you will, but, in doing so, you bring in a universal scepticism. You ask the mind to bring into doubt all its knowledge of the outward world. Surely Christian apologists do not desire this result. And the case standing thus, it is fairly a question whether we should admit, as part of our knowledge, even an individual event, which is professedly a violation of this order of nature. We may fairly ask whether this is not asking the mind to act contrary to its own structure. We assume, it may be said, the principle a hundred times to prove the fact of the exception.

The admission of individual exceptions to the order of nature, recognised as such, is of course a different thing from denying or limiting that order in a general way. The interruption of our usual ways of knowing or inferring takes place only at that point where the miracle is asserted. Those who hold the will to be self-determining may bring forward its decisions, as events not having a place [1] in the series of cause and effect, but which are still universally considered knowable by us. I do not purpose to

[1] See 'Aids to Faith,' Mansel's 'Essay on Miracles,' Art. XVI.

enter upon the metaphysical question of the freedom of the will. But I would remark that we have here no exception to the truth that human knowledge can advance only where generalizations can be traced and found to hold good. It is only by bringing human action under the reign of law, to some extent at least, that one man can be made a channel of information to another. Precisely as man's conduct is irreducible, in the matter of speech, to rules— I mean rules in the experimental, not the moral sense—is human testimony uncertain. For it is by such rules only that we learn when to believe. If we adopt the first-cause arguments we have, of course, in the case of our alleged knowledge of the Deity, another instance in which we avowedly admit as knowable something out of the order of nature. It should be remarked, that the point here raised is not quite the same as that which came up when we were considering creation as an analogue for miracles.

What we had to consider then was—Is there a First Cause? What we have to consider now is— Can man's mind know a First Cause? And on this last point I have in my first essay put forth the opinion that there was nothing to justify us in saying that a self-existent being might not become a cause of finite beings; nothing, that is to say, to prove that a first cause might not be relatively manifested to us.

To reach to the proof of such a being is beyond our powers of inference, at least by reasoning from causation. But to deny that it may exist, and be the origin, indeed of any or of all finite things, is also beyond our power. We are at liberty to believe this on the strength, say, of a natural tendency in the mind, supposed to be the work of an intelligent and moral author of nature. If we do admit it, then miracles are of course consistently admissible to any extent. The self existent being who underlies the system of caused phenomena may appear, so to speak, upon the surface anywhere; or, to express myself otherwise, the various trains of causation may at many points terminate in him. On this supposition, indeed, it may be asked, Would not the uncertainty in our knowledge of which you have spoken arise? An answer might be found in the Divine veracity. Professor Birks has I believe somewhere spoken of the argument for the existence of animals in the geological eras as resting ultimately on the truthfulness of God. He might have extended the remark to all our knowledge. An Almighty Being could of course deceive us in anything, if he were so disposed. Oddly enough, some notion of this kind has actually been suggested, as an explanation of miracles.[1] It has been thought that what give rise to the idea of a miracle might be only an im-

---

[1] See article on 'Miracles' in 'Smith's Dictionary of the Bible.'

pression on our minds, not something in the external order of things.

I will not pursue this subject further. It is, in truth, perplexed, as all subjects must be which touch upon the Infinite. We may, however, I think, say that the objection which we have been considering is not negatively conclusive against all knowledge of miracles. It may be thought by some more philosophical, more logically consistent, to look upon any anomalous event as a case of unknown law. Even if we admit this, we are not therefore called upon to reject any well-attested narrative whatever. It has been said that 'no testimony can reach to the supernatural: testimony can only prove an extraordinary and perhaps inexplicable occurrence or phenomenon; that it is due to supernatural causes is entirely dependent on the previous belief and assumption of the parties.'[1] This is true, but it is equally true, and true for the same reasons, that no theory as to the impossibility or non-knowability of the supernatural, can be an absolute bar to our believing any given narrative. The event narrated may always be a case of unknown law. Neither of the *à priori* objections deserves to be thought such a bar, and in truth they are not the objections which have most weight at the present day. Even as to the reception of wonderful facts as strictly miraculous, men

[1] 'Essays and Reviews.' Essay by Prof. Baden Powell.

incline more and more to abstain from resting their conclusions upon *à priori* grounds. They are more and more ready to listen to experience as their teacher. They shape and reshape their opinions according to the indications of observation. Foremost among the intellectual characteristics of the age is an immense accumulation of well-observed facts, and a disposition to frame speculative views by generalization upon them. But when we approach the subject of miracles from this side, we are again met by grave objections. We have not to encounter the sweeping canons of the *à priori* method, but we have, it is said, against us a long increasing presumption. More and more has the supernatural been reduced to the natural, and accordingly an expectation has arisen that any appearance of an infraction of the laws of nature, well attested as to facts, will in the end prove to be really due to a defect in our knowledge of nature or, in other words, that it is a case of unknown law. And, again, two special growths of the modern scientific mind, viz., a stricter mode of examining historical evidence, and a better understanding of men's ways of thinking in past times, have done a great deal to discredit the wonderful stories of antiquity. These converging lines of exclusion threaten to shut out the argument from miracles. The latter threatens to reduce the Scripture miracles to a residuum, which the former would explain as natural events. If it be true, as is often said, that religious scepticism has increased in England of late years, that increase I believe is mainly due to the mental influences which I have just described; and not to the influence of Germany, nor to reaction, from the Oxford Tract, or from the Ritualistic movement; nor yet I trust to an impaired sense of the value of moral or religious truth. We will now leave the consideration of the *à priori* objections, and examine the argument before us with special reference to these modern ways of thinking.

PART III.

The evidential argument rested upon two positions: the one that there is adequate evidence for the miracles of the Gospel; the other that there is not adequate evidence for any other miracles. The latter position was as essential as the former. The accounts of Christ's miracles have come down to us in company with a multitude of such accounts. If the former are to maintain the character of special Divine interferences, the latter must be discredited. We will begin with the consideration of the latter, for in this way a broad view of the miraculous and its evidence will be obtained, and we will subsequently examine how far the case of the Gospel is peculiar. The evidential writers by no means neglected this side of their argument. Bishop Douglas wrote his 'Criterion' expressly to prove that no miracles, except those of the Scriptures, were true. Paley, indeed, advanced a more guarded position, viz. 'that there is not satisfactory evidence that persons professing to be the original witnesses of other miracles, in their nature as certain as the "evangelical," have passed their lives in labours, dangers, and sufferings, voluntarily undergone in attestation of the accounts which they delivered, and properly in consequence of their belief in those accounts, and that they also submitted from the same motives to new rules of conduct.' He maintains that he has such evidence in the case of the Gospel. He denies that it exists elsewhere. But though he makes the special strength of the evidential case to consist in possessing martyr testimony, and makes this the chief point of comparison between the Gospel miracles and others, still he argues in a way to throw total discredit upon all other miracles, and indeed his argument needs as much if it is to be really evidential. He at once sets aside several classes of miraculous narratives as not worthy to be compared with the accounts of the Gospels, and a review of these particular exceptions, as well as of the general proposition just stated, will give us a tolerably comprehensive view of most of the principles involved in the credibility of a miraculous story, as we are now considering it.

First, then, we will consider Paley's general proposition. It goes upon the principle that sincerity and earnestness of faith are the great guarantee of credibility. If a man shows clearly by his conduct that he himself believes in a miracle, say the resurrection of Christ, of which he professes to be a witness, you are to believe him. How far, as a matter of fact, Paley has the kind of testimony which he claims to have, we will inquire hereafter. Let us now scrutinise the principle involved. Is it sound? Does it allow enough for human fallibility in exciting circumstances? The martyr may be the witness whose honesty is best established, but is he therefore the best witness? Are not men who die for their convictions often men more zealous than discriminating—moved, it may be, by noble feelings, but ill fitted to weigh evidence or interpret strange phenomena, often not of a judicial cast of mind, but apt, on the contrary, to contract ardent beliefs upon slender grounds? Macaulay, I think, has said that a cautious temper and a subtle intellect are not the stuff of which martyrs are made. But they are the materials that make a good judge of evidence and phenomena. Paley, and indeed all his school, seem to think that the great point is to show the sincerity of the first believers. They seem by an insensible self-deception to have transferred themselves into the position of these witnesses, and to have thought these first Christians must have looked upon things as they themselves would have done. They seem to have thought of these men, not as uncultivated Orientals of the first century, but as educated Englishmen of the eighteenth—men, like Paley himself, cool, observant, reflective, with judgments little disturbed by feeling, not likely to be deceived; and witnesses therefore worthy to be received, as to matters of fact, however strange those matters might be, so only they were sincere. These evidential writers argued as though Christian belief had been at the outset a mere inference from physical data. 'In whatever degree,' says Paley, 'or in whatever part the religion was argumentative, when it came to the question—" Is the carpenter's son of Nazareth the person whom we are to receive and obey?" there was nothing but the miracles attributed to him by which his pretensions could be maintained for a moment.'[1] This may be good reasoning from Paley's point of view; but before it proves anything as to the first believers, we must ascertain to what extent their faith was a matter of argument at all. It was much less so I believe than Paley implies. It was quite possible that they would come to very

---

[1] Paley's 'Evidences.' Proposition I. ch. vi.

positive conclusions upon grounds which they had not sifted as he would have done, and still less as a modern man of science would have done. History, and especially that of the East, has many instances of religious enthusiasts ready to sacrifice everything for a faith resting upon no argumentative evidence. I will quote one instance from Gibbon.[1] A leader of the Carmathians, a fanatical sect of Moslems, was summoned to surrender by the officers of the Caliph. 'Your Master,' said he, 'is at the head of thirty thousand soldiers; three such men as these are wanting in his host.' At the same instant, turning to three of his companions, he commanded the first to plunge a dagger into his breast, the second to leap into the Tigris, and the third to cast himself headlong down a precipice. They obeyed him without a murmur. To take an illustration from Christian history, no one I suppose will doubt that St. Francis of Assisi was sincere when he offered to walk into the furnace to convert the Soldan; nor yet will anyone believe that he attained this deadly sincerity of faith by the study of evidences. No one can study the history of the religions of the world, and their devotees, without seeing that rational argument has had but a subordinate part in generating religious faith. In the actual case of the Apostles there were clearly other

[1] Gibbon's 'Decline and Fall of the Roman Empire,' chap. lii.

influences swaying their minds to belief besides the miracles, such as the prevailing expectation of a Messiah, the influence of an exalted character in Christ, the attraction of the evangelical doctrine. In such a case the intensity of the believer's conviction, even as to matters of fact, which he takes himself to have seen, is not a measure of his credibility. This position I shall further illustrate hereafter. Meanwhile my contention is that we should value rather the cool, intelligent, unprejudiced, candid witness. Strength of belief is not of value beyond such an amount as is implied by mere honesty.

I will now enumerate the cases of miraculous narratives which Paley[1] at once puts aside :—

First on the score of fault in the evidence, he rejects :—

(1). Accounts written some ages after the event.

(2). Accounts written in countries distant from the scene of the event.

(3). Transient rumours which soon die away.

(4). Naked history, unsupported by any known facts, apparently resulting from the marvels.

(5). Accounts wanting in particularity as to time, place, person, &c.

(6). Accounts merely received with an otiose assent, not producing any strong effect upon those who profess to have received and believe them.

[1] Paley's 'Evidences,' Part II.

(7). Accounts in support of some religion already dominant, or opinion already formed.

Next, upon the score of ambiguity in the alleged facts, he rejects—

(8). Miraculous accounts, that may have arisen from false perception.

(9). Tentative miracles, that is, cases of success out of many trials.

(10). Cases in which the supposed miracle may be naturally explained.

(11). Cases in which what seems to be miraculous may be only exaggeration of some remarkable coincidence or appearance.

If we review these exceptions, we shall I think see that they may be classed with reference to the principles involved under three heads, as follows:—

First head. Want of trustworthy information in the writers.

(1). Accounts long subsequent.

(2). Accounts from distant places.

(5). Accounts wanting particularity.

(7). Accounts in which the narrator is biassed by some previous opinion.

(11). Accounts explicable by supposed exaggeration.

Second head. Want of corroboration.

(3). Transient rumours.

(4). Bare statements.

(6). Accounts received merely with an otiose assent.

In none of these cases are there visible effects of belief.

Third head. Cases in which the alleged miracles are truly described, as the facts were apprehended by the observers, but in which there still may be no miracle.

(8). Cases of false perception.

(9). Tentative miracles.

(10). Results of natural causes, which are not known to the observers.

I will try to estimate the credibility of these different kinds of histories, not as Paley has done, in comparison with those of the Gospel, but absolutely. Under the first head, we have just objections. Accounts coming from distant times and places (1) and (2) are not to be trusted. Those wanting in particularity (5) are weak, but not so weak as (1) and (2). Details are *primâ facie* evidence of accurate information, but they may be simulated; and, further, in uncritical times, true narratives may easily want them. Accounts in which a previous bias of opinion is suspected (7) are open to objection, but not to unconditional rejection. They should be carefully examined. It is also to be observed that under this head we must take account, not only of the influence of a dominant religion, or of a government, or of social patronage, as Paley has done, but also of all causes of strong prejudice in such a matter, as, for instance, admiration for an exalted character, the sway of earnest teaching, the contagion of enthusiasm, the attraction of a doctrine in some important particulars suited to the hearers. All these things predispose to a belief in the miraculous, as I shall endeavour to illustrate. (11). We must be on our guard against exaggeration. It is particularly to be looked for where the influences just named are at work. And indeed the love of the marvellous, or the mere desire to give effect to a story, will lead to it, unless the narrators have very well-trained minds.[1]

Under the second head we have reasoning really the same in principle as that of the general proposition. Transient rumours, bare history, carelessly received accounts, are not, Paley tells us, to be put in comparison with the histories of the Gospel, for the latter have martyr testimony, whilst the former were never earnestly believed. In the case of the Gospel we see results which prove earnest faith; in the other cases we have no such effects. How far this is a fair account of the Christian evidences we shall, as I have said, inquire by and by. But I may at once repeat my remark that Paley over-

---

[1] For the effects of scientific training in this matter, see Galton's 'English Men of Science,' p. 141.

rated the value of strong persuasion in a witness, and that the best witness is the observant, intelligent conscientious man. We might have the testimony of such witnesses in any of the cases last named, and that testimony would be worth more than that of excitable men carried away by the force of their convictions, even though the latter should 'turn the world upside down.'

Under the third head we have, first, false perception (8).

Here no doubt is a source of error. Indeed, Paley has made too little of it. He accounts for such cases by temporary insanity. Now it is certain that visions are seen by men, who in all other respects are sane. Dr. Hibbert, in his work upon apparitions, has given at length such a case— that of Nicolai, a bookseller at Berlin. Sir Walter Scott, in his 'Letters on Demonology,' and Professor Huxley, in his elementary work on physiology, have also given instances. Neither is Paley justified in saying that the like delusion may not fall upon many persons at once, nor yet that one sense may not confirm the errors of another. Dr. Hibbert relates a story of a whole ship's crew, except the captain being deceived by a chance resemblance between a floating piece of wreck and a dead companion, and supposing it to be his ghost. The accounts of modern spiritualism allege cases in which the apparition is seen by several, and also *felt*.[1] If we are allowed to go back to times as distant as those of the New Testament, we might instance the prodigies related by Josephus as preceding the fall of Jerusalem, among which are visions occurring to many at once.

Paley of course is justified in saying that there must be a difference between the explanation of such cases and other cases in which a permanent physical effect remains, as in anomalous cures. But it is a mistake to imply that these last are irreducible to natural law.

Next tentative miracles (9).

These are cases in which there are some successes out of many failures. The accounts record the former, but are silent as to the latter. From Paley's remarks, we are led to think that he looked upon these events as 'fortunate experiments,' things to be 'explained by the power of accident.'[2] He instances cures by relics, and at the tombs of saints, and by the king's touch. Paley was too acute a man to see in fortune or 'accident' a real cause of events. What he meant was, I presume, that in the few cases of cure there were natural causes of recovery at work, but unobserved—perhaps indeed

---

[1] 'Quarterly Journal of Science,' W. Crookes, January 1874.
[2] Paley's 'Evidences,' Prop. II., Ch. 1.

obscure, and not recognised as such causes. I shall hereafter notice more particularly the cures which he has instanced. Meanwhile I will make this remark. If the cures, however few, do appear unaccountable from known physical causes, the inference is that they arose from some cause not hitherto known, and the fact that success was very partial should be attributed to the feebleness of this cause, except in very peculiar cases.

Lastly, we have to consider the cases which seemed to be miracles to the observers, but which are explicable now, or at least admit the hope of future explanation (10).

As I have said already, the tendency of modern thought would extend this class much further than Paley thought of. It would indeed be hard to persuade a man of science in these days that he had a miracle before him in any case. However anomalous the phenomena, he would begin trying to reduce them to known laws, and failing this he would try to make new laws to take them in. And there is much in the past progress and present state of knowledge to justify such proceedings. There was a time when the comet, the eclipse, the rainbow, the lightning, the wind, the pestilence, the famine, nay, the daily motions of the sun and moon, were all explained by special personal agency. Even now at first hearing it might seem inexplicable to many that a man should pass[1] his hand unharmed through molten metal, or speak[2] intelligibly without a tongue, that stones[3] should fall from the sky, or fishes[4] come up alive from the bowels of the earth, that showers of blood[5] should seem to fall, or that a great river should appear as though turned into blood. Yet all these things science can explain. There seems no limit to such explanations. Perhaps still in the present state of knowledge there may be many conceivable events so out of the known course of nature that we could not think of them otherwise than as supernatural. We are not ready to receive as natural the wonders of the Arabian Nights' Entertainments. But the miracles, with which we have to do in the evidential argument, are not wonders so extravagant.

Whatever miraculous histories Paley could not bring within his eleven excepted classes he disposed of by his general proposition as to martyr testimony. For the lack of this, if for no other reason, they could not be set in competition with the Gospel narra-

---

[1] Prof. Tyndall's 'Heat a Mode of Motion,' chap. v., Art. CC.
[2] See statements on this point farther on.
[3] Lockyer's 'Elementary Lessons in Astronomy,' Art. CCCXVI.
[4] Sir C. Lyell's 'Principles of Geology,' vol. i., chap. xvii., p. 393, 10th edition.
[5] Blood prodigies. 'The Insect World,' by Louis Figuier, English translation, p. 193. Chapman and Hall, 1868. 'Footnotes from the Page of Nature,' by the Rev. Hugh Macmillan, published by Macmillan & Co., London, 1861, p. 140 and onwards.

tives. On this general reasoning he mainly relied. To prove a general negative, or even to make a show of doing so, would be of course impossible, except by such general propositions. The only specific cases which he examines are those brought forward by Hume. With something of the art of a controversialist, he takes it for granted that these must be the strongest. They are the miracles at the tomb of the Abbé Paris in the last century; two cures wrought by the Emperor Vespasian, and recorded by Tacitus; and a story told by the Cardinal de Retz, of a man at Saragossa who lost a leg and had it miraculously restored. Of the first case, I will speak hereafter; as to the others, Paley sets up the hypothesis of fraud. He brings them under the head of stories circulated in the interest of a dominant religion (7).

To the adverse presumption thus established we may oppose the publicity and notoriety of the affair. In the case of the Vespasian cures, we may urge that they were wrought on a person well known, and before many witnesses, and continued to be affirmed when nothing was to be gained thereby. As to the Saragossa miracle, Mr. Lecky[1] tells us that much has been written upon it, and that the Spanish divines consider it remarkably well attested.

[1] See note at p. 154, vol. i., Lecky's 'History of the Rise and Influence of Rationalism.'

This is, however, more incredible than the others. These latter were very possibly instances of mental effects of which I shall speak presently.

As a matter of fact, these cases adduced by Hume, and considered by Paley, are not the most plausible cases of the supernatural which can be found in history. I will presently bring forward various histories that have at least the appearance of the supernatural, and one or two at least will I think be found better attested than Hume's cases. But I shall not maintain that any of them will really pass the ordeal of all Paley's exceptions, even as I have revised those exceptions. My purpose in bringing these cases forward will rather be to give a general view of a good many seemingly miraculous stories, with the idea of so suggesting principles, mental or physical, that may explain their origin. I believe that Paley's argument will be found inadequate for the purposes of modern controversy. But the weakness will appear, not when we are considering the rival cases, but when we come to apply to the Gospel accounts themselves the tests by which other miracles were disposed of.

To some minds, this last proceeding may seem irreverent. Would you test the narratives of Scripture, it may be asked, in the same way that you would test others? The answer is plain, that we must do so in an evidential argument. We cannot assume that accounts of miracles found in Scripture must be true, and those found elsewhere must be false. Plainly, in our present discussion, this would be begging the question. And, indeed, in any case, it would be unphilosophical as regards the negative proposition. Such a way of regarding the matter was popular in England forty years ago, but even then it was impugned by Dr. Maitland, in one of the essays of his work 'Eruvin.' An argument in its favour has, I know, been put forward. The Gospel miracles, it has been said, have an evidential value. There is in their case a purpose obvious on *à priori* grounds which countervails the antecedent improbability of such events, and, if you admit them, you must admit all the Scripture miracles. But in any story without this presumption on its side the antecedent improbability prevails. There is here far too much of that judging what God will do, and how he will do it, which all cautious thinkers now avoid. The evidential writers were no doubt justified when they said that man needed light upon religious subjects, and that our notions of the goodness of God would lead us to expect that he would in some way provide that light. But they made an assumption when they said or implied that this could be done only by a miraculous revelation. The growth of the moral faculty and of our knowledge of the universe are at least conceivable alternatives. Douglas and

Warburton might speak confidently on such a point, but thoughtful men of these days would be less bold. I may quote Dr. Newman as a remarkable instance of awakening to the untenableness of this position as to non-scriptural miracles. In early life he wrote an essay upon Scripture miracles, discrediting others. In later life he wrote an essay on ecclesiastical miracles, admitting them.

PART IV.

I will now give, as I proposed, some examples of narratives, which seem at least to relate the miraculous.

None of the fathers of the Primitive Church has a higher reputation for piety and ability than St. Augustine of Hippo; perhaps, indeed, none so high. Now it is noteworthy that his testimony to the occurrence of miracles in his own time is remarkably strong. In his great work, 'De Civitate Dei,' lib. xxii. cap. viii., he has given us a collection of accounts of supposed miracles. The first is the history of a blind man cured at Milan by the relics of the martyrs Gervasius and Protasius. Augustine tells us that he himself was there at the time, and adds that an immense number of people were witnesses. The miracle is attested also by St. Ambrose and by Paulinus his secretary. It has been skilfully defended by Dr. Newman[1] as satisfying the tests of Paley, Douglas, and Leslie. The evidence is that of writers of high character, present at the time and place. The fact was cognisable by the senses, and open to the verification of the public. The man himself remained a monument of its reality. The account was published at once, and with effect, in opposition to a powerful religious party. The Empress, who had been trying to seize a church for the Arians, gave way. The man himself dedicated his life to the service of religion.

Augustine's next story is that of the case of a man named Innocentius, who was suffering severely from fistula. Augustine tells us that the patient feared greatly the pain of the operation, which the medical men declared to be necessary. He himself witnessed the earnest supplication which Innocentius made to God for relief, when he was informed of this necessity, and he was also present on the day following, when, to the astonishment of the medical men, they found, upon proceeding to operate, that the fistula was gone. The whole scene is described with great liveliness of feeling.

[1] 'Essay on the Miracles of Early Ecclesiastical History,' chap. v., Sect. VIII.

Other accounts follow. Cures from cancer, gout, paralysis, calculus, and, what is more extraordinary still, no less than five restorations from death. In none of these latter, however, is any great interval said to have elapsed between death and revival. One story is told less miraculous than those just named, but which will recall an incident in the Gospels. A poor tailor is relieved in distress upon prayer to certain martyrs, by finding on the shore a fish in whose stomach was a valuable ring. St. Augustine himself was much struck with the great number of these miracles. He tells us that when he saw that these signs of Divine power, like those of old time, were frequent, he caused accounts of such things to be drawn up and to be read publicly. In two years, in his own diocese of Hippo, nearly seventy such miracles were recorded, and many he believed had missed of record. In the neighbouring province of Calama, an incomparably greater number had taken place.

I would next refer to Bede's history of our own English Church in its infancy. This work contains very many miraculous accounts It may be said that Bede lived in superstitious and credulous times. I may reply that he himself was probably the most learned and pious man of those times. His miracles are mostly cures by relics, or at the tombs of saints; for instance, the ninth and four following chapters of his third book are full of accounts of cures wrought by the relics of Oswald, a pious king of Northumbria. These stories are not peculiarly fantastic or incredible. They are of the usual character of such accounts—recoveries from fever, blindness, paralysis, and the like, and their date is in Bede's own time, or a little before. Bede, I allow, is not generally particular as to circumstances or authorities. But he does give us his authority in the case of several wonders wrought by a Bishop John, viz. the Bishop's deacon, who was, Bede tells us, living in his own time, and of whom he speaks as 'reverendissimus ac veracissimus.'

St. Francis of Assissi, the founder of the Order of the Friars Minor or Franciscans, has been said to be the greatest of the mediæval saints. And indeed we may see much to give him this pre-eminence, whether we look at the extent of his influence, the wonders related of his life, or, what is a much more just ground of esteem, the exalted beauty and goodness of his character. Miracles in abundance are related of him, even by his earliest biographers, and some of the first magnitude, as curing the paralytic, giving of sight to the blind, even raising the dead. The most celebrated of all these miracles, perhaps indeed the most celebrated miracle in the entire history of the Church since the days of the Apostles, is the receiving by the saint of the stigmata, or marks of the wounds of Christ. It happens also to be remarkably well attested. M. Chavin de Malan, one of the modern biographers of St. Francis, is ready to renounce all faith in human testimony if this miracle be not established. Other historians have, however, I must say, come to a different conclusion. Especially Professor Karl Hase, of the University of Jena, has appended to his life of the saint a special discussion of this miracle, in which he decides against its authenticity. I am acquainted with this book through the French translation of M. Charles Berthoud, and I purpose to insert here, first the principal historical evidences for the miracle, and then the criticisms of Professor Hase upon them. We shall thus, I think, be placed in a good position for forming an opinion upon the whole. I will arrange the testimonies according to their dates.

1. We have extant a letter written by Elias of Cortona, a companion of the saint in the latter part of his life, and his successor in the government of the Order. The letter is printed in the history of the Franciscans by Luke Waddington. This author wrote a full and minute history of the Order in the first half of the seventeenth century. He professed to publish the letter in question as a copy from the original, preserved in a convent of the Franciscans at Valenciennes, then a town of Belgium. It was written by Elias on occasion of the death of the

saint, to announce that event to the absent brethren. It relates that St. Francis, not long before his death (non diu ante mortem), appeared as if he had been crucified. It speaks of the marks (puncturas) of the nails in the hands and feet, and of their showing the blackness of nails.

2. Thomas de Celano, also one of the companions of the saint, wrote his history within three years of his death at the command of the then Pope, Gregory IX. This would be in the year 1229. The book was printed for the first time in the Bollandist collection,[1] but evidence of its existence almost at the date in question exists, as we shall see. Celano tells us that St. Francis was in religious retirement on Mount Aumna (Alvernia), a desolate mountain in the Apennines, about two years before his death, and that he sought a sign of God's disposition towards him by opening a service-book. The book thrice opened at the passion of Christ, and this led the saint to believe that he should be conformed to the sufferings of his master. Soon after, he saw a vision of a seraph, as it were a man fastened to a cross in the usual manner with six wings. Two wings were raised above the head, two were stretched out in flight, two covered the body. Whilst the mind of St. Francis was filled with the emotions

---

[1] 'Acta Sanctorum.' Die Quartâ Octobris, de S. Francisco, Con-

which this vision raised, there began to appear in his body the marks known as the stigmata, *i. e.* wounds in the hands and feet, as if by crucifixion, and also a wound in the side. Celano speaks of the appearance of nails in the wounds. The heads of the nails appeared on one side of the hands and feet, and their points on the other. Celano particularly tells us that the heads of the nails were upon the inside of the hands, and upon the top of the feet. St. Francis was alone, when this wonder befell him, and he did all in his power to conceal the marks. It was his custom to reveal the secret rarely or to no one (raro aut nulli). This conduct seems to have arisen partly from humility and partly from prudence. As to the wound in the side, Elias only is said to have seen it during the Saint's life, and Ruffinus to have touched it. But blood occasionally issued from it, and stained the clothes of the Saint in a manner which those who attended upon him observed. But at the death of the Saint we hear of a concourse of people to see the dead body, and of their beholding not merely the wounds in the hands and feet but also, as it were, nails themselves in the wounds, and also the wound in the side. The brethren and disciples (fratres et filii) were allowed to kiss the stigmata. The people thought it a great privilege to kiss or even to see these marks. St. Francis died about an hour after sunset on Saturday, and during the night there was a great concourse of people. In the morning the corpse was carried, amidst a great multitude of people, first to be seen by St. Clare and her nuns, and then to the tomb in which it was for a time to rest.

(3). Three of the brethren, Leo, Ruffinus, and Angelo, wrote another life of the Saint, a sort of supplement to that of Celano, in the year 1247, that is, about twenty years after his death. They also had been companions of St. Francis. Leo had been his confessor. Their work also was first printed in the Bollandist collection. Their account of his receiving the stigmata is substantially the same as Celano's. St. Francis is said to have concealed the marks as much as he could, but he could not hinder their being seen at least by his familiar companions. After his death all the brethren, and very many secular persons (omnes fratres et sæculares quam plurimi) saw them plainly. The appearance of nails and the blackness of iron are mentioned; also miracles in attestation.

(4). Bonaventura, Cardinal and Saint, also wrote a life of St. Francis. It is true that he had not known the Saint personally, and did not write before the year 1263. But there are still circumstances which give a value to his work as evidence. He was a man of the highest character. Of him it was said, that in Bonaventura 'Adam seemed not to have sinned.' Certainly he was not a man likely to be guilty of any wilful deception. Again, he was the general of the Order of the Franciscans, and would have access to every means of information which was to be had in his day, and that was the generation immediately following St. Francis, when numbers who knew him were alive. Indeed, Bonaventura had himself been presented to the Saint as a child, and is said to have been cured of a sickness by him. This biographer visited Assissi, and, we may suppose, gathered information from first-hand sources. His book has long been before the public. He speaks of the religious retirement on Mount Alvernia. It was a forty days' fast in honour of the archangel St. Michael, immediately before the Archangel's Feast in 1226. Bonaventura speaks of the religious excitement of the Saint at the time, and of some wonderful circumstances attending it, as of his being lifted up on high (in altum). He tells us of the book being thrice opened at the passion of Christ, and of the Saint's thence concluding that he was to be made like unto Christ in his sufferings. St. Francis was praying on the side of the mountain alone, about the time of the feast of the exaltation of the cross (Sept. 14), when he saw the vision of the seraph. That vision is described as in the earlier accounts. The seraph is said to fly to a place in the air near to the Saint. He concludes, God revealing it (Deo revelante), that he was to be altogether conformed to the likeness of Christ crucified, not by martyrdom of the flesh, but by burning of the mind (se non per martyrium carnis sed per incendium mentis totum in Christi crucifixi similitudinem transformandum). Presently the stigmata began to appear. They are described as before. We read of the actual appearance of nails, and of the blackness of the iron (nigredinem). The truth of the fact is said to be attested both by sight and touch. We are told that it clearly appeared both in life and death ('luculente apparuit,' 'in vitâ et morte.') The stigmata on St. Francis are said to have resembled the marks which he saw upon the seraph, and here, as in Celano, the nail-heads are said to have been inside the hands.

A further account is given explaining how the vision came to be known to the brethren in spite of the reserve of St. Francis. He was in great doubt whether he should make it known, and consulted some of his companions. One of them conjecturing that he had something wonderful to relate, induced him to declare it, by the consideration that it might have befallen him to the end, that its being known should be for the good of others. But St. Francis is said by Bonaventura, as well as by the other biographers, to have concealed the marks; some, however (aliqui), did see them in his hands and feet even in his life, and afterwards confirmed their testimony upon oath. Bonaventura tells us that some cardinals were among those who thus saw them, and also that he himself heard Pope Alexander IV. say, when preaching to the people, that he had seen them. After the death of St. Francis more than fifty of the brethren, St. Clare and her nuns, and also a great number of laymen (quam plurimi), beheld these marks, and many kissed and handled them. Bonaventura speaks of the wound in the side in the same way as Celano.

The accounts now given are the oldest authorities on which we can depend. The Bollandist collector, following Waddington, quotes also another life of St. Francis attributed to a John or Thomas de Ceprano, who was not thought to be a companion of St. Francis, or indeed a Franciscan, but a layman of the Pope's Court. He believes this life to have been written between 1230 and 1241 because it speaks of Gregory IX. as living, and he finds it quoted by Vincentius Bellovacensis, a French writer of the middle of the thirteenth century. But a good deal that has been said of it seems, as he points out, properly to apply to the life by Celano. He has not published it in his collection, nor can it be relied upon. He gives the following testimonies from contemporary writers, who were not Franciscans, and may therefore be thought more free from partiality. Lucas Tudensis, a Spanish Bishop, wrote a book against the Albigenses about the year 1231, and in this book he appeals to the stigmata of St. Francis, as proving that Christ was fastened to the cross by four nails, and was wounded on the right side. He follows Celano closely. This is important, as proving the existence of Celano's history at this early period. And it has also some value as an independent confirmation; for the Bishop had visited Elias in Italy, and so had at least opportunity for independent knowledge. He also adds, what is not in Celano, something about the testimony of many religious and also lay people.

Vincentius Bellovacensis, a Dominican of France, wrote a book called 'Speculum historiæ,' before the middle of the thirteenth century, in which the stigmata of St. Francis are spoken of.

Matthew Paris, a Benedictine monk and a well-known English historian, writing in the first half of the thirteenth century, and certainly with no partiality to the Franciscans, speaks of the stigmata. But his account differs from those already given. He makes the stigmata to appear only fifteen days before the death of St. Francis, and speaks of a great concourse of people coming together to see them. Amongst the crowd were some cardinals. They are represented as asking St. Francis as to the prodigy, and he as addressing them in return. Matthew Paris, writing in England, might not have good information.

Jacobus de Vorago, who lived and died in the thirteenth century, writes of the stigmata, and briefly gives the heads of the story, the vision of the seraph having the appearance of a man upon the cross, the marks arising in the body of St. Francis, his concealing them, their being seen by some during his life, and by many after his death.

Popes Gregory IX. and Alexander IV., both contemporaries and friends of St. Francis, strenuously maintained the truth of the stigmata. The Bishop of Olmutz, and a Dominican friar in Moldavia, had denied this. Gregory IX., writing about 1237, severely rebuked them both. The Roman Catholic Church instituted a feast on Sept. 17 in honour of this great miracle.

So much for the evidence. I will now speak of the adverse criticisms of Professor Hase. He admits the genuineness of the letter of Elias, and also of the three lives, that of Celano, the Three Brethren (Tres Socii), and Bonaventura. But he brings forward the following objections to the truth of their accounts :—

1. There is a perceptible growth in the accounts, as is common with wonderful stories. The language of Elias is rather vague and obscure, and he says nothing of the vision. This was needed to explain the origin of the marks. Accordingly, we have it in

Celano and the Tres Socii. It was further needful to explain how, if St. Francis were so reserved upon the subject, the vision came to be known. This accordingly we find explained by a new narrative in Bonaventura.

2. There is some discrepancy, the Professor thinks, upon an important point—the date of the occurrence. The three histories speak of two years before the Saint's death. The letter of Elias says 'not long before his death' ('non diu ante mortem'). If we call to mind that St. Francis died at forty-five, we shall not think that this latter expression agrees well with the time of two years. Professor Hase brings forward the precise statement of Matthew Paris, about fifteen days, as better agreeing with that of Elias.

3. Neither the Popes in their letters, nor the historians in their histories, distinctly say that they had themselves seen these marks. Yet according to the accounts, some of them, as Pope Alexander IV. and Ruffinus, had done so. Elias and Ruffinus alone had knowledge of the side-wound during the Saint's life.

4. The stigmata were, it seems, denied by some contemporaries, as the Bishop of Olmutz and the Dominican friar.

Professor Hase himself puts forward the conjecture either that Elias started the story in the letter already quoted, and that the immediate companions of St. Francis acquiesced in the deception, in order to magnify the reputation of the Saint, or that Elias actually marked the corpse on the night after death, so as to deceive others. To support this idea he adduces the fact that Elias proved to be a scheming and unprincipled man, and he also points out a certain haste in the burial, and evidence of a wish upon the part of Elias that the corpse should not be seen by the people when it was removed, about four years later, from its temporary tomb to what was meant to be its last resting-place, the Church of San Francisco.

The hypothesis of Professor Hase does not seem to me credible in the face of the testimony which has been adduced. With regard to his criticisms, I would make the following remarks. The additions to the account in the three successive lives are not so serious as to throw doubt upon the whole; the words of Elias as to the time are not precise, and must not be pressed too much; the testimony of Matthew Paris cannot be relied upon, as he was writing at a distance. We are not to expect in the attestation of the Popes or historians of those days the formal precision of depositions in a court of justice. The limitation of the testimony to Elias and Ruffinus concerns only the wound in the side, and that during the Saint's life; and even here we have some other evidence from the staining of the Saint's clothes. If the miracle were denied at the time, this was done by people at a distance, and apparently not on critical but upon theological grounds, and perhaps to some extent from the prejudice of the Dominicans against the Franciscans. The wish to avoid giving the people access to the corpse may be naturally explained from a fear of those melancholy scenes which have on such occasions arisen from the eagerness of the people to possess themselves of some relic of a departed saint. Lastly, Elias is represented by Waddington as falling away after his elevation, and it is hard to understand how he could get others to join him in the fraud. On the whole, I do not see that the Professor has adequately supported his view, and I am disposed myself to think the account well attested. Principal Tulloch, I must say, in an article in 'Good Words,' January 1, 1867, came to a different conclusion. He followed Hase. The question of course remains, can the event be naturally explained? We shall see, by and by, that there are many accounts of persons being marked with the wounds of Christ. There is one, indeed, of our own day, that of the Belgian ecstatic, Louise Lateau. One of our ablest physiological writers, Dr. Carpenter, in his recent work, ' Mental Physiology,' regards these phenomena as quite capable of natural explanation. In the accounts of

St. Francis, we see that intense absorption in the contemplation of Christ's passion which is supposed to produce the effects. The vision of the seraph, which can of course be explained, and the resulting conviction that the Saint was to be transformed into the likeness of Christ crucified, were exactly the antecedents likely to be followed by such a result. It has, indeed, been objected that in the case of St. Francis we have not merely the five wounds of Christ impressed upon the body, but also the appearance of what seemed to be nails in form and colour. We may reply that it is difficult to set a limit to this power of a mental impression over the bodily frame. Marks which have often been produced in unborn children, as is commonly thought by impressions on the mind of the mother, seem analogous even to this extreme case of St. Francis. I ought, however, to add, that so far as I have been able to learn, medical authorities oppose the popular idea that these marks are caused by ideas in the mind of the mother.[1]

The Reformation, it has been said, was unfavourable to a belief in any form of the miraculous except the diabolic. We see, however, that eminent divines were still found, in the reformed churches, who believed in the continuance of miracles. Bax-

[1] See 'Elements of Physiology,' by J. Müller, translation by W. Baly, Part IV., p. 1404.

ter, Grotius, Bengel, may be named. Grotius, in his commentary on Mark xvi. 17, refers to many patristic miracles, but does not speak of any similar events in modern times. But Baxter and Bengel give examples of the supernatural in their own days. In the second part of the 'Saint's Everlasting Rest,' Baxter considers the miracles of the Gospel as Christian evidences, and he adduces in support modern cases which he distinguishes from the evangelical miracles, and speaks of rather as wonderful acts of Providence, but which he still asserts to be supernatural. He tells us that when he was minister at Bridgnorth, there fell from the sky in several parts of England a sort of grain like withered wheat corn, but not so long. The skin was of a dark colour, and when this was pulled off the grain tasted somewhat sharp and hot. Baxter himself tasted it, and kept some a long time. It fell, he tells us, upon the roof of his own church, and his own house. He is very full and emphatic in asserting the power of prayer to raise up the sick, when all human means fail, and asserts that this had been his own case more than once or twice or ten times. He refers also to the case of Myconius, who, when supposed to be dying of consumption, was restored upon the earnest prayer of Luther, then at a distance, and lived six years. It is remarkable that Luther was most confident of his recovery. Also the case of

Baynam, who felt no pain in the fires of martyrdom; and that of Bishop Farrar, who said, as he went to the stake, 'If I stir in the fire, believe not my doctrine,' and who did remain unmoved. He quotes also the story of Theodorus, a martyr in the time of the apostate Julian, who when tortured lost all sense of pain, and had a vision of a heavenly figure, as it were a young man ministering to his relief. I may mention here that Dr. Hibbert, in his work upon apparitions, refers to this last history, and considers it in connection with one or two similar cases that have no bearing on religion. Dr. Hibbert[1] seems to think these accounts explicable by some revulsion of the nervous system. Dr. Carpenter also speaks of certain conditions of the nervous system as leading to a cessation of pain even under torture, and instances Damien sleeping on the rack.

Baxter, I must add, is copious in his testimonies to the diabolic form of the supernatural. Of these and of other non-christian wonders I will say something by and by. But before leaving this author, I may add that he seems to have thought some of the miracles alleged by Papists to be true. He mentions, for instance, that Carolus Piso had related of a deaf patient that she was cured at the shrine of Our Lady of Loretto.

[1] Dr. Hibbert's 'Philosophy of Apparitions,' p. 369; Carpenter's 'Principles of Physiology,' p. 121.

In Bengel's 'Gnomon' there will be found, among the remarks upon St. Mark xvi. 17, 18, the following extraordinary account. There was present at church in Leonberg, a town of Wirtemburg, on the thirteenth Sunday after Trinity, in the year 1644, a girl of twenty years of age, so disabled as to be scarcely able to creep along upon crutches. She had been thus disabled for nine years. As the Dean Raumier was from the pulpit dwelling on the miraculous power of the name of Jesus, she was suddenly raised up and restored to the use of her limbs. This happened in the presence of Duke Eberhard III. and his courtiers, and was committed to the public records, which are above all suspicion. Bengel's son Ernest, in his edition of the 'Gnomon,' gives the very words of the Dean, and he adds another supposed case of the supernatural. At Lavingen, on Nov. 26, in the year 1606, there was born Joseph Jenisch, of the noble stock of the Kellers. He was without a tongue. But still in consequence, as was supposed, of the earnest prayers of his family, he was able, before he finished his first year, to name distinctly the members of his family. He was dedicated to the ministry, and for forty years discharged the sacred office at Böblingen and Münchingen.

This last case, it is now well known, involves nothing supernatural. The celebrated case of the African confessors called attention to this tongueless speech, and it is now known that though the loss of part of the tongue may prevent speech, that of the whole does not.[1]

The cures wrought at the tomb of the Abbé Paris, in the early part of last century, have already been referred to in connection with this subject. A detailed account of eight of these cures was published by a M. Montgeron. This gentleman, it may be observed, supplies the kind of testimony which Paley especially preferred, that of a convert and a martyr. He passed himself through a marked change of life, in consequence of what he saw at the tomb, and he ventured to present his book to King Louis XIV., for which act he was sent to the Bastille. The accounts in question have been valued by others, because the wonders which they relate were subjected to a strict medical investigation, took place in a great seat of modern civilisation, and were opposed to the reigning powers in Church and State. A notice from a hostile quarter appeared in a pastoral of the Archbishop of Sens. Bishop Douglas has carefully examined Montgeron's accounts, comparing them with the Archbishop's statements. Four cures he admits, viz., Margaret

---

[1] Dr. J. H. Newman, note on p. 383 of his two 'Essays on Scripture Miracles,' 2nd edit. London, Pickering, 1870; Prof. Huxley, 'Lessons on Elementary Physiology,' p. 207; Milman's Edition of 'Gibbon,' vol. iv. p. 336.

Thibault and Margaret Francis Duchesne cured of dropsy, Serjeant and Hardouin of paralysis; and it may be added that these recoveries, as he states them, are manifestly too sudden and too immediately connected with the excitement at the tomb to be looked upon as tentative, *i. e.* cases in which recovery took place without any real connection with what happened at the tomb. The Bishop was a hostile critic, a writer ostensibly engaged in discrediting all miracles except those of the Gospels. He explains the facts by the influence of mental excitement, and to support this view he quotes many examples of this kind of influence upon the body. When quoting examples of the efficacy of the royal touch, he mentions that he had himself known a man who professed to have been cured thereby. As comparatively modern and well-known instances of such cures by mental influence, he quotes the cures performed by Mr. Greatrakes, of Waterford, by stroking with the hand; Sir Richard Bulkley cured of rupture by one of the French prophets; Madame de la Fosse, cured of a long-standing issue of blood by supplication to the host when it was being carried in procession.

Among no body of modern Christians has a higher tone of piety prevailed than among the Moravian Brethren. Paley, in the work which we have now specially in view, has paid them a compliment, not the less to be valued because it was seemingly undesigned. When speaking of the life of the first Christians, he says that it probably resembled theirs.[1] Now it is worthy of notice that the resemblance extends to the alleged existence of the miraculous. In a history of the Brethren, by M. Bost, of Geneva, we have the following extract from the words of Count Zinzendorf, the early founder and ruler of the sect. He speaks of their having experienced the following wonderful occurrences :—' The discovery of things, persons, and circumstances, which could not humanly have been discovered; the healing of maladies in themselves incurable, such as cancers and consumptions, when the patient was in the agonies of death, and all by means of prayer or of a single word; wild beasts stopped at the moment of attack, by the word of the Lord, without any external aid or their having themselves received any hurt.' These statements are, I allow, uncircumstantial, but still the high character of Count Zinzendorf makes them worthy of attention.

The narrative which I am about to relate has some degree of particularity as to names, places, and dates.

Soon after the foundation of the first settlement of the Brethren by Count Zinzendorf at Herrnhut, there arose an awakening among the descendants of

[1] Paley's 'Evidences,' Part I. chap. i.

the old Protestant church of Bohemia, which had been almost crushed and exterminated. The new Brethren were much persecuted, and experienced some wonderful deliverances and escapes. Among these the following may be quoted as approaching the miraculous, and also as having some resemblance to narratives in the Acts of the Apostles. It is given by M. Bost, on the authority of an autobiography of the hero, David Nitschman, who died at Bethlehem, in Pennsylvania, in the eighty-fourth year of his age, in the year 1758. The circumstances are also alluded to in a history of the Brethren by Mr. Latrobe.

Nitschman and some of his party were cast into prison, and chained two and two. He, however, was ironed apart. He relates as follows:—'On Thursday evening I told my brethren that I had thoughts of leaving them that night. And "I too," instantly added David Schneider; "I mean to go with you." We had to wait till eleven. Not knowing how I should be able to get rid of my irons, I laid my hand upon the padlock which fastened them, to try and open it with a knife, and behold it was opened! I began to weep for joy, and I said to Schneider, "Now I see it is the will of God that I should go." We removed the irons from our feet, we took leave of the brethren in profound silence, and crossed the court to see if we could find a ladder.

I went as far as the principal passage, which was secured by two doors, and I found the first open and the second likewise. This was a second sign that we were to go. Being out of the castle, we hung our irons on the wall, and we crossed the garden to reach my dwelling, where we waited awhile that I might tell my wife how she should go when I sent one to fetch her.'

Nitschman thus escaped on the night of the 25th of January, 1725, and after being awhile in Silesia, he reached Herrnhut on March 3. Nitschman also relates that on an earlier occasion he was kept in prison three days without any nourishment, and did not suffer hunger.

M. Bost relates other escapes perhaps not so wonderful. The following, however, is singular:—A man, named André Beyer, was in prison with a Brother named David Fritsch. Their imprisonment was to be made more severe, but on the day before this was to be done Fritsch accidentally pushed the door of his prison, the great chain stretched across it outside gave way, the door opened, they saw no sentinels, went forth, and escaped. I do not pretend that there is anything in this account, or yet in the former, which could be at all put forward as a breach of a law of nature, but they are stories of very exceptional events in connection with religion. There are many others in the history of the Moravians, as happy choices by lot, warnings by dreams, or otherwise.

Another body of men, to whom Paley compared the primitive Christians, were the English Methodists of last century. In their case also accounts of visions, prophecies, strange providences, expulsions of evil spirits, wonderful cures, are also to be met with. Bishop Lavington, in his 'Enthusiasm of Methodists and Papists Compared,' has very fully and with much detail pointed out the resemblance between the wonderful things related of remarkable religious characters in those two bodies of Christians in some respects so remote. And, indeed, he extends the analogy to the Montanists and heathens. A less hostile writer, Mr. Southey, also tells us that Wesley claimed the power of working miracles.[1] He believed that he had himself been miraculously recovered from a fever. He had restored a dying man. The meetings of his followers were, it is well known, sometimes attended with great excitement, issuing in some strange physical results, as tremblings, screamings, swoons, convulsions; and it is worthy of notice that these effects showed their epidemic character by sometimes seizing upon persons present, whose minds were not under the influence of Wesley's teaching.[2] There is a story of a Quaker

---

[1] 'Southey's Life,' vol. i. p. 385; Southey quotes 'Wesley's Journal,' vol. iii.

[2] Southey's 'Life of Wesley,' vol. i. p. 212.

who was caught by the contagion at one of the meetings, whilst he was inveighing against what he called 'the dissimulation of the creatures.' A singular story is also related by Southey (as well as Bishop Lavington) of a woman who was thought to be possessed, and was certainly fearfully agitated. This woman told those around her that Wesley was coming galloping to see her when he really was doing so, but was yet three miles off, and she had no natural means of knowing of his coming.[1] Coleridge, in a note upon this anecdote, declares that an extensive inquiry had convinced him of the actual occurrence of such apparent anomalies.

As I have said already, these accounts have not been given because they seem to me by any means to compel the admission of the miraculous. I have no idea of so disproving the negative part of the evidential argument. I quote them to introduce some views as to the origin of such accounts. If we review them the following observation will be made. Wherever and whenever religious faith and earnestness are unusually strong, and the views of modern science are little understood or entertained ; whenever, in fact, you have Christians resembling the first believers, then miraculous, or at least wonderful, stories spring up, sometimes in numbers. We have already seen this illustrated in very different ages, and countries, and forms, of the Christian faith. Our ex-

[1] Southey's 'Life of Wesley,' vol. i. p. 254.

amples include the early church, the early British church, the mediæval church, the Puritans, the Moravians, the early Methodists. The range might have been immensely extended. The Bollandist collection alone, of the lives of the saints, has been computed to relate about 25,000 miracles.[1] And the inference from this observation I think would be that an exalted feeling of the personal action of God in the world, and perhaps of other supernatural beings as well, favours, nay often generates, a belief in miracles, just as a perception of natural law checks it. Mr. Lecky, from a wider review, has come to a similar conclusion in a more general form.[2] Obviously this view helps to explain several of the classes of wonderful stories which we have had to consider. The tendency in question would help to gain credit for exaggerations, and bias men in favour of reports of miracles. It may also, in company with general religious excitement, have promoted cases of false perception, visions, voices, dreams, and the like. Indeed, these latter are at all times more common than some persons may suppose. Neander[3] quotes Origen and Tertullian to the effect that visions either in sleep or waking were in their days the most common causes of conversion. I believe that I have

[1] Lecky's 'History of Rationalism,' vol. i.
[2] Lecky's 'History of European Civilisation,' p. 370 and onwards; 'History of Rationalism,' chap. ii.
[3] Neander's 'Church History,' English Trans., vol. i. p. 102.

somewhere read the same of South India at the present day. There are, I should think, in England itself few clergymen who have had much to do with the poor who have not had stories of visions related to them. Such, at least, has been my own experience. Further, it may reasonably be supposed that at such times remarkable acts of God's providence do occur, especially in answer to prayer, or to meet some emergency. We can hardly deny this, if we believe in God's moral government of the world. And that government I am at present assuming. I make no doubt that the Almighty does use the course of nature as an instrument for the ends of that government. The question before us is, Does he ever break through that order for those ends? No doubt some of the special providences which I am admitting would seem to be such interferences in the eyes of excited believers. We inquire, Are there also events which have that appearance in the judgment of observant and impartial persons? Now, if we turn again to the narratives just given, the wonderful cures and bodily effects will be seen to be the most plausible cases of such interference. There is here less room for delusion of the mind and the senses than in many alleged miracles. Such delusion will produce wonders, as we know from the tricks of a clever conjuror. But here, as Paley has justly pointed out, is a permanent effect, which it could not produce. It is, I think, needful to suppose some unknown, or at least ill-understood, powers of nature to explain these cases. I will presently give examples so well attested as to the facts, and yet so extraordinary, as to seem to require this supposition. But as some of the things which I am about to say may seem incredible, and as there may be in the minds of some a natural prejudice against such suppositions as that which I am going to advocate, let me, by way of preface, cite some instances in which men of science have been led to reject wonderful accounts, when well attested, merely because they were inexplicable, and yet all has subsequently proved to be true. Mr. Robert Chambers, in a little pamphlet, entitled 'Testimony: its Posture in the Scientific World,' collected several such instances. A committee of the French Academy last century rejected three nearly contemporary accounts of the fall of meteoric stones. The Royal Medical and Chirurgical Society of London received with contemptuous incredulity an account of an amputation performed without pain upon a mesmerised patient. Mr Hallam and Mr. Rogers were even treated with rudeness for venturing to describe in England mesmeric phenomena which they had witnessed in France. Gibbon thought that no one could believe in the tongueless speech of the African confessors, save those who also believed in their orthodoxy. A strange story was told in France last century about three balls of fire being seen at the points of the cross on a church when thunder was near. The scientific world rejected the account, but Franklin's discovery that lightning was due to electricity explained the matter. Other examples might be added. I ask, Have we not to learn from such cases diffidence in rejecting an account merely because, in the present state of science, it cannot be explained? Should we not be ready to admit at least as an alternative to the supposition of its falsehood the other supposition of which I have spoken?

The learning and the piety, the genius and the persecutions, of the Port Royalists have given a deep interest to their history. Among its incidents are many miracles, and one especially as well attested as any in ecclesiastical history. Mrs. Schimmelpenninck[1] is able to refer to a long list of authorities—Besogne, Clemencet, Gilbert, Perrier, Pascal, 'Necrologie,' 'Manuel de Port Royal,' ' Histoire du Miracle de la Sainte Épine,' 'Mémoires de Fontaine,' 'Notes de Nicole aux Le tres Provinciales,' Racine 'Histoire Port Royal,' Choiseul 'Mémoires sur la Religion,' 'Attestation des Grands Vicaires de Paris.' I shall quote only a few to whom I have myself referred, but they will, I think, be sufficient to show the strength of the case.

[1] 'Port Royal: Its Saints,' by Mrs. Schimmelpenninck, p. 68.

The story is briefly this. Marguerite Perrier, niece to the celebrated Blaise Pascal, was placed at the convent of Port Royal with her eldest sister for her education in the year 1653. She was afflicted for three years and a-half with a fistula lachrymalis in the corner of the left eye. It became of the size of a nut. The bones of the nose became carious, and perforated to the palate. The left eye became less in size, and the sense of smell was lost. A very offensive discharge came from the sore. The child was under the care of M. Dalencé, an able surgeon, who had proposed, as a last desperate attempt at remedy, to cauterise the fistula. The consent of her father had been asked, and he was indeed intending to be present. At this crisis, a thorn, said to have been part of the crown of Christ in his passion, was sent to Port Royal, and exhibited to the nuns and other inmates on March 24, 1656. The wound of Marguerite was touched with this thorn, and within a quarter of an hour all signs of her disease had disappeared.

I find this story in the histories of Du Fosse, Fontaine, and Clemencet. The two former were contemporary, and Du Fosse knew the young lady intimately. She was then eleven years old, and lived, according to Fontaine, until the year 1733. Clemencet is a writer of later date, of the early part of the next century, but of much research. I would quote also the following testimonies.

The girl had an aunt among the nuns, La Sœur Jacqueline de Sainte Euphémie. We find a letter written by her to the child's mother preserved in the 'Recueil des plusieurs pièces pour servir à l'histoire de Port Royal,' Utrecht. This letter was begun on March 26, 1656, but not finished until eight days after. It gives full particulars as to the cure. We have also preserved among the letters of the justly esteemed abbess of Port Royal, the Mère Angelique, one written to the Queen of Poland about the beginning of the May following this event, and relating the story at length. In the genuineness of both these letters, M. Sainte-Beuve, an acute critic, opposed to the marvellous view of the matter, has full confidence. We have also a tract published by Pascal himself at Paris in 1656, in answer to a publication of the Jesuits hostile to the miracle.[1] Pascal gives the essential circumstances, as stated above. He rests, indeed, the defence of Port Royal upon this miracle.

He mentions several other wonderful cures which the holy thorn was the means of causing at Port Royal. But it had not this effect elsewhere. He notices the following objections :—The elder

[1] 'Œuvres de Pascal.'

sister Perrier had, it was said, been substituted for the younger. The one shown as in health was not the one who had been really afflicted. In answer, both were produced. Again, it was said that the cure was incomplete, and that the disease had returned, but this was disproved by the examination of M. Dalencé and another eminent surgeon. Also it was said that the disease had only changed its seat, and that the child was otherwise afflicted; but this was also disproved by M. Guillard, an eminent surgeon, and by M. Felix, first surgeon to the king.

The accounts of the writers whom I have quoted do not, I ought to say, minutely agree. There is something of that addition of striking particulars which we generally see in successive narratives of any wonderful events. Thus M. Fontaine gives a much more lively and dramatic account of the discovery of the cure by the medical men than that which we find in the letter of the Sœur Jacqueline. But all the accounts do agree in the main points. All, for instance, attest the severity of the disease. The letter just named expressly describes how M. Dalencé ascertained the perforated condition of the bone. Pascal is explicit as to the symptoms, the carious state of the bone, the frequent and offensive discharges, &c. And this is I think the main point. The subsequently healthy state of the child is abundantly and incontestably established. Clemencet, indeed, relates that several distinguished physicians, Charles Bonoard, first physician to the king, Jean Hamon and Isaac Eusebe Renaudot; and also surgeons Pierre Cressé, Martin Dalencé, and Etienne Guillard, attested the miracle from their knowledge of the case *before* as well as *after* the cure, and this attestation is found in other histories as well as his.

Certainly there can be no doubt as to the state of things after the cure. The truth of the story was investigated by M. Felix, the king's first surgeon, sent by a hostile court, and he confirmed the report. An investigation was also made by the Grand Vicars of the Archbishop of Paris with a like result. In fact, the miracle was believed in not only by the friends but also by the enemies of Port Royal, and actually caused a change in the conduct of the court towards the convent. The only question is, it seems to me, as to the nature of the previous disease. Accordingly, M. Sainte-Beuve[1] offers the explanation that the complaint was really not fistula lachrymalis but tumor lachrymalis (tumeur lacrymale), causing an obstruction in the lachrymal duct which drains the surface of the eye, and that the pressure of the holy thorn on the tumour caused its dispersion in a natural way.

[1] 'Port Royal,' C. A. Sainte-Beuve.

But I do not see how this hypothesis can be made to agree with the authentic accounts of the malady.

The next case is that of Miss Fancourt. It is a history which excited much attention about forty-four years ago.

Miss Fancourt was a young lady, the daughter of a clergyman living in London. She had been suffering severely for eight years from what was thought to be disease of the hip. She had been under the care of different medical men, and had undergone various treatment without recovery. She was instantaneously cured under the following circumstances:—A pious friend, who had made her case the subject of very earnest prayer, solemnly asked her whether she believed that Christ had power to heal her. She answered that she did. He bade her rise from her couch and walk. She actually did so, and was permanently restored.

This wonderful occurrence was much discussed at the time, and various opinions concerning it were advocated by men of learning and ability. These opinions have been ably contrasted by Professor Baden Powell in his work called the 'Order of Nature.' The well-known Dr. Maitland, in an essay in his book called 'Eruvin,' maintained the miraculous view of the matter; and the Rev. Thomas Boys, also a clergyman of the Church of England, advocated the same view, and published a book called 'The Suppressed Evidence,' a work that has aided me, in order to prove the continuance of miraculous powers in Christ's Church. On the contrary, the editor of the 'Christian Observer,' in the number of that magazine for November 1830, opposed this view. Apparently his grounds were purely theological. He was determined to look upon all miracles out of Scripture as merely natural wonders, but seemingly not from any difference which he could trace in the facts themselves or the evidence for them, but from theological views, such as the need of evidential purpose to make a real miracle in his opinion credible, the peculiar character of Scripture history, antipathy to Popish miracles, and the like. The facts of the case before us he fully allows. He gives a letter, signed 'H. S. C. H.,' containing a statement of these facts drawn up by Miss Fancourt herself, and also a letter from her father to a friend. In the latter the father states that the flesh of the restored limb had been, previous to the cure, loose and flabby, but that after the cure it was found to be firm and strong. He adds also that there had been a flexure of the spine, and an enlargement of the collar-bone on one side, and that these symptoms also had disappeared. These particulars he gives on the authority of his wife.

Admitting these facts, the editor explains them by the power of mental excitement. It will be noticed that he here follows the example of Bishop Douglas, and, like that prelate, he seeks to support his view by other cases which must he thinks be thus explained. He refers to two modern instances— 1. A wonderful cure of a Mrs. Ann Mattingly, attested by a number of affidavits published at Washington, March 10, 1824. 2. The case of Mrs. Stuart, cured at the convent of St. Joseph, Ranelagh, in the diocese of Dublin, published by Dr. Murray, Bishop of Dublin, 1823. It would seem that though a strong Protestant he did not fully share Paley's distrust of miraculous narratives published in the interest of an Established religion, and above all of the Popish religion.

Professor Powell himself, in accordance with his well-known views, favoured a natural explanation, viz., 'that the apparent spinal or hip disease was due entirely to the deceptive effect of hysterical affection, simulating the supposed disorder, and which was at once removed when the hysteria was subdued.' He refers to a letter from Mr. Travers, an eminent surgeon, who was consulted in the case, and who 'after some doubt at length explained it in the way just stated.' He also refers to a notice of the case by Sir Benjamin Brodie in a small volume called 'Lectures on Local Nervous Affections.' This book is a collection of cases in which hysteria simulated local injury or disease, and it is true that

Sir Benjamin speaks of Miss Fancourt's illness as an instance. But I feel bound to say that his notice seems to me cursory. He does not appear to have had any knowledge of the case except from the report of the 'Christian Observer.' He simply speaks of it as plainly an 'hysterical affection simulating disease of the hip-joint,' and does not notice the circumstances stated in the father's letter as to the spine and collar-bone. Dr. Maitland refers to other eminent medical men who thought the case inexplicable.

In the number of 'Macmillan's Magazine' for April 1871, there is an account by an eminent medical man, Dr. Day, of a Belgian ecstatic, Louise Lateau. Dr. Day does not speak as an eye-witness. He takes the particulars from an account published by Dr. Lefebvre, Professor of General Pathology and Therapeutics at the University of Louvain. Dr. Lefebvre himself had long and carefully examined the case. The facts, indeed, have been so minutely and scientifically investigated, and the absence of fraud has been so strictly tested, that there cannot, I should think, be any doubt as to the truth of the mere phenomena. They are briefly as follows :— Louise Lateau was a peasant girl of pious but not enthusiastic character, who after a severe illness received without external cause marks resembling those known as the stigmata, and already spoken of in the case of St. Francis. In her case there were marks similar to those commonly associated with the crucifixion upon both sides of the hands and of the feet, a mark upon the left side of the chest, and also pricks in a zone going round the head between the hair and eyebrows. But there was not the appearance of nails. From these marks blood issued every Friday. Further, about a quarter of a year after these appearances, an ecstatic state began to recur every Friday. In this state Louise Lateau saw visions of our Lord's Passion, and remained perfectly insensible to outward things, even under the most severe tests.

Dr. Lefebvre considered these phenomena inexplicable in the present state of medical science. But in a number of the 'Lancet,' published immediately after the account in 'Macmillan's Magazine,' it is maintained that these phenomena, however strange, can be explained by the action of the mind, when its attention is automatically, and therefore very long and very powerfully, directed to a particular part of the body. A singular case is mentioned in which a severe injury to the fingers of a child was followed by inflammation and sloughing in the corresponding parts of the mother's fingers. Dr. Carpenter, in his 'Mental Physiology,'[1] has also mentioned this case, and added another similar case on the authority of Dr. Tuke.

[1] Carpenter's 'Principles of Mental Physiology,' p. 682.

The imaginary cold experienced by some subjects in displays of electro-biology has been known to produce actual chilblains.

The article in 'Macmillan's Magazine' tells us that there are on record in all about seventy alleged cases of receiving the stigmata, beginning with that of St. Francis.

I have cited these three cases because, as it seems to me, they are adequately attested, and seem to prove that religious feeling may produce bodily effects which in ignorant times would certainly have been accounted miraculous, and which may, I think, be fairly compared with the miracles of the New Testament. With a little research, other cases might, I have no doubt, be added. But as enough may have been said upon this point, I will pass on to another which is of great importance in our subject.

The cases which I have brought prominently forward have all been connected with the influence of the Christian religion. Incidentally, reference has been made to other analogous cases which had no such connection; which, in fact, had sometimes no connection with any religion.

I would now expressly call attention to the fact, as a very important point, that wonderful bodily effects are produced by mental influences other than religious. Of this fact we have already had one example in the Vespasian cures. It is evidently important in our present inquiry, because it tends to deprive the cause of these anomalous cures, be it what it may, of a strictly religious character. I will illustrate it further, by a reference to the cures by the king's touch, of which mention has been already made. We have, indeed, a great deal of evidence that such cures really occurred. I will give some. Dr. Tooker, who lived in the reign of Elizabeth, and was made Dean of Lichfield, wrote a book upon the subject, entitled 'Charisma sive Donum Sanationis.' In Chapter VIII. he gives the names and abodes of some persons whom he knew to have been cured, and he tells us that he had by inquiries found the cures to be real and permanent. He says that the cured were of all ranks, ages, and sexes, and he adds the instructive remark that he had found in the applicants for relief 'incredibilem ardorem et fidem adipiscendæ salutis.'

Mr. Richard Wiseman was a principal surgeon in the army of Charles I., and serjeant-surgeon to Charles II. He has left a collection of surgical treatises, amongst which there is one on the king's evil. It opens with a notice of cures by the king's touch, from which I extract the following passage:—

'I myself have been a frequent eye-witness of many hundreds of cures performed by His Majesty's touch alone, without any assistance of chirurgery, and those many of them such as had tired out the endeavours of able chirurgeons, before they came thither. It were needless to recite what I myself have seen, and what I have received acknowledgment of by letter, not only from several parts of this nation, but also from Ireland, Scotland, Jersey, and Guernsey.' He mentions certain objections. The improvement in health might, it was said, be the effect of the journey and change of air. He brings forward in reply the case of Londoners who had been cured. Some attributed the cures to the effect of imagination; but this explanation, Wiseman remarks, would not apply to the case of infants who had been cured. Others connected the benefit with the piece of gold usually given on the occasion, and cases were cited in which, when this gift had been parted with, the recovery did not last. Our author admits this fact, but says that the relapse did not always follow, and further asserts that Charles I. performed cures when he gave only silver pieces and indeed sometimes nothing at all. He tells us that like miracles of healing were performed by the blood of Charles I. preserved after his execution upon chips of wood and handkerchiefs. I ought perhaps to add that he does not give the names of the cured of whom he speaks. We are here reminded of 'the special miracles' wrought at Ephesus by the hands of Paul, 'so that from his body were brought unto the sick handkerchiefs or aprons, and the diseases departed from them, and the evil spirits went out of them' (Acts xix. 12); and again of the sick laid out upon their beds, 'that at the least the shadow of Peter passing by might overshadow some of them' (Acts v. 15).

I have referred already to the testimony which Bishop Douglas, in his work 'The Criterion,' bears to the reality of some of these cures. I may add that, besides referring to the writers from whom I have myself quoted, he also cites Mr. Dickens, serjeant-surgeon to Queen Anne. Of this gentleman the Bishop expresses a high opinion, and he tells us that Mr. Dickens had full opportunity of testing the truth, as those who were to be touched were first examined by him. He made no secret of bearing witness to the certainty of some of the cures.

I will now quote the explanation of those cures from extraordinary mental impressions, either religious or secular, given by an eminent living physiologist. The natural agency supposed will be seen to be the same as that suggested in the quotation from the 'Lancet,' and even those who may not be willing to accept this explanation must allow that it is sound in principle, being an attempt at legitimate generalisation from a great number of observed facts. The following quotation is from Dr. Carpenter's 'Principles of Human Physiology.' The author has been speaking of certain extraordinary effects upon

DR. CARPENTER'S EXPLANATION.

the body from a fixed attention of the mind, and he adds as follows :—

'Now the effects which are producible by the voluntary or determinate direction of the consciousness to the result are doubtless no less producible by that involuntary fixation of the attention upon it, which is consequent upon the eager expectation of benefit from some curative method in which implicit confidence is placed. It is to such a state that we may fairly attribute most, if not all, the cures which have been worked through what is popularly called the imagination. The cures are real facts, however they may be explained, and there is scarcely a malady in which amendment has not been produced not merely in the estimation of the patient but in the more trustworthy opinion of medical observers, by practices which can have had no other effect than to direct the attention of the sufferer, and keep alive his confident expectation of the cure. The charming away of warts by spells of the most vulgar kind, the imposition of the royal hands for the cure of the evil, the pawings and strokings of Valentine Greatrakes, the manipulations practised with the metallic tractors, the invocations of Prince Hohenlohe *et hoc genus omne*, not omitting the globulistic administrations of the infinitesimal doctors, and the manipulations of the mesmerists of our own times, have all worked to the same end, and have all alike been successful. It is unquestionable that in all such cases the benefit derived is in direct proportion to the faith of the sufferer in the means employed, and thus we see that a couple of bread pills will produce copious purgation, and a dose of red poppy syrup will serve as a powerful narcotic, if the patient have entertained a sufficiently confident expectation of such a result.' He goes on to speak of ill effects following in like manner. In a note, the case of Pascal's niece is mentioned and spoken of as well attested. Similar views are expressed and further illustrated in Dr. Carpenter's more recent book, 'Principles of Mental Physiology,' p. 685. The case of Marguerite Perrier is there given at some length.

We have had before us wonderful effects on the body arising from influences of the mind which have no connection with religion. It is hardly needful to say that we have also accounts of all other kinds of marvels with which religion, or at least the Christian religion, has nothing to do. We have such accounts in connection with other religions, as Buddhism and Muhammedanism, with magic, with fairy superstitions, with apparitions of the dead, with important political events, as, for instance, the death of Julius Cæsar. Now, a vast majority of these stories we can at once put aside. Their evidence is obviously weak. But it is not so always. We have stories in which we must either allow some unknown agency or confess that our ordinary rules for judging of evidence are at fault. The early history of John Wesley supplies a ghost story, which must I think be looked upon as such a puzzle. In the collection of accounts by which Glanvil has sought to uphold the belief in witchcraft there are circumstances equally perplexing.

Mr. Lecky[1] has truly said that there is an enormous amount of evidence which once satisfied acute and practised judges in support of the marvels of witchcraft. When every allowance has been made for the effects of prepossession and credulity, I think that we must see something more than mere delusion. On this point I cannot altogether agree with the eminent writer to whom I have referred. We must, I think, allow the working of ill-understood natural agencies of which it is my purpose next to speak in connection with events of our own day. I will begin by referring to a remarkable outbreak of epidemic insanity which took place at Morzine, a commune in Savoy, about 1857. It throws much light on a large class of New Testament miracles, the cases of demoniacal possession, and I think also on the origin of many stories of witchcraft. We have here the personation of evil spirits, prophecies of attacks and recoveries, perception of things and persons at extraordinary distances, speaking in unknown

---

[1] See Lecky's 'History of Rationalism,' chap. i. p. 2.

tongues, wonderful strength and activity of body and mind. Dr. Constans, the physician sent by the French Government to deal with the epidemic, endeavours to divest the history of all appearance of the supernatural, and no doubt many of his explanations may be accepted. Seeming possession may be a form of insanity; prophecies may fulfil themselves; a few words of a strange language originally heard by accident, and little noticed at the time, may be subsequently remembered and uttered in an abnormal state of mind, and may pass for speaking with unknown tongues; a perception of what is passing miles away may be put down, in the last resort, as somnambulism. All this may be done, and rightly done. But it must be owned that if this age be content to rest in such explanations, other times would have seen in these things the work of supernatural powers. I may add, as of further bearing upon our subject, that a state of excitement was induced among the people in which still greater prodigies were gravely attested.[1]

I have spoken of these phenomena as especially allied to what we read in the New Testament of possession by evil spirits. This will, I think, be felt by anyone who reads the accounts. In a recent work upon 'Our Lord's Miracles of Healing,' written

---

[1] See Dr. A. Constans: 'Relation sur une Épidémie d'Hystéro-Démonopathie;' also 'Cornhill Magazine,' April 1865.

by a clergyman, the Rev. T. W. Belcher, who had been in early life a medical man, and written certainly in no rationalistic spirit, the writer mentions that he had attended a lady suffering from mental disease, whose symptoms resembled those of the demoniacs in the Gospels.

Mention has been made of somnambulism. This exceptional nervous state has long been known as arising in peculiar cases. But of late years our knowledge of it has been greatly increased by the discovery that a state essentially the same may be artificially brought about with many persons. I allude to what is popularly known as electro-biology or animal magnetism.

The late Mr. Braid, of Manchester, used to bring on in those on whom he operated a state which he called hypnotism, a kind of artificial somnambulism, and his researches threw much light upon the subject.

Here, too, we have many phenomena which in past days would have been taken for the supernatural. Serjeant Cox,[1] in a recent work on psychology, has collected many details. We hear of what seems to be sight when the eyes were closed, or the objects distant, or otherwise not naturally

---

[1] 'What am I? a Popular Introduction to Mental Philosophy and Psychology,' by Edward W. Cox, Barrister-at-law. Longmans & Co., London, 1874.

visible. We have great exaltation of the emotions and intellectual powers, and further a stimulation of particular faculties by touching certain parts of the head. We find the patient brought under the control of another person, technically said to be *en rapport*. We find that it is even in the power of the latter to suggest to the mind of the former ideas which, though utterly false, shall pass as experienced facts; for instance, to make him take a glass of water for wine. We have insight into the thoughts of others. Lastly, we have cures, even of such diseases as paralysis, cancer, and consumption. These cures, however, have a strong appearance of coming under the explanation of Dr. Carpenter, already given. Indeed, Serjeant Cox gives the same explanation, with an addition due to his own views of the physical cause of these phenomena. He supposes that the direction of the mind to the diseased part causes a *flow of nerve force* to it. He cites as an example the cure of Miss Martineau, the well-known authoress, by these means, from an ulcer which the most eminent medical men had pronounced incurable and fatal.

Allied, yet dissimilar, to somnambulism, is trance. Here we have great mental elevation, at times prolonged fasting, simulated death, and what is perhaps stranger than all, according to Serjeant Cox, cases of resistance to the action of heat. This state has also a feature peculiarly fitted to give rise to stories of the supernatural, viz., the acting at times with wonderful effect of some character far superior to the patient. Nothing would be more likely to suggest ideas of inspiration or possession.

In connection with these phenomena of trance and somnambulism I may refer to the yet wider subject of 'unconscious cerebration.' This is the name which Dr. Carpenter has given to that unconscious action of the mind, of which we have very many examples, not only in abnormal states, as delirium, but also in our ordinary healthy life, as in sleep, or in the performance of habitual acts, such as reading or walking.[1] One form of this kind of action has no doubt played an important part in religious history, viz., the mysterious voices which the mind sometimes seems to hear speaking it knows not whence.

I may add that Dr. Carpenter, who is a cautious and thoroughly scientific writer, does allow some of the wonderful phenomena just mentioned, as the cases of suggestion of ideas to a hypnotised patient, great exaltation of the sense perceptions, power of reading the thoughts of others, cures, and other effects on the bodily functions. He also allows that if nerve force be a form of energy, its action at a distance, so that one brain should affect another far

[1] See Essays by F. P. Cobbe, 'Unconscious Cerebration,' p. 316.

away, cannot be said *à priori* to be impossible, but it would need very good evidence for its proof.[1]

There is yet one more class of phenomena in these days of which I would here speak. I allude to what is called spiritualism. I am far from advocating the belief that the phenomena in question are really caused by the spirits of the dead. This belief certainly needs confirmation. But it must, I think, be allowed that we have good evidence for facts, which our present physical and mental science does not explain, and which in former ages would have been thought supernatural. No one can, I think, read the report of the committee of the Dialectical Society on the subject, or the publications of Mr. Crookes, in his 'Quarterly Journal of Science,' without admitting so much. We have, indeed, here the seeming supernatural in varied and difficult forms. We hear of mysterious sounds, movements of heavy bodies without mechanical means, imparting of information in inexplicable ways, apparitions visible to many, sensible also to the touch, performing physical acts some of which, as the introduction of solid bodies into closed rooms, seem impossible. These phenomena are attested, in many cases, by men not only of high character and social position, but also of undoubted scientific cultivation. It is interesting to notice how some of the most striking of the eccle-

[1] See 'Mental Physiology,' p. 633.

siastical wonders are reproduced, as, for instance, the levitation or miraculous transference of the human body. In the number of his Journal for January of this year, Mr. Crookes has treated this last point at length. He has instanced no less than forty saints of the Roman Catholic Church who are related to have been thus raised or carried through the air. He might have carried his analogies even further than he has done. We have similar accounts, not only as he tells us as to Romish saints, and as to Pythagoras or Apolonius of Tyana, but also in Buddhist legends, in the witch cases as those of Glanvil, and still more recently in the Morzine phenomena.[1] There must, one would say, be some unknown principle, either psychical or physical, to account for kindred narratives springing up in quarters so remote; and surely we may add the reflection, that with such accounts so attested at the present day amongst ourselves, it must be hard to establish an exclusive case for the miraculous in Judæa eighteen centuries ago. Of course, as we shall more fully point out hereafter, if we do admit the agency of the spirits of the dead, then the theological inferences from what is thought to be supernatural fall to the ground.

If we review what has now been brought forward as to non-evangelical wonders we shall not, I sup-

[1] Tylor's 'Primitive Culture,' vol. i. p. 135.

pose, think that any true miracle has been *proved*, but we shall, I think, allow that a well-supported case has been made out for wonderful bodily effects, especially cures from mental influence. Further, it appears that this influence does often exist in cases of religious excitement. But at the same time it is by no means confined to such cases. A connection is also to be traced between the faith of those healed and their recovery. So far we may speak confidently. And this conclusion is of great importance, because it affects a class of miracles which, as I have pointed out, are especially verifiable. We may also deem it probable that there are ill-understood powers of nature which at times simulate the miraculous. We have a strong ground for such belief in the abnormal perceptions of the somnambulist and the table-turnings of the spiritualist.

PART V.

Leaving now our notice of these wonders with the conclusions just given, we come to the question, How stand the narratives of the Gospels when they are judged as we have been judging other wonderful accounts? Do they establish an exclusive case of the miraculous? Can they escape the various tests as to evidence, and the various hypotheses of natural explanation, by which other marvels are disposed of or explained? This, I need scarcely remind my reader, is the great point in our inquiry. Paley maintains that the Gospel narratives have this advantage over all other miraculous histories. But I doubt his conclusion. Let us go in order through his various exceptions, arranging them according to my own classification, and also modifying them, and estimating their force as I have thought just. And with these revisions, let us apply them to the case of the Christian miracles.

First class of exceptions. Want of trustworthy information.

(1). Accounts written long subsequent to the event. Paley tells us that 'ours is contemporary history.'[1] If it be meant that the narratives of our present Gospels were drawn up at the time of the events which they record, the assertion cannot be maintained. The external evidence of the existence of these narratives is but weak for a long time after, say, for a hundred years. With St. Matthew and St. Mark,[2] there may be internal evidence for a date not later than the age of the Apostles. But there[3]

[1] Paley's 'Evidences,' Prop. II. chap. i.
[2] St. Matthew, chap. xxiv. v. 34, 35; St. Mark, chap. xiii. v. 30; St. Mark, chap. xv. v. 21; with Romans, chap. xvi. v. 13.
[3] St. Matthew, chap. xxvii. v. 8; chap. xxviii. v. 15.

is also evidence against an origin contemporary with the events. St. Luke's history is avowedly drawn from second-hand sources—see Preface, St. Luke i. 1-4. St. John's has marks of a date later than the death of Christ—see St. John xix. 27; xxi. 19, 23. The want of reference in the apostolic epistles would be inexplicable if the histories were really contemporary. Nor do I know that this is maintained by anyone. Paley himself admits the reverse.[1]

(2). Accounts from distant places.

'In the case of Christianity,' says Paley, 'Judæa, which was the scene of the transaction, was the centre of the Mission. The story was published in the place in which it was acted.[2] The church of Christ was first planted at Jerusalem.' This assertion does not prove that our present Gospels, or indeed any of them, were first published at Jerusalem; nor in fact is there any proof. 'The story' is an ambiguous expression. An adversary might grant that something very wonderful as to Christ was believed by the first Christians at Jerusalem, but not all the miraculous accounts of the Gospels. These, he might say, may be of later growth. It is the nature of all movements, which strongly agitate the mind, especially among an uncultivated people, to generate such growth of legend.

(5). Accounts wanting in particularity.

---

[1] Paley's 'Evidences,' chap. viii.
[2] Prop. II. chap. i. head 2.

Paley[1] instances the account of St. Paul's voyage and shipwreck in the twenty-seventh chapter of the Acts, and that of the cure and examination of the blind man in the ninth chapter of St. John's Gospel, as examples of circumstantial narratives. The former account certainly has this character. And further I believe that the researches of modern times have fully established its accuracy.[2] But it is no part of the Gospels. All that its confirmation proves is that the writer of the Acts was either a companion of St. Paul on the occasion, or at least had access to an account written by such a companion. The narrative in St. John is not, I think, so justly brought forward as circumstantial. Neither the name of the sufferer nor the place or date of the cure are given. In fact, there is no name given in connection with the particulars except the name of Christ and of the pool of Siloam, and in reference to the last[3] a mistake is made. As a rule, the narratives of the Gospels are not characterised by particularity. We have often vague general summaries, as St. Luke iv. 40, St. Matthew iv. 24. Some of the cases of wonderful cures, which I have quoted, have come down to us with more circumstantial details than any in the Gospels.[4]

[1] 'Evidences,' Prop. II. chap. i. head 5.
[2] See 'Voyage and Shipwreck of St. Paul,' by Smith, of Jordan Hill.
[3] See 'Davidson's Introduction to the New Testament,' vol. ii. p. 428.
[4] Innocentius, Mademoiselle Perrier, Miss Fancourt.

(7). Accounts in which the writer is biassed by some previous opinion.

Paley objects to accounts 'in affirmance of opinions already formed.'[1] He very decidedly contrasts the histories of the Gospels with such accounts. He writes :— 'They' (the miracles) 'produced a change; they established a society upon the spot adhering to the belief of them; they made converts, and those who were converted gave up to the testimony their most fixed opinions and most favourite prejudices. They who acted and suffered in the cause, acted and suffered for the miracles, for there was no anterior persuasion to induce them, no prior reverence, prejudice, or partiality to take hold of. Jesus had not one follower when he set up his claim—his miracles gave birth to his sect.'

I have already said that Paley, in my judgment, overrates the part which the miracles had in the origin of Christian belief. Here and in other places he speaks as though he thought that the first disciples had been reluctantly won over by the sheer force of miraculous evidence. To think thus is, for reasons which I have given already, to misunderstand the times. Very possibly, that mental condition, which gave effect to the argument from miracles, viz., the general but not universal recognition of the laws of nature, may have prevailed in Paley's time, but it

---

[1] Paley's 'Evidences,' Prop. II. chap. i. head 7.

certainly did not in that of the first Christians. The men of those days had plenty of ways of explaining the supernatural without ascribing it to God. There were other influences at work. The Gospels themselves do not represent the miracles as producing conviction on any large scale, but the reverse.[1] The striking progress of Christianity was not in Galilee or Jerusalem in Christ's own day, but afterwards, and elsewhere. It has been well said that it was not the sight of the miracles but the report thereof which wrought conversion. And lastly, we must bear in mind that Paley's remarks cannot with confidence be said to apply to what is related in the Gospels. Those accounts were certainly written a good many years after the events, say thirty at least, and when they were written the writers, be they who they may, were Christians strongly influenced by their faith, and so disposed to believe the miraculous as to Christ.

(11). Accounts explicable by exaggeration.

Paley puts aside histories [2] 'in which the variation of a small circumstance may have transformed some extraordinary appearance or some critical coincidence of events into a miracle.' The miracles of the Gospels can by no possibility be explained away in this manner. He adduces the feeding of

---
[1] St. John, chap. xii. v. 37.
[2] 'Evidences,' Prop. II. chap. i. head 4.

the five thousand, and the raising of Lazarus, and of the widow of Nain's son, as instances thus inexplicable. It would be more just to say that some of the miracles of the Gospels cannot thus be explained away. Others may. The two great draughts of fishes, the stater found in the fish's mouth, the withering of the fig-tree, the st'lling of the tempest, may be only such critical coincidences, not in reality breaches of the laws of nature. Stress has been laid upon the cures wrought at a distance, but there is here necessarily no more of the miraculous than in the recovery of Myconius from apparent consumption, simultaneous with the earnest prayer of his friend Luther then at a distance. None of these things need, in fact, to be thought more than special providences, as distinguished from miracles proper. The account of the feeding of the five thousand is a case in which exaggeration of some particulars, and omission of others, might play an important part. The story would be materially less miraculous if few or hardly any of the multitude partook, if religious enthusiasm or other nervous influence sustained them, if their number was much less, or if others besides the disciples contributed to their repast. The story of the raising of the widow's son is not more miraculous than that of some of the resurrections in Augustine's 'de Civitate.' To the history of Lazarus I shall refer hereafter.

Second class of exceptions. Want of corroboration.

(3). Transient rumours.

(4). Bare statements of history.

(6). Accounts received with a careless assent.

I will take all these together.

The advantage which the Gospels are alleged to have over such narratives is that they were earnestly believed, and that what they profess to describe, viz., Christ's life, did produce a great effect in the world.

What I have said when speaking of class (7) applies to the cases now before us. The rapid growth of primitive Christianity does not appear to have arisen from the sight of Christ's miracles. It is not so represented in the Gospels themselves. It was confessedly brought about to a great extent by the preaching of persons who, like Paul and Apollos, were not original witnesses of the miracles. The earnest belief of persons who were not actual witnesses is not a strong evidence for matters of fact. Of course, Christ's own life must have made some earnest disciples. But as the Gospels were confessedly written a good many years after his death, the question arises do they correctly describe the events which caused this first belief? All that we can strictly infer on their behalf, from the consideration before us, is this,—the events which they profess to describe must have been of such a nature that, in conjunction with certain other influences, such as the expectation of a messiah, and the moral power of Christ's character and teaching, they did produce, in a comparatively small number of the spectators, a firm belief in his divine character. This I allow does put a difference between them and the accounts classified above. We must, however, bear in mind that we have other miraculous accounts in which an effect did follow, as, for instance, the cure of the blind man at Milan and of Mademoiselle Perrier, and further in these last cases it was an effect upon hostile minds.

Third class of exceptions. Natural explanation.

(8). Cases of false perception.

(9). Tentative miracles.

(10). Results of natural causes which are not known to the observers.

These also we will take together.

It must, I think, be allowed that if we set aside accounts such as those which I have brought forward of visions and cures as explicable under (8) or (10), then we cannot fairly urge for evidential purposes many of the New Testament miracles. Under (8) I may instance the visions of Zacharias and of the Virgin Mary, the voice from heaven at Christ's baptism, and that mentioned by St. John, the apparitions of departed saints after the crucifixion, the appearances of angels after the resurrection; under (10), the expulsions of evil spirits, the cures of deafness, lameness, blindness, fever, paralysis, leprosy, which make up so much of the miraculous in the Gospel histories. This of course is not withdrawing the claim of the alleged miracles to be thought facts in the case of the cures and subjectively experienced in the case of the visions and sounds. I, for one, have no doubt that Christ did work very wonderful cures. Only I contend that if you will not allow other similar cures to be infractions of the course of nature, but will explain them, say, by extraordinary mental influence, then, to be consistent, you ought to admit the like explanation in the case of Christ. You may not be willing from your own convictions as to Christ's character to adopt this explanation, but you ought not to forbid an adversary to do so. I would here point out the history of the cure of the woman afflicted with an issue of blood as favouring this view. The impression there given is that of a cure performed not by a conscious act of Christ's will, but by an influence proceeding from him in a way only imperfectly known to himself.[1]

The need of faith in those to be cured, when it is considered in connection with what we have seen in other cases of the effect of strong faith and consequent expectancy, does also favour this view of Christ's miracles. And I may add that I see no-

[1] Luke, chap. viii. v. 43-48; Mark, chap. v. v. 25-34.

thing derogatory to Our Lord's character in such an admission. A power working through the laws of nature seems to me more analogous to the divine than a power breaking in upon those laws. But I do allow that this view does not suit the evidential argument.

When I was speaking of tentative miracles I pointed out that the true account of the matter was not vaguely to refer the effect to accident, but to admit the working of obscure unnoticed causes in the few cases of success. Paley[1] tells us that 'no solution of the kind is applicable to the miracles of the Gospels. There is nothing in the narrative which can induce or even allow us to believe that Christ attempted cures in many cases, and succeeded in a few, or that he ever made the attempt in vain;' and again 'Christ never pronounced the word but the effect followed.'

This, I think, is going beyond what the narratives impartially considered justify, or at all events beyond what an evidential writer is entitled to assume in controversy with a sceptic. It is quite true that the Gospels never mention a failure or an imperfect cure. But, on the other hand, it is not expressly said that such never occurred. There is no record of subsequent examination by persons of good medical knowledge. It is not according to the

[1] Paley's 'Evidences,' Prop. II. chap. i.

analogy of such histories that we should hear of failures. When St Augustine is relating the cures performed by the relics of St. Stephen he says nothing of any applicants who failed to derive benefit. Yet we can hardly doubt that there were some, whilst at the same time we do not doubt his good faith. If, as was certainly the case with St. Luke, the evangelists composed their narratives at second hand, they might well have never heard of any imperfect success. Perhaps, if you regard the Gospels as miraculously free from any of the imperfections which beset the compositions even of good and well-informed men, and as presenting accordingly a perfect image of the transactions which they record, you may build something upon their silence. But this is a way of regarding them inadmissible in an evidential argument; and further one which seems to me at variance with their phenomena. One thing they do say, which implies a condition of success, and therefore a possibility of failure. They speak of faith as needed in the recipient of benefit. On one occasion we read [1] that 'he could there do no mighty work save that he laid his hands upon a few sick folk and healed them.' And this inability apparently arose from a want of faith in the people. Lastly, if we do suppose that 'Christ never pronounced the word but the effect followed,' all may still be

---

[1] See Mark, chap. vi. v. 5 ; Matthew, chap. xiii. v. 58.

explained by supposing that with him the restorative power of mental influence was at a wonderful height.

I have now gone through Paley's canons of exception, and applied them to the Gospels. I have endeavoured to do so strictly and impartially. In that attempt I may have written in a way to hurt the feelings of many Christians. This I certainly would not do unless I believed that thorough candour in the matter is necessary if my reasoning is to have influence with the class of people for whom it is designed —men of shaken faith. I repeat that this seems to me the only fair course. If you maintain, for instance, that the vision seen by Colonel Gardiner, or the sound heard by Lord Herbert of Cherbury, was subjective, why not the vision or the voice at the baptism of Christ? In an evidential argument, at all events, we cannot look upon the miracles of Scripture as a privileged class, exempt from criticism or explanation. It is well known that it has ever been one of the difficulties of Protestant, and especially of evidential, writers, to say when miracles ceased in the Church. As Middleton abundantly showed, we continue to have accounts as wonderful as those of the first days, long after the times of the Apostles. We have only to turn to the Roman Catholic Church to find them even in these days. Now it is, I say, an arbitrary thing to set aside these accounts by certain canons of criticism, and yet refrain from applying these canons to the histories of the Gospels.

Paley[1] himself has not overlooked this objection. He treats it thus. 'Having thus enumerated several exceptions, which may justly be taken to relations of miracles, it is necessary, when we read the Scriptures, to bear in our minds this general remark, that although there be miracles recorded in the New Testament which fall within some or other of the exceptions here assigned, yet that they are united with others to which none of the same exceptions extend, and that their credibility stands upon this union.'

Paley here again has gone too far. The extent to which the conjunction of an event with a true miracle would help to make the former credible as a miracle is simply this. It would greatly diminish the *à priori* improbability of the event being a miracle. Although I have not admitted as conclusive what were expressly called in this essay the *à priori* objections, still I have allowed that the general course of modern discovery has established a presumption against miracles. And this presumption the conjunction in question diminishes. If we do admit one true miracle in the Gospel histories, we must be more ready to admit another. If the event be really well attested, and not naturally explicable, the most reasonable course may be to look upon it as a miracle. But this does not take away

---

[1] Paley's 'Evidences,' Prop. II. end chap. i.

the application of all Paley's exceptions. It does not take away the exceptions from natural explanation, or yet from weakness of evidence. If, for instance, we admit the resurrection of Christ, we are not therefore to pronounce all his cures miraculous if any of them appear capable of an explanation applied in other cases, such as that of mental influence. Nor yet are we to admit any account in the Gospels if the evidence for it, apart from any presumption against miracles, appears to be weak.

It remains now only to notice the general proposition by which Paley seeks to set aside any other non-christian wonders which may not be included in the sweep of his eleven exceptions. To these he applies this final distinction :—' That there is not satisfactory evidence that persons pretending to be original witnesses of the miracles passed their lives in labours, dangers, and sufferings, voluntarily undertaken and undergone in attestation of the accounts, which they delivered, and properly on account of their belief in the truth of those accounts.' I have already given my reasons for estimating much less highly than Paley the value of this kind of testimony. The question now to be before us is, How far the Gospels have this witness? How far they are really distinguished in this respect from all other miraculous histories?

The first proposition in Paley's 'Evidences' is, that the miracles of the Gospels have this martyr testimony. He devotes the first nine chapters of the work to prove this proposition. He argues from the *à priori* probabilities of the case, from profane testimony, from sacred testimony, direct and indirect, and he certainly does establish the fact that many believers of the first age must have suffered for their faith, and also must have undergone a change of life from its influence. But he does not make it equally clear that those early Christians suffered as witnesses to the miracles of which we read in our Gospels. The twelve men of his ideal case are, after all, not produced. The nearest approach which he is able to make is in what he brings forward[1] from the early chapters of the Acts of the Apostles, and concerns principally the resurrection of Christ. We read there of the Apostles testifying to the resurrection, exaltation, and office of Christ in the face of threats and persecution. Now the latter part of this work, 'the Acts,' is no doubt of high historical authority. Paley himself, in his 'Horæ Paulinæ,' has, by comparing the Acts and St. Paul's Epistles, made out a very strong case for believing that the Pauline Acts, chs. xiii. to xxviii., were written by an actor in the transactions described, or at the least by one who had a manuscript written by such an actor. And this conclusion has been further confirmed by modern investigations into the account

---

[1] Paley's 'Evidences,' chap. iv. ; Acts, chap. v.

of St. Paul's journey to Rome. But this does not prove, nor indeed make it at all probable, that the writer of the early chapters of the Acts, with which we are now concerned, was a member of the early Jerusalem Church, and an eyewitness of what is there described. It would not do so on the hypothesis that the book was, all of it, the original composition of one man. And when these earlier chapters are compared with St. Paul's Epistles, we not only have not the same amount of confirmation which perhaps from the nature of the case we could not have, but we have also more of serious difficulties, and that even in the narrative parts. For examples I may refer to the description of the gift of tongues, the acquaintance of the early Christians at Jerusalem with St. Paul, and the doings of that Apostle immediately after his conversion. I do not purpose to go into the somewhat difficult question of the genuineness and authenticity of 'the Acts,' but I do feel bound to allow that, for the reason just mentioned, the early chapters of the book do not seem to me to possess the high historical authority which certainly does belong to the later. But still we cannot well doubt that some of the earthly companions of Christ did face danger and suffering for their faith in him. The Galatian Epistle alone proves that Peter, John, and James, were in very early days prominent preachers of Christianity at Jerusalem; and if so, they must have been at times in danger, although their Christianity was less anti-Jewish than that of St. Paul. But the question remains, how far this faith of theirs was faith in what we now read in the Gospels? Is the story which Christians have now the story which they had then? Paley[1] has argued that it was, from four general considerations: (1) 'the recognition of the account in its principal parts by a series of succeeding writers'; (2) 'the total absence of any account of the origin of the religion substantially different from ours'; (3) 'the early and extensive practice of rites and institutions which result from our account'; (4) 'our account bearing in its construction proof that it is an account of facts which were known and believed at the time.' He allows that these considerations give only a presumption that our history is 'in general' the original story, and I do not suppose that anyone who considers the discrepancies of our four accounts, and the slenderness of the recognition of their particulars in any other writing until about the year A.D. 145, would venture to claim more. Paley instances the resurrection as a miracle, which we may conclude was part of the original story, and this I think must be allowed. Apart from the above reasoning, we have strong testimony to this last point from Epistles of St. Paul, whose genuineness scarcely any will question—

[1] Paley's 'Evidences,' chap. vii.

those to the Romans, Galatians, and Corinthians. Of the resurrection we will speak separately. As to the other miracles of the Gospels there remains a difficulty under the head which we are now considering. Our present Gospels are not found at the beginning of the religion. Paley [1] himself admits that 'the Gospels were not the original cause of Christian history being believed, but were themselves among the consequences of that belief.' Is it not then a vital question, how far their narratives are a faithful account of that first history? Is what we read in them, what the first Christians at least believed that they saw? Paley's general considerations, as he himself [2] admits, do not guarantee the details, and without a knowledge of these we cannot judge how far natural explanation would apply. To establish these details—the particular cases, that is to say, of miracle, we have to enter on the great question of the authorship and credibility of the Gospels. Paley allows this at the beginning of Chapter viii., and in this and in the following chapter he has treated the subject briefly, but with his usual perspicuity. It will, however, I presume, be allowed that his treatment is not equal to the wants of the present day. He did little more than condense Lardner's 'Credi-

---

[1] Paley's 'Evidences,' chap. vii. Part I. p. 71, edition by Rev. D. S. Wayland, London, 1837.
[2] Ibid., p. 74.

bility of the Gospel.' No doubt Lardner's was a great work, but biblical criticism has made immense advances since his day. We have come now, indeed, upon one of the great battle-fields of modern criticism. It is not my purpose to enter on the discussion as to the origin of the Gospels. I would leave this wide and difficult subject to those whose studies specially qualify them for it. I will offer here only a few remarks pointing to considerations that especially concern our subject.

The recognition of the four Gospels is general and explicit at the end of the second century. The earliest express testimonies, that of Irenæus and of the Muratorian Fragment, cannot, however, be pushed back much, if at all, farther than the fourth quarter of the century. But certainly this general recognition argues an earlier belief. We cannot suppose that these books could in a short time have gained credit over an area including places so remote as Lyons, Rome, Carthage, Alexandria, and Antioch. On the other hand, it must be borne in mind that the writers of that age were altogether uncritical. Indeed, the age was so. Irenæus[1] gives fanciful reasons why there should be exactly four Gospels, viz. that there are four quarters of the world, four principal spirits or winds, four successive dispensations to man, four forms of the cherubim. These last, indeed, he

[1] 'Irenæus adversus Hæreses,' lib. iii. cap. xi.

connects with the peculiar character as well as number of the Gospels. So with regard to the Old Testament, he accepts the legend of the making of the Septuagint translation by seventy translators, who worked quite independently and yet exactly agreed in their rendering,[1] and also the still wilder story about Ezra rewriting the Old Testament,[2] when it had been lost. The Muratorian Fragment[3] contains a legend as to the writing of St. John's Gospel. We cannot put full confidence in the judgment of such writers. Nearly a century and a-half parts their time from that of Christ. An evil practice existed among Christians in those times of putting forth books under feigned names, generally the names of eminent Christians, as Barnabas or Clemens Romanus. We have even a letter (probably of the early part of the third century) attributed to Christ himself, which seems to have imposed upon Eusebius.[4] Can we then, I repeat, rely upon such writers as Irenæus? Had they the accumen, impartiality, and research which, even in their day, the settlement of the true authorship of the Gospels may have required? Nor does the general acceptance of the Gospels in their day appear of so much weight when we call to mind

---

[1] 'Irenæus adversus Hæreses,' lib. iii. cap. xxv.
[2] Ibid., cap. xxi., xxii.
[3] See Muratorian Fragment, published by Prof. Westcott in his work on the canon of the New Testament.
[4] See Eusebius' 'Ecclesiastical History,' Book I. chap. xiii.

that by that time ecclesiastical organisation had become strong in the Church. Are not ecclesiastical judgments in such matters influenced by the supposed interests of orthodoxy? With such an example before us, as the acceptance of a forgery, like the decretals of Isidore, at a later time I allow, can we doubt this tendency? Now when we try to pass over the interval of which I have spoken, and trace back the recognition of our Gospels to apostolic or sub-apostolic times, great difficulties meet us. The remains of Christian writers during that time are few and often fragmentary. Often, as with the Ignatian Epistles, they have been much corrupted. The date and authorship of others, as of the Clementine Homilies and the letter to Diognetus, are uncertain. Those early writers had a loose, inaccurate way of quoting; there were other accounts either written or oral of Christ's words and acts besides our Gospels, from which they might, and in some cases certainly did, quote. The manuscripts of our own Gospels may have varied much, as we see from the Codex Bezæ. Hence, a mere coincidence between an ancient writer and the words of our Gospels,[1] is not conclusive of real quotation. Nor indeed, on the other hand, are variations in the words very conclusive against it.[2] Lastly, although it may

---

[1] See Prof. Westcott's 'Canon of the New Testament,' p. 49.
[2] Prof. Westcott's 'Introduction to the Study of the New Testament,' chap. iii.

be that our Gospels were much read during the latter part of that time, and also used in public worship, it does not appear that they were venerated during the greater part of this time as canonical writings have been venerated since, or indeed as the Old Testament was venerated then. This fact is of importance, as making credible a tampering with those histories, which later times would not have allowed. As an evidence for it, I may quote the following words from Papias [1] in the early part of the second century :—'I do not think that I derived so much benefit from books as from the living voice of those that are still surviving.' These words point to a state of things in which oral tradition was still an authority at least as much esteemed as any written document. All these circumstances combined have left us little conclusive evidence. Some stress has been laid upon heretical testimony. The work attributed to Hippolytus, Bishop of Portus A.D. 200–230, has been quoted to prove acquaintance with the Gospel of St. John on the part of Basilides 125 A.D. and Valentinus 140 A.D. But the evidence suffers much from the loose way of quotation.[2] Indeed, we have but two writers upon whom much stress can be laid. We have in them something more than

---

[1] Eusebius' 'Ecclesiastical History,' Book III. chap. xxxix., Cruse's Translation.

[2] See Davidson's 'Introduction to the Study of the New Testament,' p. 388 and onward.

those resemblances of language which at the most prove only the existence and not the authorship of the books. We have express mention of works which may presumably be identified with our present Gospels. I speak of Justin Martyr and Papias. The former speaks of certain accounts of the life of Christ, which he calls 'Memoirs of the Apostles,' and which he attributes to the Apostles and their immediate followers. I shall not pretend to discuss the question how far these 'Memoirs' can be identified with our Gospels. I will state only my own belief that the Synoptic Gospels were among them, whilst it is also clear that Justin quoted from other authorities as to the words and life of Christ; and I do not see why one or more of these may not have been written accounts. The preface to St. Luke's Gospel shows the early existence of such. The claim of the Fourth Gospel to be one of the 'Memoirs' cannot, I think, be clearly made out. This, indeed, I understand Professor Westcott to allow.[1] There are words strikingly alike in Justin and the Gospel, but not, so far as I can see from the references in Otto's Justin, a case of an identical passage. Mere resemblance, as I have pointed out, is not enough for proof; and further there is a good deal to be urged from what Justin says as to Christ and his life against his having used the Fourth Gospel.

[1] See 'Canon of the New Testament,' 3rd edition, p. 150.

This is shown by Dr. Davidson. See his 'Introduction to the Study of the New Testament,' vol. ii. p. 374 and onwards. Papias speaks distinctly of two accounts, one written by St. Matthew, the other by St. Mark. The first, he tells us, was written originally in the Hebrew, i.e. Syro-Chaldean language, and interpreted by everyone as he could. His statement as to the language is, I believe, confirmed by all old writers. The question here is how to identify this Hebrew book with our Greek Gospel? The internal evidence of our St. Matthew's Gospel is against that gospel being a translation from the Hebrew.[1] St. Mark,[2] Papias tells us, drew his information from St. Peter. 'What he wrote, he wrote with great accuracy, but not, however, in the order in which it was spoken or done by our Lord, for he neither heard nor followed our Lord.' This alleged want of arrangement has been urged to prove that the original Gospel of St. Mark cannot be ours. But this does not seem conclusive. The Gospel, I may add, is generally thought to have traces of the style of an eye-witness. On the other hand, there is in our present Synoptic Gospels strong internal evidence against their being independent works, as we might expect them to be, if one represented the tradition of

---

[1] See Alford's 'Greek Testament,' Prolegomena.

[2] 'Eusebius,' Book III. chap. xxxix., Cruse's translation. I suppose that the testimony which has been alleged from Papias to the Johannine authorship of the Fourth Gospel will not be pressed.

St. Peter, another that of St. Matthew. It is well known that they have in the order and events of the narrative much in common, and still more in the sayings of Christ. The language, even at times, is identical, especially in the record of Christ's sayings.[1] Perhaps about two-fifths are common matter, and in the case of St. Mark but very little, about twenty-four verses, fails to have a parallel in St. Matthew or in St. Luke. Further also, when these latter verbally agree, St. Mark invariably agrees with them also. It seems clear that they must have borrowed from a common source, oral or written, or from one another. On the contrary, a striking difference exists between the Synoptics, on the one hand, and the Fourth Gospel on the other. We see this in the facts of the narrative, in the style and matter of Christ's sayings, in the view of his person and work.

I do not pretend that the above is anything but a very brief summary of the principal points in a great controversy. It is, however, I think, enough to show that we have not a strong case for attributing our present Gospels to their reputed authors, and a still less strong case for attributing them to eye-

---

[1] See Prof. Westcott's 'Introduction to the Study of the Gospels,' 4th edit. pp. 190-196, for a pretty full statement on these points. This subject has exercised the ingenuity of many writers, beginning in our country with Bishop Marsh. Among recent writers, I would refer to Mr. Smith, of Jordan Hill, as original in some of his ways of treatment : 'Dissertation on the Origin and Connection of the Gospels.'

witnesses of Christ's life. We will take this last point as that which most concerns us now, and is most easily treated. In the case of St. Matthew there is the difficulty of identifying our present Gospel with the Hebrew original. With St. Mark we have the testimony of Papias that he was not an eye-witness of Christ's life. With St. Luke this is acknowledged. There remains only St. John. This Gospel is for our present purpose the most important, because its miracles are, as a rule, more decidedly supernatural, that is, less presumably explicable in a natural way than those of the Synoptics. Thus we have the cure of a man who had an infirmity thirty-eight years, the giving of sight to a man born blind, the raising of Lazarus when he had been dead four days. But the Johannine authorship of the Fourth Gospel I do not think that we could expect an adversary to admit. He would probably meet us by some such remarks as the following : 'The historical evidence for this Gospel is weaker than that for the Synoptics. You cannot fairly quote Justin Martyr or Papias on its behalf. The internal evidence offers serious difficulties. The greater departure from nature in the miracles is of itself an unfavourable sign ; it suggests, at least, that growth of the story so common in successive accounts of wonderful things. Then there is an appearance of a doctrinal rather than historical purpose, as, for

II. THE AUTHORSHIP OF THE GOSPELS. 235

instance, in the narration of miracles apparently as introduction to discourses; there is a narration of things, which it is strange that the Synoptics omit, as the raising of Lazarus; there is a discrepancy from them as to facts, as in the day of the crucifixion, and the abode of Lazarus and his sisters, the period and the scene of Christ's ministry; there are discourses attributed to Christ differing both in style and matter from those in the Synoptics; there is a style of language and of thought in the Gospel which we should not expect from St. John, from what we read of him in the other Gospels and the Epistles of St. Paul, or from the Apocalypse.' I for one could not say that all such objections have so far been adequately answered, nor do I know that the defenders of Johannine authorship have anything to set against them from internal evidence which might not be plausibly explained on the supposition of the Gospel being written by one acquainted with St. John. Upon the whole, in the present state of the controversy, I do not think that the Fourth Gospel can be relied upon for evidential purposes. It does not seem to me right to refuse to recognise these difficulties merely because we feel the spiritual beauty of the Gospel, or hold it part of the canon.

There are other tests of the authenticity of a narrative besides those which Paley's exceptions have brought before us. They may be comprehensively described as consistency in its statements one with another and with what we know of its subject from other sources. If the Gospels be thus tried, it is well known that a number of discrepancies are found. Still as regards the Synoptics, a case of general untrustworthiness is not made out. Strauss worked this mode of attack with great skill and industry. No doubt his criticisms make up a very strong objection to the infallibility of the narratives or even their great accuracy. But still his conclusion that they were largely myths generated partly by the action of Old Testament ideas has not been widely accepted. It could, I think, be plausibly applied only to very few New Testament accounts, as, for instance, that of the magi. Nay, I think that we may fairly claim that he has not lowered the historical authority of much the greater part of the Synoptics even to that of legend, that is to say, of imaginative accounts with a basis of historical truth. It is difficult to imagine that the recorded sayings of Christ could have been invented for him, and often those in the Gospels cohere with miraculous narratives, as in the healing of the paralytic—St. Luke v. 18-26, St. Mark ii. 3-12. Indeed, a knowledge of Christ's sayings in the Evangelists plainly makes for a knowledge of his works also. The argument from discrepancy does appear to me stronger against the Fourth Gospel, as I have already said.

I will not dwell longer on these criticisms, but endeavour now to sum up our results in their bearing on the evidential argument. In the first place, I would repeat that this argument involves two positions. You have to establish the evangelical miracles and to discredit others. I have specially considered the reasoning of Paley, because I think that it is the ablest specimen of such argument in our language. His main allegation on behalf of the Gospel miracles is the possession of martyr testimony. I have endeavoured to show that such testimony was not of so high a value as he assumes, and further that it is a question whether the particular miracles recorded in our Gospels possess it. Paley urged certain rules of exception against other miraculous narratives. The first class of these exceptions—(1) not being written at the time, (2) or on the spot, (5) want of particularity, (7) bias in the writers, (11) liability to explanation as exaggerations, are objections which, if we are to be impartial, we must largely apply to the narratives of the New Testament. I cannot allow Paley's reason for not applying them. Now if we do so no miracle except the resurrection of Christ will, I believe, escape. The second class of exceptions— (3) transient rumours, (4) bare statements of history, (6) carelessly believed accounts, also apply to the evangelical miracles with the like exception in some degree. There is a want of corroboration which is the ground of these objections. Putting aside the resurrection, we cannot well show that any one of the alleged miracles of Christ had much to do with the great fact brought forward in corroboration, viz. the origin of his Church. The case may require that something wonderful occurred in Christ's life, but this is vague. Lastly, our third batch of exceptions, (8) false perception, (9) so-called tentative miracles, (10) natural explanation, are likewise valid against many New Testament accounts. It is allowed that the witnesses of whatever did occur were uneducated men, or at all events strangers to modern science. We find two of the principal of them spoken of in the Acts as ignorant and unlearned men. We learn from sources beyond question that the first Christians were believers in dreams, magic, angelic and diabolic interference even with physical phenomena, that they made inaccurate quotations and uncritical applications of Scripture, of whose authority, at the same time, they cherished the highest ideas; that, in short, they do not seem to have been accurate observers or reasoners according to our notion, and that their minds were filled with those ideas of personal supernatural agency which, as I have said, favour the springing up of miraculous accounts just as a belief in natural law discourages them. That want of accuracy which, as I have said in my consideration of further tests, the discrepancies of the

Gospels prove, is of importance in judging as to the last class of exceptions, (8), (9), (10). In finally deciding whether an event be a miracle, precision in the account of the circumstances is of great importance. A particular easily overlooked by an excited spectator, without scientific training, might suggest the explanation to a Faraday or a Tyndall. The cures of the New Testament are justly brought forward as having the best claim to be thought miracles. But they were not so fully investigated as the cases of Mademoiselle Perrier or Miss Fancourt. In pronouncing upon the absolute truth of the Gospel accounts, we are bound to bear in mind that the first and second class of our exceptions are not conclusive against it, they only weaken the evidence, and also that the third class spare the fact, though they take away its character as a miracle. But when we revert to the evidential view of the matter, viz. the comparative credibility of these and other miracles, we are obliged to allow that other stories, as, for instance, the cure of Innocentius, that of the blind man at Milan, the cure mentioned by Bengel, and that of Pascal's niece, have equal claims to be believed. The resurrection of Christ, however, remains outstanding as an exception to these conclusions. Let us now carefully examine this stronghold of the evidential argument.

PART VI.

First, I will state certain considerations which give peculiar weight to the miracle of the resurrection of Christ as a part of the Christian evidences, and in doing so I will refer to the exceptions of Paley which they concern.

In the first place, we remark that the resurrection of Christ, as it is understood by the New Testament writers, has a clear and strong claim to be thought a miracle in the strict sense of the word. It can hardly be thought reducible to natural law. The mere resuscitation of a man thought to be dead is common enough. But this, at most, is only restoration to a mortal life. Here is something more. It is the transformation of a presumed corpse into a spiritual body—an organism of a new kind. Again, we have many stories of apparitions of the dead; but none that I know of in which the apparition was thought to be a transformed corpse. As Paley justly remarks, all accounts of spectres leave the body in the grave.[1] In short, the alleged event is unique, (9), (10), (11).

Next, the fact is attested, more or less explicitly, by almost every early Christian writing, (1), (2), (3). We have detailed accounts of the discovery of the

[1] Except Matthew, chap. xxvii. ver. 52, 53.

resurrection in each of the four Gospels, and an account of interviews between the risen Christ and his disciples, not only in them, but in the Acts. We have also in the early part of the Acts records of speeches by the apostles, principally Peter, bearing witness to the resurrection.[1] We have a record of particular appearances in the First Epistle to the Corinthians. Mention is also made of the resurrection in Romans i. 4, Galatians i. 1, Ephesians i. 20, Philippians iii. 10, Colossians i. 18, 1 Thessalonians iv. 14, 1 Peter i. 3. There is evidence from early Christian writers for the genuineness of some of the Epistles which is not open to the doubt which, as I have said, must be allowed as to apparent quotations from the Gospels. No one, I believe, will question that of Romans, Galatians, and the two Corinthian Epistles.[2] The Revelation of St. John also, a book whose authorship is well attested, distinctly teaches this fact of the resurrection (Rev. i. 18); and, indeed, a belief therein may be said to underlie a great part of New Testament teaching. It is, for instance, assumed in the looking for Christ's return, and in the belief of his intercession in heaven. Paley[3] did not go much too far when he wrote as follows: 'Every piece of Scripture recognises the resurrection. Every epistle of every apostle; every author

---

[1] Acts, chaps. i. ii. iii. iv. v. x. [2] See Baur's Work on St. Paul.
[3] Paley's 'Evidences,' Part II. chap. viii.

contemporary with the apostles, of the age immediately succeeding the apostles; every writing from that age to the present, genuine or spurious, on the side of Christianity or against it, concur in representing the resurrection of Christ as an article of his history received without doubt or disagreement by all who called themselves Christians,[1] as alleged from the beginning by the propagators of the institution, and alleged as the centre of their testimony.' We cannot doubt that it was firmly believed by the first Christians.

Next, there is corroboration at least of the fact of belief in this event from the first. We have this in facts of history which all must admit. If we allow the fact of this belief, then the faith and earnestness of the first Christians are naturally explained. It is allowed on all hands that Jesus Christ was put to death as a malefactor. Great discouragement to his disciples must have followed. Yet there must have been a revival of faith. Independent of the Acts and the Epistles, the spread of the religion proves this revival. There is no explanation of this

---

[1] I do not see the force in the difference of the views of Christ's resurrection taken by St. Paul, which Dr. Davidson seems to see ('Introduction to New Testament,' vol. ii. p. 40). St. Paul might spiritualise the idea of resurrection, and so apply it to conversion, as in Romans, chap. vi. ver. 4; Coloss. chap. iii. ver. 1, without losing hold of the objective fact. It is not clear that the Corinthians, spoken of in chap. xv. 1st Epistle, extended their denial of the resurrection to that of Christ.

continued or renewed faith in Christ so adequate as the belief, at least of the disciples, in the resurrection. The mere beauty of Christian morality is not sufficient. If a religion is to spread as Christianity did in such an age, it must have something for the self-caring instincts of man, some hope to set before him. It is one great office of religion to conciliate those instincts with the higher principles of his nature. Now, if we take away the resurrection there is nothing left, in what is distinctively Christian, to do this work. Where, in that case, would be the looking for Christ's coming again? or of his judgment? or of his rewarding the believer? A strong persuasion of this event at the time is evidently needed to explain what we know of the period. And herein is a corroboration, just as in Leslie's acts or monuments set up at the time. An event thus attested has a root in history, (3), (4), (6).

Lastly, we have in this case a good approach to that martyr testimony upon which, beyond anything else, Paley rests his case. There is at least a presumption that persons who took themselves to be original witnesses of Christ's resurrection, exposed themselves to danger in that capacity. If we trust the early chapters of the Acts,[1] this is expressly proved. And even if we do not, as I have pointed out, the Galatian Epistle, whose genuineness will

---

[1] Acts, chap. iv. ver. 10; chap. v. ver. 30.

hardly be disputed, gives a high presumption for something of the kind, a presumption confirmed by 1 Thessalonians ii. 14, 15, and Hebrews x. 34.

These remarks may suffice to point out the strong points in the histories of Christ's resurrection as a part of Christian evidences. We will now turn to the consideration of various objections.

In the first place, a question has been raised whether Christ died upon the cross at all. He was not long enough, by any means, upon the cross to bring about death from that cause in a natural way.[1] And hence it has been conjectured that he did not die in the manner usually supposed, but that he may only have sunk into a swoon. If so, the subsequent interviews with his disciples, which gave rise to the traditions in the Gospels, may have had nothing really supernatural about them. But this view has many serious difficulties. It requires the supposition of confederates unknown to us. The young men spoken of in the accounts of the resurrection have been taken for such. But this idea of a prolonged life with secret friends is altogether at variance with these accounts. Who could these friends be, or how can we think that they, or still more Christ, deceived the disciples? If we accept the authority of the fourth Gospel, then we must think that the spear wound would in all probability have been fatal, if

---

[1] See article Crucifixion, Smith's 'Dictionary.'

Christ had not died before. And without this the acceleration of death may be accounted for by previous fatigue and suffering of body and mind.

Leaving this conjecture, we have now to turn to more serious criticism. We certainly have external evidence enough to prove that the first Christians earnestly believed in the resurrection of Christ. Of this there cannot be a reasonable doubt. But it is a fair question, whether they did so upon grounds which would have satisfied us. To make this vital point clear it is needful, first, to examine with careful criticism the accounts of the New Testament, with a view to showing upon what particulars we can insist; and then to consider whether these particulars would in our eyes establish the truth of this great miracle. We begin with the first work. We have to examine and compare the accounts in the four Gospels, and what is said in the first chapter of the Acts and in the fifteenth chapter of First Corinthians as to the risen Saviour. The other references to the resurrection in the New Testament are too general for our purpose. I have said to compare, for indeed a great part of our work will be to trace out the discrepancies in the narratives, and to judge how far they invalidate the testimony. That task is the more incumbent upon us, because the discrepancies are really greater here than in the average of the history, and have been strenuously maintained to prove that the accounts are quite inconsistent, and cannot be esteemed more than 'uncertain and very varied reports.'[1] For distinctness' sake we will consider, separately and in succession—1st, the accounts of the discovery of the resurrection; 2nd, the accounts of Christ's subsequent appearances. I will arrange the points of difference in the accounts of the first discovery in order.

1. All the evangelists represent the tomb of Christ as being found empty early on the third day by female disciples; but they give the names of these women very differently. In St. Matthew they are Mary Magdalene and the other Mary. In St. Mark they are Mary Magdalene, Mary mother of James, and Salome. In St. Luke they are women which came with him from Galilee; afterwards Mary Magdalene and Joanna and Mary the mother of James are mentioned among those women who report what had happened at the tomb to the apostles, and who are apparently, though not of necessity, the same as the party said to have visited the tomb. Lastly, in St. John we have only Mary Magdalene.

2. The women provide spices to anoint Christ's body; but in St. Mark they do this on the Saturday evening, in St. Luke on the Friday afternoon.

---

[1] See 'Life of Jesus,' critically examined by Dr. D. F. Strauss, Part III. chap. iv., § 138, p. 344, authorised English translation. Chapman Brothers, London, 1846.

3. They come to the sepulchre at different times according to different evangelists. In St. Matthew it is 'as it began to dawn' (τῇ ἐπιφωσκούσῃ); in St. Mark it is 'at the rising of the sun' (ἀνατείλαντος τοῦ ἡλίου); in St. Luke it is 'very early in the morning' (ὄρθρου βαθέος); in St. John, 'when it was yet dark' (σκοτίας ἔτι οὔσης).

4. They see visions of angels; but the visions differ. In St. Matthew we hear of one angel outside the sepulchre, apparently sitting on the stone which he had rolled from the tomb's mouth. In St. Mark we have one young man inside sitting. In St. Luke two men inside, but standing. In St. John two angels sitting are seen by Mary Magdalene, but not till her second visit to the tomb and the departure of the two apostles whom she had summoned.

5. The angels speak to the women, but in different ways. In St. Matthew and St. Mark they tell the women of the resurrection, bid them not to fear, and charge them to acquaint the disciples. In St. Luke they do not speak words of encouragement, nor charge the women to tell the disciples, but they remind them how Christ had spoken in Galilee of his death and resurrection. The tone has something of rebuke—'Why seek ye the living among the dead?' In St. John they merely ask Mary Magdalene why she weeps.

6. The conduct of the women is differently de-

scribed. In St. Matthew they leave the sepulchre with fear and great joy, and run to tell the disciples. In St. Mark they are afraid, and tell no one. In St. Luke they tell the eleven and the rest. In St. John Mary Magdalene tells St. Peter and St. John that ' they have taken away the Lord out of the sepulchre, and *we* know not where they have laid him,' words in which the plural form ' we know not ' (οὐκ οἴδαμεν) is to be noticed; and subsequently, after her interview with Christ at her second visit, she announces this appearance also to the disciples.

All these variations are patent on the face of the narratives. I will next speak of one less obvious, which it will take a little time to point out, but which it is, I believe, more difficult for the harmonists to explain. Partly on account of this difficulty, and partly for another reason, I wish to speak of it at some length. It concerns the fact of our Lord appearing to Mary Magdalene *first*. Now I think that the first appearance of the risen Lord would be a prominent, striking feature in the history of his resurrection: not one of those subordinate details about which we might reasonably look for some confusion or error. Let us then carefully examine what is said as to this point. St. Matthew tells us that as Mary Magdalene and the other Mary were returning from the sepulchre, Christ himself met them, and charged them to tell his disciples to go to

Galilee, where they should see him. Now in St. Mark, or at least in the last twelve verses of the received text of St. Mark, we read expressly that Christ appeared *first* to Mary Magdalene; and we find also that the first appearance mentioned in St. John's Gospel is to her. The account of this last-mentioned interview differs essentially from that in St. Matthew. Yet how are we to make it different from this meeting with the two Marys mentioned in the first Gospel? We might suppose that Mary Magdalene separated from her companions, and that the plural is still kept to in St. Matthew because there were other women whom he has not named— a supposition, however, not agreeing well with St. Matthew's words. It would allow of Mary Magdalene seeing our Lord when by herself, as in St. John; but it brings in other difficulties. St. John makes our Lord's interview with Mary Magdalene to occur after her announcement to St. Peter and St. John, and after they had visited the sepulchre upon her report. Now the natural meaning of St. Matthew's words does not favour our supposing that Mary Magdalene parted with her companions until after they had been at the sepulchre, until, in fact, they were running to acquaint the disciples. If so, it seems difficult to understand how she should have had time to fetch Peter and John, and to have afterwards a first interview with Christ before the interview mentioned in St. Matthew with the women hastening from the sepulchre. Again, we may reason thus from other points in the narratives.

In St. Luke xxiv. 12, we read that St. Peter ran to inspect the tomb after the report of the women. About this verse, however, there are critical doubts. It is omitted by Tischendorf, marked doubtful by Tregelles, retained by Alford. It is in the oldest manuscripts—the Sinaitic, Vatican, Alexandrian. Even if we give it up there is still a reference to such a visit by some of the disciples at verse 24 of the same chapter. It seems probable that this is the same visit as that described by St. John. The language of St. Luke xxiv. 12, is very similar to that in St. John xx. 6, 7. Further, it is not easy to suppose two visits, one by St. Peter and St. John on the report of Mary Magdalene, another by some of the disciples (amongst whom, if we take the received text, is Peter) on the report of some women, to all appearance Mary Magdalene among the rest (St. Luke xxiv. 10, 22, 24). In St. Mark we find the women charged to tell Peter and the disciples. If the visits be the same, then the appearance to Mary Magdalene in St. John must have been *after* not *before* the announcement of the women to the disciples. We lose our only way of explaining the apparent contradiction pointed out above, viz. the reconciliation by supposing that Mary Magdalene parted from her comrades; that they carried their news to other of the apostles than Peter and John, although they had been specially told to acquaint Peter (St. Mark xvi. 7); and that whilst they were thus engaged she had time to fetch these two apostles and have the interview with our Lord described in St. John.

This becomes plainly impossible as the interview between our Lord and her in St. John is now made to follow the announcement of the women to the disciples, and therefore, according to St. Matthew, their seeing Christ. We have a distinct opposition between St. Matthew's account of Christ's meeting the women and St. Mark's statement of his first appearing to Mary Magdalene. The latter, I allow, is a text of questioned genuineness, but it has, as I have pointed out, a support from St. John. It is hard to suppose a meeting with other women before the appearance to Mary Magdalene in St. John.

Again, suppose that we give up the identity of these visits to the tomb by disciples in St. Luke and St. John, and allow the priority of the appearance to Mary Magdalene, we have still other difficulties. In that case the visit of Peter and John to the tomb must also have gone before Christ's meeting the women hastening to the disciples, and, therefore, before their announcement to the apostles. If so, John must have already believed (St. John

xx. 8). Why, then, should the story of the women appear as idle tales and be disbelieved (St. Luke xxiv. 11)? or why should Peter, or at least some of them, go again to the tomb?

The point of difficulty raised in the above reasoning turns upon reconciling the priority of the appearance to Mary Magdalene with other particulars. But it will have been noticed that if we drop this point altogether, there would remain a difficulty in the fact that St. Matthew and St. Luke seem to conjoin Mary Magdalene with others in announcing the resurrection to the apostles; St. Mark at least represents her as commissioned along with two others so to do; whilst St. John makes her alone acquaint Peter and John, though I allow that in this Gospel too she uses a plural form, 'we know not,' when speaking to the apostles.

What I have now said may suffice as to the discrepancies in the Gospel accounts of the discovery of the resurrection of Christ. It is clear that they cannot all be accurate accounts of the same events; but the supposition offers itself that they may be accurate accounts of different parts of a combination of events occurring on the resurrection day. Can we then imagine any consistent combination of events which will thus verify all the accounts? This is what the harmonists have endeavoured to do, but I believe unsuccessfully. I will bring forward an example of their schemes—that of Mr. Greswell. I choose his because I do not know a better (Rev. E. Greswell, 'Dissertations on the Gospels,' vi.). Mr. Greswell supposes two parties of women, the one that of Salome spoken of by Matthew and Mark; the other that of Joanna spoken of by Luke. By this supposition he reconciles several discrepancies, the differences in the names of the women in Matthew and Mark as compared with Luke; the different times of preparing the spices, Friday afternoon and Saturday evening; the differences in the visions of angels; above all, the marked difference in the words spoken by the angels. Next he makes Mary Magdalene to go back to Peter and John as soon as the approaching women see the stone removed from the mouth of the sepulchre and men around it. Thus he explains how Mary Magdalene alone is mentioned in St. John. Mark's account he supposes to be supplementary to Matthew's, and thus he explains how we read in the second Evangelist of an angel inside the tomb. The difference as to time which is most marked between Mark and John he accounts for by supposing that the words 'at the rising of the sun' in Mark applies to the arrival of the women at the tomb, the 'yet dark' of John to their setting out from home. The silence of the women in Mark, which contrasts with their announcement in St. Luke, he explains by supposing that it refers only to strangers, not to their friends. The difficulty about the first appearance, he disposes of, by first rejecting on fair critical grounds the words, 'And as they went to tell his disciples,' Matt. xxviii. 9, and then boldly removing the rest of the verses, Matt. xxviii. 9, 10, 'Behold Jesus met them, saying,' &c., out of their place. He would understand them to refer to matter subsequent to that of verses 11–15 in the same chapter; in fact, to an appearance of Christ some days later than the resurrection. Such are his expedients. The last is obviously violent; so, too, it is contrary, at all events, to the most natural understanding of St. Luke to suppose that 'the women' spoken of from ch. xxiii. 55 to ch. xxiv. 10, are not the persons enumerated in the last verse. Now if they be, Mr. Greswell's theory of two parties is untenable. The explanation as to the times also is forced. The words to which the different notes of time in Mark and John are affixed are the same in meaning—$\H{\epsilon}\rho\chi o\nu\tau\alpha\iota\ \H{\epsilon}\pi\H{\iota}\ \tau\H{o}\ \mu\nu\eta\mu\epsilon\H{\iota}o\nu$ in St. Mark, $\H{\epsilon}\rho\chi\epsilon\tau\alpha\iota$ . . . . $\epsilon\H{\iota}\varsigma\ \tau\H{o}\ \mu\nu\eta\mu\epsilon\H{\iota}o\nu$ in St. John. Why should they mean in one place 'set out from home,' in the other 'reach the sepulchre'? The idea of Mark's account being meant as a supplement to Matthew's, and that of the silence of the women in his account referring only to strangers, are plainly expedients. In fact, the whole explanation is unsatisfactory. It is of course difficult to set limits to human ingenuity and to say what might not be done by cutting out verses, perhaps on doubtful critical grounds, giving unnatural meanings to words and supposing improbable combinations of circumstances. But I do venture to say that apart from the influence of theories of Scripture inspiration, a candid man would reject the idea that any combination of events which we can now conjecture would harmonise these accounts. Neither are we at liberty to say with Dean Alford[1] that if we knew all the circumstances we should have such a combination. This can only be surmise. On the whole, then, I should conclude that we have real inconsistency.

I will next say something as to the appearances subsequent to the first discovery. In St. Matthew we have a second appearance of Christ in Galilee to the eleven at an appointed place upon a mountain. In St. Mark we find in the last twelve verses of our received text brief notices, first of an appearance to Mary Magdalene; next to two disciples when walking into the country; lastly to the eleven. In St. Luke we have first what seems to be the appearance to the two disciples spoken of in St. Mark, then another to Peter, then to the eleven. In St. John we find first the appearance to Mary Magdalene, then an appearance to ten of the apostles, then to the eleven, lastly to Peter, Thomas, Nathaniel, John, James, and two other disciples when fishing

---

[1] Alford's Commentary, Matthew, chap. xxviii. verses 1-10.

in Galilee. This appearance John calls the third. Furthermore, in the Acts, we learn that our Lord did not ascend on the day of his resurrection as we might have concluded from St. Luke. The ascension did not take place for forty days, and we hear in a general way of appearances of Christ, and of conversations between him and his disciples during that interval. Finally, in St. Paul's First Epistle to the Corinthians, ch. xv., we have six appearances of the risen Lord enumerated seemingly in order of time—first to Cephas, next to the twelve, then to above five hundred brethren at once, next to James, fifthly to all the apostles, lastly to St. Paul himself. These accounts obviously differ a good deal, and difficulties may be raised as to the place, the order, the circumstances of these appearances. These difficulties we will now examine.

It has been said that in distinct interviews there is an appearance of leave-taking, which is opposed to subsequent interviews. It has been thought that St. Matthew's account of the appearance in Galilee was in this way inconsistent with the account of the ascension in the Acts, which is evidently there meant to be the last interview. In like manner, St. Mark has an account which seems to be that of the last interview, and which, if it be, does not agree with the account in the Acts of the Ascension. In St. Luke also we need to interpolate an interval of forty days between the 43rd and 44th verses of the twenty-fourth chapter in order to bring it into harmony with the Acts. No doubt there is in all this a difficulty, but it does not amount to a precise contradiction. We are not bound to suppose that either St. Matthew's or St. Mark's account is really that of the last interview, nor yet to refuse the interpolation of time in St. Luke. A better supported case of contradiction, but in a minor circumstance, is to be found with reference to the meeting of the two disciples, when returned from Emmaus, with the apostles and other disciples. If we suppose, as I think that we must, that the same meeting is spoken of both by St. Mark and St. Luke we have this opposition. In St. Mark the other disciples do not believe, whilst in St. Luke they meet the two with an assurance that the Lord is risen. A difficulty has been raised as to the locality of the appearances. Both in St. Matthew and St. Mark the angels direct the disciples to go to Galilee there to meet the Lord, and in St. Matthew Christ also himself gives the same direction. In St. Luke, on the other hand, the Lord bids them remain at Jerusalem until 'endowed with power from on high'—a charge which is repeated in the Acts, and there interpreted to refer to the descent of the Holy Ghost on the day of Pentecost. But this difficulty disappears if we suppose the charge mentioned in St. Luke and in the Acts to have been given on the day of the ascension. The earlier direction was, we know, given on the day of the resurrection. The interval is long enough to admit of the disciples obeying it and returning to Jerusalem. But it has been said, again, that if the disciples were thus charged immediately after the resurrection to go to Galilee, there to see the Lord, it is singular that we should hear of an appearance to the eleven in Jerusalem, at least eight days afterwards as we do in St. John. But if we allow this interview, the interval left for the journey to Galilee before the ascension is still long enough. That the disciples did visit Galilee before the ascension is confirmed by St. John's account of the appearance at the sea of Tiberias, and also I think by St. Paul's mention of an appearance to above five hundred brethren at once. For it is a very reasonable conjecture that this last appearance is the same as that on the mountain in Galilee. The number five hundred is greater than that of the disciples at that time in Jerusalem—Acts ch. i. 15. But as our Lord's ministry had been chiefly in Galilee there were probably more disciples there, and the fact of the appearance being previously appointed would probably cause a numerous assembly. It is true that the account in St. Matthew gives us the idea that it applies only to the apostles. But I do not think that this circumstance in so brief an account prevents us from supposing that others were present. Finally, a difficulty has been found in arranging the accounts. St. John speaks of the appearance to the seven disciples at the sea of Tiberias as the third to his disciples (τοῖς μαθηταῖς αὐτοῦ—John ch. xxi. 14.) To all appearance we have before this an appearance to Mary Magdalene, to other women, to Peter, to the two disciples on the road to Emmaus, to the ten without Thomas, to the eleven eight days later. No admissible supposition can, I believe, reduce the number of these previous appearances to two. But the difficulty is avoided if we suppose St. John to mean by 'shewed himself to his disciples' an appearance only to several of them at once. This is quite credible. In any case the mistake is not serious. To sum up this part of our inquiry we may, I think, say that the apparent inconsistencies here are more explicable than those with reference to the first discovery, and that certainly they are not sufficient ground for rejecting the accounts. But still we must, I think, allow the presence of error. It seems natural to find some inaccuracies and inconsistencies in accounts of an event so exciting and from writers who were certainly not accurate in their ways of thinking and writing. The detection even of several such mistakes would by no means justify us in setting aside their witness altogether. But at the same time it does impair our confidence in the details. It seems well attested that the disciples found the tomb empty on the third day and that they firmly believed that Christ repeatedly appeared to one or more of their number. These conclusions have I think a confirmation from St. Paul's First Epistle to the Corinthians. We have there express assertion of the latter point, and at least an indirect testimony to the former. Christ is said to have risen again on 'the third day.' That is plainly the date at which the accounts of the resurrection had their rise. We cannot put their origin later—in Galilee, as Strauss suggests. But if they began on the third day the tomb must have been empty then, or the presence of the corpse would at once have stopped the reports. So much, I think, we may claim. At the same time, we must allow that some error and confusion have crept into the accounts.

Such seems to me the fair conclusion from comparison. It may be asked, Can criticism detect in any other way unfavourable signs? Do we, for instance, seem to see a growth of the story in the later writers? or can we trace in their additional particulars the working of any motives which would lead to additions? This is an important inquiry when error is allowed. If, as there seems reason to do, we take the accounts of St. Matthew and of the first eight verses in St. Mark's last chapter to be the oldest accounts, there certainly does seem to be some development. In those first accounts we have only two appearances. In the rest of St. Mark's last chapter we have brief notices of three more. In Luke we have also three, not all new, but more in detail. St. John has something further that is new—the convincing of Thomas, and the appearance at the sea of Tiberias. If we pass on to the Acts we have still more told us. In fact, such accounts as that in John xxi., and such statements as that in Acts ch. i. 3, and ch. x. 41, give the idea of something beyond a brief appearance, something like a partial renewal of the intercourse of natural life, and it cannot be denied that some of the details thus progressively introduced seem fitted to meet doubts; such are the showing of the hands and feet and the invitation to feel the body first mentioned by St. Luke, the convincing of Thomas added by St. John, the intercourse of forty days with its 'many infallible proofs' of which we hear in the Acts. If we suppose that the first Gospel was written by St. Matthew, it seems singular that he should have said nothing of the two striking and convincing appearances to the assembled apostles at Jerusalem, since he must have been present, and it is further singular that in his account of the Galilee appearance some, seemingly apostles, are said to doubt, although we are almost obliged to believe that these Jerusalem appearances had already taken place. We call to mind also that, in examining the discrepancies, one that perplexed us most was between St. Matthew's account of our Lord meeting the women, and the appearance to Mary Magdalene spoken of in the last twelve verses of St. Mark and in St. John. There is an appearance of opposition between St. Matthew and the later writers. On the other hand, as we have seen when examining the evidence as to the genuineness of the Gospels, we are by no means bound to believe that the first was written by St. Matthew at least as we possess it. We certainly cannot think that the accounts of the later Jerusalem appearances were subsequent inventions merely because they do not appear in St. Matthew and the undisputed part of St. Mark. For in the First Epistle to the Corinthians, which is probably older than any of the Gospels, we have mention of several appearances, some of which may reasonably be identified with those at Jerusalem, as that to 'the twelve' with St. Luke's and St. John's account of the apostles seeing Christ on the resurrection day, and that to 'all the apostles' with the interview before the ascension. But though we cannot for any reason, found here more than elsewhere, put aside the alleged fact of those appearances, still some persons may suspect that details have been added. It is thoroughly in keeping with experience that wonderful and startling accounts should acquire additions by repetition.

I will now leave the criticism of the accounts of the resurrection, and will proceed to the second branch of our inquiry. Are the accounts admitted, so far as we have been led to think them firmly established, sufficient to establish the miracle of the resurrection?

I have pointed out that the resurrection, as understood by the first Christians, has an unusually strong claim to be thought a miracle. It is, in fact, the transformation of a corpse into a wholly new organism. But it must be borne in mind that what we have actually in evidence amounts only to this: 1st. The disappearance of the body from the tomb by the morning of the third day. 2nd. The alleged testimony of certain angels and young men that Christ had risen. 3rd. Reported appearances of Christ himself. It is not said that any human eye witnessed the actual change. A natural explanation is therefore possible by combining two hypotheses—1st, that the body was in some way removed unknown to the disciples; 2nd, that the appearances of Christ and of the angels and young men are to be classed with ordinary accounts of apparitions. We will examine the credibility of each of these hypotheses.

The first has obvious difficulties. I should not rely upon the watch mentioned in St. Matthew as conclusive against it. This account has, I allow, critical difficulties. It is not mentioned by the other evangelists, or in the speeches of the apostles narrated in the Acts on the subject of the resurrection. This is singular when we consider its confirmatory character. It is hard to understand how the chief priests and Pharisees should have known that Christ had prophesied his resurrection, since he had not done so openly; and his private sayings to his disciples on the subject do not seem to have been understood: or, again, how these chief priests, whose leaders were Sadducees, should have believed the report of the soldiers, as the account seems to make them do: or, yet again, how the soldiers should venture to publish the story put into their mouths when the influence of the chief priests with Pilate was so doubtful, as it plainly was. I have said that I cannot regard these histories of the evangelists as free from all error, and certainly this particular part of St. Matthew has a greater appearance of addition than the corresponding parts of the other narratives. We have, for instance, more prodigies at the crucifixion. Further, the account in question has somewhat of an appearance of an answer to the Jewish report of the body being removed by the disciples. Again, even if we do hold to this account of the watch, we must remember that it was not set till the Saturday evening. And, finally, if the guards were really accessible to bribes from the chief priests, why might they not have been induced to allow the removal of the body by Joseph of Arimathæa, Nicodemus, or some other friends of Jesus who may not have thought Christ dead ? Upon the whole, I do not think that this account can be relied on as sufficient proof that the body was not removed in a natural way. But still it is hard to conjecture who could have removed it, and yet concealed the fact from the disciples. With our imperfect knowledge of the times and the actors, we cannot speak positively; but certainly there is here a serious objection to the supposition before us. I may add that even if we look upon the story of the guard as only an invention of later days to meet the Jewish report of the body having been stolen, still even that report concedes the fact that the body was missing.

I go on to the second hypothesis. The reported appearances of angels and of Christ may be looked upon as ordinary accounts of apparitions. Several features in the narratives have been pointed out as giving plausibility to this view. The appearances begin with the women, who were most liable to be deceived ; and, especially, the first appearance of Christ is to Mary Magdalene, who had been of unsound mind. The appearances seem purposeless and irregular. Thus, in St. Matthew the angels charge the women to tell the disciples to meet our Lord in Galilee, and immediately afterwards our Lord himself appears and repeats the direction.

The appearance of our Lord seems changed, and is not readily recognised. In St. Matthew xxviii. 17, 'some doubt;' in St. Mark [1] we hear of 'another form' (ἐν ἑτέρᾳ μορφῇ); in St. Luke the two disciples do not recognise the Lord on the way to Emmaus, and when he stands in the midst of the eleven and the rest they take him for a spirit; in St. John, Mary Magdalene at first thinks that he is the gardener, and the seven disciples at the sea of Tiberias do not recognise him for a time. No appearances were vouchsafed to any but disciples—'Not to all the people, but to witnesses chosen before of God, even to us who did eat and drink with him after he rose from the dead;'[2] all were not satisfied.[3] There are, it is well known, innumerable accounts of apparitions of the dead even to this day. Some, indeed, go the length of describing the apparition as heard speaking, or felt, or performing physical acts. That the disciples were at the time in question in a state favourable to such visions we might infer, not only from their general mental character and the excitement attending the crucifixion, but also from what is said in St. Matthew xxvii. 52, 53:—'And the graves were opened, and many bodies of saints which slept arose and came out of the graves after his resurrection, and went into the holy city and appeared unto many.' And also from the account given of them

---

[1] St. Mark, chap. xvi. ver. 12.   [2] Acts, chap. x. ver. 41.
[3] Matthew, chap. xxviii. ver. 17.

in the early chapters of the Acts. Among people in this state of mind the idea that Christ had risen, once started by the women and confirmed by the emptiness of the tomb, and possibly, as Strauss conjectures, by a supposed application of Old Testament texts, might spread such visions epidemically. Lastly, the manner in which St. Paul speaks of the appearances of the risen Saviour has been appealed to on behalf of this view.[1] He classes the other appearances with one to himself, presumably with the vision at his conversion. As this last occurred after the ascension, it is maintained that it was a vision, not a bodily return of Christ to this earth.

What, I ask, can be brought against these indications? The details of the appearances in St. John and St. Luke, and 'the eating and drinking with the disciples' spoken of by St. Peter (Acts x. 41), and the 'many infallible signs' mentioned in the same book (Acts i. 3), at once occur to us. These things do seem at first sight quite incompatible with the theory of mere apparitions. But it is true that stories, having equally the appearance of a renewal of the intercourse of natural life between the dead and the living, do somehow spring up even to this day. Even now we hear of apparitions[2] 'eating and drinking,' and inviting handling. We

[1] 1 Corinthians, chap. xv. ver. 8.
[2] 'Quarterly Journal of Science,' Jan. 1875.

ought also to remember that the writer of the third Gospel and of the Acts of the Apostles was not an eye-witness. The testimony of the fourth Gospel, if its genuineness were beyond doubt, would certainly be eye-witness testimony. I would not be understood to say myself that it is not St. John's, but as the controversy respecting that gospel now stands, I could not expect an adversary to admit that it is. Even if he should admit another view, popular with some,[1] if he should allow the Gospel to be St. John's, and account for the peculiarity of the conversations there attributed to Christ by supposing that the evangelist had blended his own thoughts with those of his Master, still he might raise this question; if the fourth Gospel cannot be trusted for the words of Christ, can it be trusted for the events of his life? But upon the other hand the confirmatory evidence of St. Paul shows that these later and fuller accounts of interviews in St. Luke and St. John cannot be later inventions; and the mere fact of repeated appearances to several persons, producing in them deep faith, is strong evidence in spite of what has been said as to their state of mind. Much stress may also be laid upon the statement of St. Paul in his First Epistle to the Corinthians xv. 6, that Christ 'was seen of above five hundred brethren at once, of whom the

---

[1] See 'The Authorship and Historical Character of the Fourth Gospel,' William Sanday, M.A. London: Macmillan, 1870.

greater part remain until this present, but some are fallen asleep.' But there are some weak points even here which ought in candour to be noticed. St. Paul was certainly not present himself: here again, then, we have not eye-witness testimony. All depends on the credibility of St. Paul's informants, whom we do not know. The words 'of whom the greater part remain until this present, but some are fallen asleep,' may be understood to show that some of the five hundred were known to the apostle, and if the twelve were among the number this was the case. But it is possible that the twelve may not have been among the five hundred, or at all events may not have been St. Paul's authority, and that accordingly the history of this appearance to five hundred may have been an account told to St. Paul by persons less worthy of confidence than the other apostles. St. Paul had many noble gifts, intellectual as well as moral, but we have no reason to believe that the power of critically sifting and weighing evidence was among the number. We have no mention of these five hundred elsewhere. If, as I have given some reason for thinking, this appearance is the same as that in St. Matthew upon the mountain in Galilee, then we might perhaps assume the testimony of the twelve; but we should still have one weak point. The first Gospel makes some seemingly of the eleven doubt:

if so, may not many of the five hundred have doubted? Finally, in any case an appearance even to so many as five hundred, though very strong evidence, is not absolutely conclusive. As I have said, we have recorded instances of illusions falling upon several persons at once.

We are now in a position to judge of the evidence of Christ's resurrection. If we set it aside we must accept two hypotheses—1, the removal of the body unknown to the disciples; 2, that the alleged appearances of Christ and the angels were really only subjective visions. These are the only explanations which our present science would allow. I have endeavoured candidly to state the probabilities and improbabilities of each hypothesis. To me it seems that each is difficult to be received, and it must be remembered that both have to be received if the resurrection is denied. What judgment, then, I ask, are we to form on the whole matter? A good deal will depend upon the convictions and sympathies with which we approach the subject. On the one hand, our evidence is certainly not demonstration. We may avoid its force by credible, though not probable, hypotheses. On the other hand, it may be truly urged that we have probability. We Christians do not rest in this matter merely on vague tradition, or habitual faith, or reverence, or religious expediency. We have a case. The ultimate question is, Does our probability rise to such a height as would decide the conduct of any fair-judging man who understood the argument? That is all in the way of proof for which we must look in one of the practical affairs of life, such as religion is. This amount of proof I claim that we have. But others, I allow, may honestly form a different opinion. When we try to make an estimate of such evidence, the measure of our belief is affected by our habits of mind, our sympathies, our hopes, fears, desires. The man of science, influenced, I must add unduly, by the increased presumption against miracles, would often need stronger evidence than we can bring forward; the religious man, on the contrary, attached to the doctrines, the consolations, and the hopes of religion, and habituated to believe in the personal action of God, would confidently accept what we have. This may not seem a very satisfactory upshot of our inquiry; but so far as I can judge it is the fair conclusion.

PART VII.

I return now to the evidential argument from miracles. We have concluded that the resurrection of Christ is its only truly firm foundation in matters of fact, and even here we cannot with absolute confidence look for assent from our adversaries. A few words more need to be said as to the argument itself before I finally offer an opinion upon its merits. Its conclusiveness depends not merely on the occurrence of the alleged miracles as matters of fact, but also upon their being miracles in the strict sense of the word. The event concerned must be clearly an infraction of the laws of nature by the will of God. Then only can we be confident in putting a meaning upon it on moral grounds. God's government of the world is thought of as carried on by general laws, but yet still as directed ultimately by his moral attributes. It is admitted that we can by no means assign his moral purpose in all the individual appointments of his providence. They are perhaps individual results of general appointments, and all that we can do is to grasp and to assign the good purpose of the general ordinance. But in a miracle we have the general ordinance set aside. There seems to be an emergency, so to speak, which makes the Almighty depart from the usual course of his government, and the grounds of that emergency we naturally look for in the consequences of the miracle. The act of God must be judged in and by itself, with reference solely to its own bearing and result. It is no longer a part of a stupendous plan of physical nature having connections and bearings of which we have possibly no idea. It stands out, isolated, an exception to the scheme of nature. The purpose of God here stands forth free from all ambiguities introduced by the thought that any particular event is but the combined result of a number of general laws which have a very wide scope. We therefore may be bold to read that purpose from purely moral considerations. It seems reasonable to suppose that the Almighty did intend the event in question to have in our eyes that meaning which our ideas of his moral and intelligent character and of its obvious effects would suggest. Thus the resurrection of Christ has been taken for an attestation of Christ's claims. But there is here still, I must point out, some of that liability to error which we, with our limited knowledge and faculties, must incur when we attempt to read the mind of God, especially in any particular appointment. For the event in question, though as regards its antecedents broken off from the great chain of past causation and therefore not mixed up with them as to its final cause, is, as regards its consequents, not so disconnected; especially its moral and intellectual results may have an enormous extent and a varied character. A miracle, for example, may attract faith in one age and repel it in another. One generation might ask for a sign, another see the hand of God sooner in the order of nature. And we, with our limited knowledge of all these issues, should speak diffidently as to the purpose of God on any such occasion. It is a bold thing, with our short range of vision, to undertake to read the mind of the Almighty. This qualification we must allow to our evidential conclusions. With this qualification the argument from a miracle stands as I have described it. But obviously, so soon as any anomalous event seems likely after all to prove an instance of natural law, it begins to lose this evidential power. It becomes blended with the common course of events where confessedly we cannot practise with the same confidence this kind of interpretation. For instance, if Christ's miracles of healing are only instances of a kind of cures by mental influence of which there have been innumerable examples—sometimes cases when false religion was the source of influence—sometimes cases with which religion of any kind had nothing to do, then they cannot be reasoned from as above. It may be true that Christ's possessing this natural power in so great a degree contributed to the establishment of his religion, and this we may look upon as an appointment of God's providence for this end. But so regarded it is not evidential proof. We might in like manner quote the fact that Mahomet had great natural eloquence, and some of his first disciples had remarkable military talents, circumstances which powerfully conduced to the spread of his religion, as appointments of Providence bearing witness to his mission. The question here offers itself, Can even the resurrection, understood in its most strictly miraculous sense as a transformation of Christ's corpse, be confidently pronounced such a miracle as we require, an event undoubtedly beyond all natural explanation.

I have said that it had a clear and strong claim so to be considered. But I would not venture to say that the claim was beyond all doubt. Science has explained so many wonderful things that he would be a bold man who would say what that is which she never will explain. The event might be unique, but still we might conceive the laws of nature so arranged after the example of Mr. Babbage's calculating machine [1] as to bring about what would seem to us such a unique event. We might also think of the resurrection as caused by the incoming of the powers of a spiritual world without real breach of continuity as the authors of 'The Unseen Universe' have done. These views still leave the resurrection an evidence of Christ's divinity by what I may call analogy. He differs from all other men. This latter reasoning may not be so conclusive as that from attestation by breach of law, but it has the advantage of avoiding the difficulties of proving such breach of law, and also the conflict with the doctrine of continuity.[2]

---

[1] See 'Unseen Universe,' art. 80; also Mr. Babbage's ninth Bridgewater Treatise.

[2] I would here offer an answer to a suggestion which might occur

There is another way also of avoiding the evidential force even of the most incontestable miracles which scientific men perhaps would not bring forward, but of which something must here be said. I allude to the hypothesis of the personal action of supernatural beings other than God. This hypothesis was, we read, the resource of our Lord's personal adversaries. It has often since been revived, and, indeed, may be found in our own day in the well-known work called 'Supernatural Religion.' Here, however, it appears rather as a logical difficulty in the argument from the Christian miracles than as a serious explanation of them. It seems to me also that the hypothesis of the book to which I have just referred, 'The Unseen Universe,' viz. that there is a universe unseen by us, yet in actual physical relation to the visible universe, would open a door to like explanations. It would, for instance, give a standing ground to the Spiritualists. In spite of the strong objection which many scientific men feel to apparitions, and the admitted failure of the evidence on their behalf in many cases, I for one cannot help thinking that there is probably under certain laws unknown to us a communication be-

to some minds, Why not deal with the argument for Christianity as with the argument for a God, combine different arguments for Christ's divinity to answer objections to his miracles? It seems to me that we should not thus escape some of the most important objections to miracles, their liability to natural explanation, and the allegation that this view is most congruous with divine action as known to us.

tween this physical universe and an unseen spiritual universe. The multitude of accounts of appearances of the dead cannot all be easily taken for subjective visions. I would instance that class of such accounts which make the apparition contemporary with the time of death when the death is at a distant place: such as the story known as the 'Beresford Ghost Story,' or the apparition to the late Lord Brougham. They seem to me to have a certain verifiable confirmation. The coincidence as to time of the death and the vision can, at all events, be verified; and if it be true, it does not agree well with the notion of a mere subjective vision. Now, if we do admit such interferences of beings who are not a part of the visible system of nature, then even such an event as the resurrection of Christ, or at least the recorded facts, might be explained without supposing a special unique interference of the Almighty himself. In any case, whether we think this explanation admissible or no, there certainly is the difficulty in question on the side of Christianity, because the Bible expressly admits the interference even with physical nature of supernatural beings hostile to God and wishing to deceive man. It has been customary to reply to this objection by pointing to the character of the Christian miracles and of the religion which they helped to establish, as quite inconsistent with this idea of their origin. Mr. Farmer, who wrote a book upon this subject last century, took up a still wider position. He contended that there never had been any real miracles, except those of divine agency. But his arguments are not convincing; he reasons too much in the *à priori* fashion as to what God would be likely to do or to permit. He dwells much upon the mischief that would follow from diabolic interference. He tells us that for God to permit an evil spirit to interrupt the course of nature would be the same thing as interrupting it himself in the alleged way. His attempt to explain away the apparent recognition of diabolic miracles in the Scriptures fails. Farmer, it may be said, has gone too far: a more cautious divine would not deny diabolic miracles altogether. He would only deny that the Gospel miracles were such, and he would, as we have said, rest his denial on the goodness and the salutary tendency of Christian doctrine. I do not know that he would in so doing be at all open to the charge of reasoning in a circle, that is, first proving the miracles by the doctrine and then the doctrine by the miracles. He might fairly contend that our own independent judgment in moral things was quite competent to pronounce the character and tendency of Christianity inconsistent with diabolic origin. But I still do not think that he would make his case complete. To do this he must, I think, in accordance with the ideas just expressed, take a rather wider view of the possible supernatural. He must not confine himself to the diabolic agency which the statements of Scripture do no doubt require him to consider. If we give up the universality of law, and admit personal supernatural agency in physical nature, we have to show that there can be no such agency, in this matter at least, except that of God on the one hand or of evil spirits on the other. Apart from the reign of law, it is not true that the aspect of nature excludes the supposition of other supernatural interference. To the polytheist we know that it suggests it, and so also, as it seems, to the modern Spiritualist.

We may ask, might not the Christian miracles have proceeded from some supernatural beings of imperfect goodness, not of unqualified wickedness? And it seems to me that in order fairly to put aside this hypothesis, we should have to try to estimate the actual results of Christianity in the world; not to consider simply its intrinsic beauty or goodness, as it was originally propounded, but its effects in man's history as corrupted and perverted by human ignorance and sinfulness; and to endeavour at least to show that it was, in spite of these abatements and qualifications to its success, after all the very best means for promoting man's good possible under the restrictions morally necessary from man's freedom at the time of its promulgation. Nothing short of this would, I think, make it worthy of a divine interference. A lower view would suggest an author less perfect, or wise, or powerful than God. I am quite aware that many instances may be pointed out in God's natural works, or in his providence, where we cannot trace this perfect adaptation to the end. But these things are seen, it must be noticed, in his natural administration. They are not, therefore, fair analogies for a supernatural interference. In this last case we might, as has been pointed out, expect to see the apparent moral purpose fully carried out. We ought to have, as I have elsewhere expressed it, Design triumphing over Law. Now I am far from saying that Christianity was not this best possible remedy for human evils; but at the same time I am so conscious of the difficulty of the inquiry, that I do not believe it possible to present our conclusion sustained by what would be in the eyes of a sceptic a convincing argument. Of course upon the assumption of uniform law in the divine action these embarrassing considerations do not enter in. No particular event can then claim that character of being an exceptional and special act of God, which gives a miracle its evidential force, and which makes it so important to show that the miracle is not the work of any creature agent. God does not appear as one of many unseen personal agents interfering with the course of the world, and we are not embarrassed to determine which interferences are his.

After these last remarks we may now draw to a close our consideration of the argument from the Christian miracles. The original question, I would once more repeat, was not whether certain events in the life of Christ, commonly taken to be miraculous, actually occurred, but whether the evidence which we have for them is so much better than that for other seemingly miraculous events that we may believe the former and reject the latter. After considering the critical tests by which other miraculous stories are put aside, and applying them to the evangelical miracles, I concluded that the resurrection of Christ himself was the only case which could fairly claim this advantage. Even as to this I was led to think that different minds would with equal honesty estimate this superiority differently. Further, we have seen that the religious interpretation of anomalous events by referring them to a direct special personal action of God, brings with it some uncertainties and difficulties. My conclusion accordingly is, that the argument from the miracles cannot in these days be relied upon as the foundation for Christian belief. This, I would once more point out, is not by any means the same thing as concluding that nothing of the nature of the true supernatural has occurred in connection with Christianity. This, I must not be understood to assert. The Christian religion, and indeed even natural religion, clearly assert a great deal of the supernatural, as that word is generally understood, though this truth, I may repeat, does not require us of necessity to set aside the doctrine of continuity, as has, I think, been shown. I would yet again repeat that it is not miracles, not even in the strictest sense of the word, which I now call in question, but the evidential argument founded upon them. That argument has not lost all its value, but it has lost some. It may claim a place, but not the first place in Christian evidences. It is auxiliary rather than fundamental, fitted, as matters stand, rather to confirm the believer than to convince the sceptic.

The question arises, If you value low the argument from miracles, upon what do you rest the truth of Christianity? Other arguments from matters of fact have been brought forward. I may mention two such arguments, one drawn from the fulfilment of prophecy, the other from the part which Christianity has actually had in the progress of man. I do not purpose here to enter on the discussion of these arguments, but I will give my own opinion. As regards the former, the cases cited are not so clear and conclusive as may, I think, be reasonably required for so important an end, and the argument is further exposed to some of the objections which beset all arguments from miracles, such as uncertainty as to the divine purpose. The latter argument also cannot be put in a fully convincing form. I allow at once that being an argument as to the divine purposes from general considerations it is not open to some of the criticisms as to miracle testimony. Further, no doubt Christianity has conferred very great blessings on mankind. But these advantages have had drawbacks from man's perversion, religious wars, and persecutions and quarrels, support to mischievous superstitions, as in the case of witchcraft, the maintenance of an oppressive and reactionary hierarchy, hindrances to the progress of thought and knowledge, consecration of secular despotisms. If we look at the matter merely in the light of history, it seems an exaggeration either to represent Christianity as the turning point of God's dealings with man, or, again, as the one grand source of human improvement. Nominally, the religion has not yet extended over much more than a fourth of mankind, and really it has effectually leavened an incomparably smaller number with its influence. So, again, we cannot deny that other very powerful agents are at work for the improvement of man's character, as the wonderful growth of natural science with its reflex influence on the human mind itself, the improvements in government, the diffusion of knowledge, the increased intercourse of nations, the growth of material resources and comfort. I cannot myself see in the evidence of history any more than in that of prophecy the strong testimony which we need. It seems to me that no argument for Christianity so definite, intelligible, and precise, was ever framed from grounds of external matter of fact as the argument of Paley. There, if anywhere, we shall find in physical events a guarantee for the teaching of our religion. But, if I am right, we find it imperfectly. What, then, is to be our course? Many earnest men, feeling these difficulties, have fallen back on ground which has no foundation in argument; at least, none I believe that can bear criticism. They have simply accepted their religion upon church authority in some shape or other. Practically, these men surrendered their judgments in the most important affair of life, under the pressure of supposed difficulty and danger. They ceased to think, lest thinking should lead them to disbelieve what they could not bear or did not dare to disbelieve. I know that this course may be adopted by minds of a very high order, as in the case of Dr. Newman. But it seems to me adapted only to a state of the human mind different from what we see now—a state with less of knowledge and maturity. With all its liability to abuse, it may be the best expedient when the education of the race is still backward, when men collectively are, so to speak, in mental infancy or boyhood. But it can be only temporary, provisional.

As knowledge grows, and thought matures, the solemn questions of religion and duty must be dealt with in a different way. In an age of active investigation and growing light, nothing will so promote absolute unbelief and indifference to all religion as bold demands on our credulity. If ever that reconciliation between science and religion so loudly called for at the present day is to take place, religious men must be content to put forth nothing to be believed by their fellow men for which they cannot give some reason, convincing so far as the nature of the case entitles us to expect. If this be a true saying, then the authority of no ecclesiastical body can be admitted as a guarantee for the truth of our religion. There remains, then, but one other foundation for religious belief; the sanction and attestation of our Moral Faculty. Here I believe that we must seek our refuge. Here we must take our stand. Serious admissions may be involved in that step. A new form may have to be given to some popular views. Upon that subject I would say a few words in another and succeeding essay.

See note on this essay at the end of the volume.

ESSAY III.

THE RELATION OF THE GOSPEL TO THE MORAL FACULTY IN MAN.

PART I.

THE net result of my inquiry in two former essays has been to leave religious truth mainly dependent upon the attestation of conscience. In my first essay, when I was seeking for evidence of the being and attributes of God, I came to the conclusion that unless we accepted as a witness our sense of right and wrong, we should not have adequate grounds for believing in the goodness of God. Again, in my second essay, after examining the miraculous evidence of Christianity, I concluded that we could not depend upon that evidence as the argumentative foundation for belief. There are, indeed, other evidences so called, as that from prophecy or from place in the Providential scheme of the world's history. But I did not think that these either would be found sufficiently strong for our main support. We are, indeed, again thrown back upon the testimony of the moral faculty. If the Gospel is to establish itself permanently in the belief of men as a special communication from God, it must be in consequence of its precepts and doctrines being witnessed to by conscience. This is not the same thing, I would remark, as saying that we are to accept the teaching of the Bible only so far as it is borne out by conscience, or some other internal verifying faculty. For independently of other arguments Christ's teaching might convince us that there was in him an intuition of moral and religious truth that entitled him to our trust and obedience when he taught things beyond any other knowledge of ours; things, indeed, which our moral faculties, however quickened and cultivated, could not intuitively recognise as true. But certainly the negative counterpart to this proposition does hold true. We may teach on Christ's authority what the conscience cannot verify, but we must not teach that which conscience distinctly disallows—the conscience, I mean, not of any particular man, but of enlightened men in general.[1] It becomes then a vital question

---

[1] This position may be displeasing to some Christians, but I do not myself see that it goes much, if at all, beyond what a much admired and trusted English theologian, Bishop Butler, has laid down at the end of the first chapter in the second part of his 'Analogy.' 'Indeed, if in revelation there be found any passages the seeming meaning of which is contrary to natural religion, we may most certainly conclude such meaning not to be the real one. But it is not any degree of a presumption against an interpretation of Scripture that

to inquire how far the teaching of Christianity is conformed to the evidence of conscience. Let us briefly examine this conformation under two heads— first, as to precepts; second, as to doctrines.

PART II.

I will begin with some consideration of what the things to be compared really are, for there is at first sight a vagueness about both. Where is the testimony of conscience to be found? How are its authoritative judgments to be recognised? This point need not detain us long. I have spoken of it already. We must freely acknowledge that conscience has borne very different witness in different ages and countries. But I have endeavoured to show that this is not a reason for disregarding her testimony. With the advance of civilisation there has been a growing consensus of opinion. Of much we may well be sure. The fact that there are uncertainties is not peculiar to that part of our knowledge which concerns moral truth. It appears here, perhaps, less than it does for the most-part

such interpretation contains a doctrine which the light of nature cannot discover or a precept which the law of nature does not oblige to.'

elsewhere. Those ages and countries which have differed in a very marked way from us in opinion as to moral questions have also differed very greatly in their notions upon other subjects. Such diversity is inseparable from the nature of a progressive mind. Our part at any given time is to make the best judgment in our power. So let us do as to the question before us.

We have next a question which will detain us longer. What is that moral teaching for which Christianity is properly responsible? There are several exclusions and qualifications which ought here to be made. In the first place, I would say that Christianity has not to justify every moral precept, example, or advice, which may be found in the Bible. No doubt she must be held strictly responsible for the precepts, example, or advice of Christ himself. So much the essential tenet of the religion, the divinity of Christ, requires. But certainly Christians are not called upon to justify all the precepts of the Old Testament as parts of permanent morality. These precepts belong to a confessedly imperfect system, to a state of belief and duty which Christianity has greatly enlarged, modified, and elevated. Christ himself has expressly recognised this truth.[1] Much less, I think, should

[1] St. Matthew, v. 17, 21, 22, 27, 28, 31, 32, 33, 34, 43, 44 ; xix. 8.

our religion be made accountable for all the actions or words of characters praised in the Old Testament, as David or Deborah ; nor, again, for all the sentiments expressed by the writers of that book, as, for example, those in the maledictory psalms. I allow, of course, that some of these characters are highly spoken of in the New Testament, and that the Old Testament is frequently quoted as of divine authority by Christ himself. Still, the moral imperfection of the Old Dispensation is distinctly recognised by him. Further, I do not think it fair to assert in the name of Christianity the infallibility of absolutely everything, even in the New Testament, upon moral subjects. It seems from that book that the apostles themselves were not always under infallible guidance, as witness the conduct of St. Peter at Antioch.[1] If we consider the writings of the New Testament impartially, we shall not think that they claim infallibility for everything which they say. For instance, when St. Paul is speaking to the Corinthians upon the subject of marriage, he seems to draw a distinction in binding power between his own judgment and that of the Lord as to that particular matter.[2] The view which he implies seems to be this. In the one case, we have an authoritative command ; in the other, the advice of an excellent and enlightened Christian, but still

---

[1] Galatians, ii. 11.   [2] 1 Cor. vii. 25.

not of one who here claimed infallibility. It would, I contend, be an exaggeration of the authority of a canonical book, however great that authority be, to carry it beyond what the writing itself implies. To apply this distinction, if St. Paul has really spoken too favourably of slavery, that is only the error of a disciple, an error, I may say, which did not spring, I am sure, from any wish to make a compromise with prevailing evil, but from an intense sense of the subordinate value of this life. Much less I think is it reasonable to bring against Christianity moral objections which may justly lie against the ecclesiastical morality or ecclesiastical institutions of times long subsequent to those of Christ. It is certainly not clear that Christ himself laid the foundation of a priesthood and hierarchy at all.[1] These things may have engrafted themselves upon the great Christian movement in the natural course of its progress. They may have in some respects aided, strengthened, consolidated that movement. But at the same time they did in the end give a new character to the religion, a character for which its founder is not to be held responsible. They diminished its deeply moral character; they made it more of a doctrinal system. Above all, they set up a vast system of priestly rule. And these changes led to religious

[1] See 'Dissertation on the Christian Ministry,' in Professor Lightfoot's book on St. Paul's Epistle to the Philippians.

strife, persecution, bondage of the human mind, but these were not the fruits of the teaching of Christ. Even the moral ideal of Christianity underwent a change.[1] Asceticism took the place of charity. But we are not to charge the extravagances of Egyptian monkery, any more than the cruelties of the Spanish Inquisition, upon the Gospel itself. Furthermore, in judging this last, there is need to be careful what we assume Christ's own words to have been. It is not right to disregard any well-supported exception of modern critics. For instance, I do not think it right that we should claim Christ's authority for the assertion that the unbeliever will be damned, upon the ground of St. Mark xvi. 16. And, lastly, we are ever to keep in mind the real character of Christ's teaching. Our Lord never delivers a complete body of commands, 'a whole duty of man.' He speaks with reference to present occasions. He brings out one side of truth at a time. He lays down principles of great depth and extent of application. But he does not expressly and in words contemplate their application to remote cases out of the experience of his hearers. He aims rather to produce a character than to deliver a code. Hence the extreme, unguarded, impracticable appearance which his teaching may sometimes appear

---

[1] See Lecky's 'History of European Morals,' vol. ii. p. 130.

to have. Kant criticised severely the precept, 'whatsoever ye would that men should do to you, do ye even so to them.'[1] No doubt the saying, considered as a precise rule of duty, is open to objection, but as a teaching of the spirit of love it is beautiful. Christ did not purpose to fence in the Christian's path on either side with 'a hard and fast line' of commandment. He aimed to put a new spirit in his followers; and herein, surely, we must see an adaptation to the changing character and circumstances of a race like that of man, spreading over the face of the globe, progressing in intellectual development and social organisation from age to age. The same peculiarity in the words of Christ accounts for what is thought by some a want of completeness in his moral teaching. Naturally, that teaching does need some complement. Christ did not profess to supersede all moral teaching which had gone before, and give a new and sufficing law in its place. He expressly allowed much of the Mosaic law. He came 'not to destroy, but to fulfil.' And the principles of his teaching will readily incorporate with themselves any sound conclusions of moral science at any time. He did not, it is true, avowedly and expressly contemplate that wonderful advance of the human mind in knowledge and in intellectual power which modern times have wit-

[1] St. Matthew, vii. 12.

nessed, and which no doubt is of the highest value to man. Had he done so, certain virtues whose importance that progress has brought strongly into light, might have been more emphasised. The love of truth for its own sake, and toleration of the errors of others, might have been more expressly taught. But as it is, they are not lost sight of. Witness the admonition of the single eye,[1] the parable of the good Samaritan,[2] the rebuke of the intolerant disciples.[3] The form of the teaching was for the days of Christ; but its spirit is for all time. A teacher who made love to God, and man, the substance of man's duty, taught for all possible conditions of our race.

If we frankly allow and fairly bear in mind the qualifications and peculiarities to which I have now called attention, I think that we shall conclude that the teaching of Christ was deeply, comprehensively, and permanently moral. No one will deny that he taught love, purity, patience, devotion to God, as powerfully as either words or examples could do. It is the permanence of his morality which, with our modern ideas of progress, is, I suppose, most likely to be questioned. Is it suited to later times? Has it grown antiquated, or even obsolete as civilisation has advanced?

[1] St. Matthew, vi. 22.   [2] Luke, x. 30–37.
[3] Luke, ix. 55.

Now, I think that some of those very precepts, which upon other grounds have been objected to, some of those sayings of Christ which, when looked at from the standpoint of our present state, have been thought extravagant, as, for instance, the injunction of unlimited almsgiving, forgiveness, submission, are really an answer to the question before us. They may fairly be said to be prospective, adapted to a progressive race. They are, at least in the letter, inapplicable now, but they seem more and more capable of a literal obedience as society approaches an ideal of moral perfection. It has been said that Christianity neglected justice, and insisted too much on charity. But surely the opposition of justice to charity is not founded on a deep view of morals. Nor would it require much thought with any Christian to conciliate the two. Charity, according to the enlightened understanding of the word, that is, a care for the general good, enjoins justice, and even penal justice, as a means thereto. There is an obvious difference between resenting injuries by private revenge and bringing the wrongdoer to justice on public grounds. To give way to criminals would not be to show kindness even to them. So, again, as to submission to authority, certainly Christ has carried the duty of the Christian far; and surely in such times as his, and among a people so turbulent as the Jews, and so apt to find pretexts for that turbulence in religion, this obligation to use peaceable means of reform was a lesson that much needed to be enforced, and it argued a deep sense of the providence of God to trust to such means. Certainly, Christ gave no sanction to injustice, either in the law or the ruler. Nothing could be more repugnant to his teaching than despotism, class privileges, slavery, harsh social arrangements, tyranny, or oppression in any shape whatever. He taught a universal brotherhood; only he allowed no violent attempts to bring about the ideal. Surely the caution was needed. I think it, however, too much to say that Christ never gave countenance to a resort to force in any case whatever. There is at least one act in his life which might be thought to do so. I allude to the cleansing of the Temple. This act has been found fault with as contrary to public order and civil obedience.[1] But we may, I think, see in it a valuable recognition of the truth, that there is even in this matter a limit to the command, an exception to the general rule, a case in which other principles take its place, a case in which submission to established authority is no longer the good man's part. It has been customary to see an absence of ritualism or of national exclu-

---

[1] By Mr. Francis Newman, if I remember rightly, as also the stress laid upon Charity by our Lord in comparison of what is said as to Justice.

siveness in the religion taught by Christ, and most persons in these days would count those features of Christianity eminent merits. But I am bound to say that their origin with Christ has been questioned. The fact that our Lord himself conformed to the Jewish law, and that his immediate disciples did the same, for some time at least, has, I suppose, been held to disprove his claim to be the founder of a religion eminently free from ceremonial observances. But something should be allowed for the gradual development of a new system, something for temporary accommodation to old practices, and ways of thinking, and to conformity to avoid needless offence. We see these principles recognised in the words and acts of Christ, as in the gradual instruction of the disciples, in his own baptism, his enjoining obedience to those in the chair of Moses, his payment of the tribute money. In the Fourth Gospel we certainly do find a highly spiritual view of worship attributed immediately to Christ. And indeed, independently of this authority, we have elsewhere evidence that Christ laid the stress of his teaching upon moral obedience, and lightly esteemed merely ceremonial acts. We may quote, for instance, the many rebukes of the Pharisees, the saying upon fasting, the preference of mercy to sacrifice, the implication that prayer is not heard for much speaking, the injunction to forgiveness before offering the gift. So, again, as to that other point, the catholicity of Christ's religion, a question has been raised whether we owe this to our Lord himself or to a movement amongst his followers, subsequent to him, headed by St. Paul. It must be allowed that his earlier efforts were directed towards 'the lost sheep of the house of Israel.' But it is also clear, even apart from the Fourth Gospel, that in the last days of his ministry he contemplated a Gentile church.[1] Asceticism, in the ordinary sense of the word, will not, I suppose, be charged against Christ. His adversaries, in his own time at all events, brought an opposite charge.[2] But perhaps a spirit dangerously opposed to our modern industrial civilisation may be found by some in his strong condemnation of the love of wealth. It must be borne in mind that he had not that civilisation to deal with. We are not to judge of the wisdom and goodness of Christ's words upon the supposition that he meant them literally to apply to our different times. Here, as in the case of the commandments which concern mental progress, we are to remember how much the form of Christ's teaching was influenced by his times. He spoke to men who, if they sought for wealth, were very likely to do so by improper means. The pursuit of wealth

---

[1] See the parables of the Marriage of the King's Son and of the Great Supper.
[2] St. Matthew, xi. 19; St. Luke, vii. 34.

by lawful means, by frugality, industry, enterprise, has no doubt in modern times conferred great benefits upon society; and such conduct the principles of Christianity certainly do not condemn. If we make the required abatements, we shall not, I think, say more than this, that Christ strongly asserted the greater importance of a future life,—a lesson which surely will not make us unprofitable here, if we keep strictly to the belief that our happiness in that future depends upon our doing our duty here. And, willing as I am to recognise the blessings of industrial progress, I would contend that the love of gain needs to be restrained, that it must be kept subordinate to higher principles, and that Christ's teaching in this matter is very valuable for this end.

Mr. Mill has charged the moral teaching of Christ with being too negative, with dealing too much in 'thou shalt not' rather than 'thou shalt.'[1] But in the face of such earnest injunctions to active benevolence as are to be found in the Gospels, this charge cannot be sustained. Both by word and example Christ taught a life of active usefulness. His ideal was not the contemplative life, not the life of the monk, or the hermit, or the quietist. He went about doing good. And that system of worship which he taught, viz., instruction in divine things,

[1] See 'Essay on Liberty,' People's Edition, p. 29.

reflection upon God and duty, and man's highest prospects, confession and repentance for sin, prayer, praise, thanksgiving, acts of Christian commemoration, and of fellowship with him and his Church, this system I say he taught, not as a substitute, but as a help to active goodness; and even those who see in worship no good except its natural reflex action upon the mind, must I think allow that such a system was purifying, elevating, strengthening. Compare it with the mysteries, sacrifices, pilgrimages, ceremonies, austerities, priestly ordinances of superstitious worship. Do we not indeed see a contrast?

Christ, it is true, brought out the passive more than the active virtues, as those words are commonly understood. We hear much of love, patience, forbearance, meekness,—less of courage, energy, perseverance. Here, again, we have an instance of the relative and incomplete character of Christ's commands. What he said took a special character from the times. The passive virtues needed most to be raised in men's esteem, and fostered in their practice. Something, too, must be allowed for the religious standpoint. We hear from Christ of humility, not magnanimity. But can we be surprised at this when we call to mind that Christ taught, not as the philosophers, with man and human society only in view, but as the messenger from God, who saw man weak and sinful, ever in relation to God, infinitely great and good. Can his teaching be said to cherish a mean or abject character in man, when it bids him always to remember that he is the child of a heavenly father? Christ may not have urged enterprise, energy, perseverance; but when he so strenuously repressed pride, sensuality, contention, did he not take out of the way the most dangerous adversaries to industrial progress? Patriotism, too, it is said, that he neglected. But is not this virtue comprehended in the Christian notion of our duty to our neighbour?

PART III.

I will go on now to my second head, the conformity of Christian doctrine to the teaching of conscience. Here, I allow, that we enter upon less certain ground. The moral faculty in man may reasonably be supposed to be a much better judge of right and wrong between man and man than between man and God. Obviously, the relation of the Creator to his creatures must be far different from that of any man to another. To take an illustration, in all civilised countries nothing has been more strenuously forbidden and checked than the taking of one man's life by another. Further, it has come to be allowed that the right to take human life, which the state claims, is limited to peculiar cases. Yet life so sacred between man and man is universally held to be at the absolute disposal of God. Ultimately, he gives, and it is for him to take away. Plainly, if life be his gift, it is his part to determine the amount of the gift. What Mr. Mill [1] has said about nature's apparent disregard of life, may be true as regards matter of fact, but, after all, it is no impeachment of God as a moral being. On the hypothesis of religion, viz., that he places us here to prepare for a future state, the only condition needed to justify any seeming abruptness in calling us hence is that the time of the summons will be upon the whole and in the end for our good. We might find other illustrations, as, for instance, an alleged appearance of want of care for veracity on the part of God,[2] inasmuch as he has left man to be so often, so long, and sometimes so mischievously, misled by the appearances of nature. The answer is of course plain that the obligation to truth exists only in a certain defined relation, that of communicating thought between two beings, and that this relation does not exist in nature between man and God. In short, we may say that no specific human

---

[1] See 'Essay on Nature,' p. 28.
[2] Lecky's 'History of European Morals,' vol. i. p. 56.

analogies will correctly represent the relations between God and man. Nor perhaps can any idea which our minds can frame. Hence, if we admit, as I think that we must admit, the validity of the moral law, even for the actions of God, we are embarrassed by questions of form and application. But we are not obliged on that account, I hold, to lay aside the thought before us. Uncertainty as to some matters of detail does not destroy the whole value of knowledge; and if the reasoning of these essays be sound, we can obtain a secure foundation for religion only by assuming that conscience does reveal, not fully I allow, but still, to some extent, really the mind of God. We have to fall back upon highly general principles; to eliminate to the best of our judgment what seems in morals due to the conditions of human life. We may safely say that in any relation between two moral beings the law of charity would hold. The ten commandments have their place only in the relations of this world; but that great commandment, the keeping of which is the fulfilling of the whole law, must hold even for the Almighty himself.

I think it worth while to mention here a distinction which does not need to be pointed out to anyone accustomed to philosophical language, but which may not be known to others. I allude to a difference between the philosophical and the popular use of the word 'reason.' Reason has been used by philosophers as a name to stand for those intuitive judgments of the mind among which the principles of the moral faculty take their place, and accordingly with them the authority of reason in matters of religion has been spoken of when that of conscience was meant. But this was, I fancy, misleading with many ordinary persons. Their notion of a thing being according to reason, was that it could be explained according to natural laws, physical or mental, could be shown to be part of the natural course of events. Now, our notorious experience of many things which cannot be thus explained, at all events at present, not to mention our just feeling that there must be in the doings of one so far above us as God, much that we cannot understand in this way, has hindered a want of conformity to reason, when thus understood, from appearing a great objection to anything in religion. But if the philosophical meaning of the word 'reason' had been thought of, if it had been distinctly understood that what was objected to was contrary to our conscience, to our natural feeling of right and wrong, the objection would have assumed a more serious and weighty appearance. We certainly have no right to refuse our belief to an event, even so contrary to the known course of nature as the general resurrection of the dead, merely on the ground of its being so contrary.

But the case stands differently with objections on moral grounds. Surely we must feel a difficulty in attributing to God conduct which, even when we have made all allowance for his peculiar relation to us, our moral feelings instinctively condemn. If my reasoning in these essays has been just, no possible evidence from miracles, or from any other source, could justify us in doing so.

Now let us consider, first, the conformity to the moral faculty of those doctrines of religion which Christianity has in common with natural religion. By these I understand the existence of a God of infinite power, wisdom, and goodness, his perfect though mysterious government of this present world, his designing for man a future state, his dealing with each individual throughout both here and hereafter as a moral ruler and a loving father, punishing or rewarding so as to secure man's lasting good. It will be noticed that the idea of punishment is here reformatory, not retributive. That seems to me the notion which the moral feeling of this age suggests. It is, I allow, inconsistent with the doctrine of the everlasting punishment of the wicked, a doctrine which I will consider at more length hereafter, but which I may say at once that I for one do not see how to defend on grounds of moral science. Our conscience may also be thought by some opposed to any sharp and determinate separation of mankind hereafter into two classes, the one happy, and the other unhappy, on the ground of their conduct in this life, because that conduct is of too mixed a character to admit of such exact discrimination. Are not the degrees of merit or demerit in individuals, it may be said, insensibly graduated? But this latter objection will, I think, upon consideration, be found to rest upon assumptions as to the uniformity and constancy of happiness and misery in the two classes which have no adequate support, even in the commonly received doctrine of future punishment, much less in the reformatory view. A distinct classification is compatible with perfect gradation in reward, retribution, or discipline. If the doctrines which Christianity and natural religion have in common, be stated as above, there is not, I think, any real question as to discrepancy between them and the witness of conscience. They are expressly made conformable to that witness. But a deeper question may still be raised, viz., whether the belief in such a God, and in his so dealing with us, does or does not give a better character to man? Strange as it may appear, this is gravely questioned. It has been thought that such a belief makes virtue selfish. It leads us to do good for what we shall gain by it, to keep from evil lest we should suffer by it. And this we are told is not so high and pure a view of human duty as that which makes us act aright merely from a wish to do so. Nay, it has even been attempted, in modern days, to preserve the moral benefits of enlightened worship, without admitting, or at least without building upon, the idea of God. Something certainly of those benefits may arise from the presenting of pure and good thoughts and examples to the mind, and the kindling and calling forth of moral sympathy, apart from the thoughts and feelings immediately directed towards God. This might be true of praise, thanksgiving, religious contemplation. There is certainly much in the universe itself to raise in the mind feelings of wonder, awe, even reverence. We see such feelings, for instance, in a mind as little influenced by religious belief as was that of the late Dr. Strauss.[1] Further, the sense of blessing, when thought of as derived only from inanimate nature, may still be cherished with profit. Nay, even in the case of prayer, that case in which the selfish ingredient of religious feeling does most largely enter, and in which we most obviously need an Almighty hearer and giver, it is still true that so far forth as the direction of the will is, that of aspiration towards moral good, the practice might be perpetuated, and that with happy effect even when the belief in a God had been relinquished. These are, I conjec-

[1] 'The Old Faith and the New,' by D. F. Strauss, authorised translation by M. Blind, 2nd edit., p. 164.

ture, the psychological principles at the bottom of the worship actually practised by the disciples of M. Comte. I admit the good so far as it goes. But I think that a further, and a very great, good is obtained by the belief in God. All the sentiments just named assume a deeper and stronger, a more living and influential, character, when our thoughts are directed towards a Being of infinite perfections as an objective reality. There is in that ideal, even if it be no more than an ideal, and if there be no direct action of that Being in response upon the soul, a power to quicken, encourage, and strengthen man's spirit in all good ways, by the admiration, love, and devotion which it calls forth. And I for one must also contend that there is in this belief in God, his protection, and care, a support which our weak nature compounded of selfish as well as generous feelings needs. I am aware that in these last words I expose myself to the imputation named a little while back of making virtue selfish. But I should contend with Butler that there is a right as well as a wrong care for self. It is but a romantic scheme of life, which does not take account of those self-caring instincts. I know that the moral reformer may hope to diminish their power, perhaps to take away their supremacy. Human nature is plastic. It has been modified greatly. Nay, if modern theories be true, it has been built up, and fashioned, and moulded, in the course of ages. It may be modified much more hereafter. However widespread and powerful are the workings of self-interest, we know that there are certainly other principles also at work in man's heart, and hereafter they may become more powerful than they are now. But it seems to me that we cannot reasonably anticipate a state of human progress in which the self-regarding instincts, including the family affections, will not be strong. Mr. Darwin's principle, the survival of those who succeed in the struggle for life, would not lead us to that expectation, since those instincts are plainly concerned in the preservation, both of the individual and the offspring. Mr. Mill has instanced the patriotism of the ancient Romans as an example of the strength which an unselfish sentiment may attain.[1] No doubt this is an instance, and others may be found of an individual virtue fostered into unusual strength. But it is plainly much short of universal benevolence. We have no reason to think that the influences which produced this as well as some other virtues in the early Romans could have brought about a complete ascendancy of unselfish feelings. And whatever those influences were, their effect was not permanent. There was a great decay of Roman virtue. The general failure of socialist[2]

---

[1] 'Essay on the Utility of Religion,' p. 107.
[2] See Mill's 'Political Economy,' book ii. chap. i.

schemes, apart from religious influences, and indeed the modifications in principle of those schemes, which their most intelligent advocates adopt, seem to prove that the permanent principles of human nature and the conditions of human life forbid us to expect a state of things in which the self-regarding sentiments, including the family affections, will be permanently subordinate to the sentiments which are wholly unselfish. At least such a state of things is not within our present horizon of prospect. Whosoever admits this, and considers how often these feelings tempt man to deal unkindly, untruly, or unjustly, with his fellow man, will acknowledge the value of a belief in a God, the righteous ruler of the world. And even if that unlooked-for state of human nature had come, even if man had learned to carry out love to his fellow man, at the cost of sacrifice to himself, still this belief in God would have its use. Would it not support and comfort us in pain, anxiety, bereavement, and especially death? To use again the words of Pope, of how large a part of mankind will it always be true that they have 'too much weakness for the stoic's part'? Can we look to see it otherwise with women or children, with the gentle or the timid? I think that we may often notice a certain gloom in the view of life taken by those who reject these ideas.[1] Surely, the cheer-

---

[1] See the character of Mr. James Mill in the Autobiography of his

fulness, hope, and comfort of religious faith are a source not of present happiness only, and that is something, but also of strength to do good, which is still further to be esteemed. This truth, indeed, seems to be admitted by Mr. Mill in his essay on Theism.[1] But I am bound to add this qualification, that faith in God has all this power for good, only in proportion as the idea of God becomes more perfectly and truly good.

I have next to say something as to the doctrines distinctively Christian, and, first, I would speak of the doctrine most characteristic of the religion, the worship of Christ. I contend that herein is one of the moral excellences of Christianity. The moral influence of worship depends, as I have just said, upon the character of the being who is worshipped, and it is one great merit of our religion that it has held up for the worship of the world a character morally worthy of that homage. I find this merit admitted by a critic as free and independent as Mr. J. S. Mill.[2] No one can deny the love, and patience, and purity, and self-sacrifice, and zeal to do good, which shine forth in the Gospel histories of Christ. I do not hold that these histories give a perfect likeness. If they are fairly and critically

Son, p. 48. Also Mr. Congreve's Essay, 'The New Religion in its Attitude towards the Old,' p. 296.
[1] See Mill's 'Essay on Theism,' part v. General Result.
[2] Ibid. p. 253.

judged, we must, I think, allow that their probable origin, their style, their discrepancies, suggest that they do not give with complete exactness the words and actions of our Lord. But still, in spite of their imperfections, we recognise an unrivalled image of goodness. It seems to me worthy of note that the most widely read, and perhaps the most deeply influential, of the many pious books which Christendom has produced, has been the 'Imitation of Christ.' I do not think it needful to dwell upon this point, for I suppose that few if any candid men would contest it. I will go on to speak of another great characteristic doctrine of the Gospel, the doctrine of grace. Understood in its broadest and deepest sense, and considered merely as setting forth an act of God to be judged of from a moral point of view, we may think of this doctrine as the assertion of God's love to man in spite of sin—the assertion that God has made in Christ a provision for the remedy of sin, and the lasting good of men. This will still appear the essential character of the doctrine, when we call to mind that there is a discrimination in the distributing of this mercy, or, in other words, in the language of theology, that justification is by faith. For this faith or condition of mercy is also said to be a grace or gift. Ultimately, then, the doctrine morally considered amounts to a belief that God is not merely a righteous judge, but also a loving father; that he has interfered in Christ for the good of the sinful. He may not, indeed, be represented as doing so to an equal extent, or with an equal efficacy for all. But there is the great and significant assertion that he has mercy for the unworthy. And if there be many who do not seem now to come within the comprehension of his grace, we, who cherish the hope of a better life, may hope to see there that even these are ultimately brought to goodness and to happiness.

This doctrine appears to me the most precious in the whole of religion. There is a great deal in our knowledge of the world and our experience of life to try our faith in the goodness of God. But here it shines out clear and bright, speaking to the heart of man, and calling him to love his heavenly father. This is beyond doubt a higher moral view of God than the bare notion of a judge. And the state of the soul, and of the life which it is fitted to produce, is a higher and a better state than that which the bare idea of a righteous law could bring about. No truthful conscience can fail to witness that we can make no claim upon God on the score of merit—that our best services are too imperfect to give a pretext for such an idea. Unquestionably that passage from a purely legal idea of our dealings with God, to the idea of grace on his part and gratitude on ours, which has so often been seen in Christians, did place them on a juster footing before God, and raise them to a higher as well as happier moral state.

I venture to claim for Christianity that it has put forth this great doctrine, the love of God to man, more powerfully than any other religion. It is, I believe, the attractiveness of this great truth which is the secret of that power which to this day is seen in evangelical revivals. It is a great thing indeed to bring home to man's heart that God does love him. And I would also maintain that we see this doctrine in unsurpassed beauty and purity in the original and unquestioned teaching of Christ. It was his reproach that he received publicans and sinners. It was his profession that he came to seek and to save that which was lost. He taught his disciples a universal kindness to their fellow men by the example of God, who maketh the sun to shine, and the rain to come down, alike upon the evil and the good. The most beautiful of all his parables describes the reception of the penitent. Among the last acts of his life was an intercession for the human instruments of his murder.

The above remarks upon the great Christian idea of grace appear to me true and just. But I am bound to add that there are views connected with this doctrine, in the minds of many Christians, which seem to me open to objection. The act of divine mercy is generally thought of as consisting of two parts—the pardon of sin upon the part of God as our sovereign, and an actual influence from him upon our spirit to make us better. I do not wish to challenge the truth of this kind of analysing of God's dealings with us. The ideas may be the best which we can at present form, but I do hold that in both cases the views popular with many Christians present a difficulty. We will begin with the first. The act of pardon on the part of God is not thought of by Christians as a mere act of grace or mercy, but is believed to be founded upon an act of Christ on behalf of man, and mainly his death. I say mainly, because a very considerable school of divines hold, not only that the death of Christ procured for sinners the forgiveness of their sins, but also that the active obedience of his life is in some way made over and attributed to them, and obtains for them divine favour in place of an actual righteousness of their own. Now there seems to me to be something in certain popular views of this reconciling of sinners to God by Christ opposed to our natural moral convictions. The simple idea that Christ the God-man died on our behalf, or in a popular sense died even in the place of man, *i.e.* for others' sins, when without sin, is certainly taught in the Scriptures, and does not present, I think, any difficulty. That he should die as a martyr to his great cause, or give up his life in some way which was, upon principles unknown to us, connected with the forgiveness of our sins, is only a height of virtue, an act of self-sacrifice, every way worthy of him and credible in him. And I must add that it has been an act fruitful of the best feelings amongst his followers. And, further, it seems to me in keeping with God's system of government that in so great an act as the reconciliation of sinners to himself, he should use some means or instrument as he does in all his acts, so far as we know. There is nothing in this inconsistent with his fatherly love, seeking the 'lost sheep.' I would wish it to be distinctly understood that it is not 'satisfaction,' *i.e.* Christ's sufferings being in some way the ground of our forgiveness, but 'penal satisfaction,' *i.e.* Christ's actually being punished in our place, to which I am about to raise an objection. Theories of the atonement, which are at least widely popular, go beyond the former. They explain the transaction upon principles which seem to me indefensible. I am aware that learned divines are cautious about such explanations. Archbishop Magee,[1] for example, seems to allow that the atoning efficacy of Christ's death cannot be explained on principles of natural reason. The explanation which I have in view, and of which I will presently speak, is often attributed to Anselm, and I must allow that this eminent prelate

---

[1] Archbishop Magee, No. xix. p. 199.

has set what seems to me an unwise example of speculation on this subject. Nevertheless, he has not given exactly the explanation to which I object. The notion which I oppose seems to be that of a transfer of punishment. So much sin calls for so much suffering; Christ is said to bear the pain in the place of the sinner, and so the sinner is, under certain conditions, allowed to escape. This transfer of suffering, or substitution of another sufferer, seems to me at variance with reasonable views of punishment. If we take the politic principle, which makes punishment reformatory to the offender or deterrent to others, that principle which I for one believe that we must, in the present stage of civilisation, think best to represent the mind of God, we see that an atonement, such as that here thought of, seems to make God indifferent whether he punishes the guilty or the innocent, so only some one is punished. That surely is not fitted to enforce obedience. Rather, it encourages hopes of escape. Nor yet, if there be any reformatory power in mere suffering upon the offender, could this have place here, for no pain is inflicted upon him. I may be told that there is a reformatory power in the manifestation of love, and I freely allow that there is, and I also believe that very many Christians have experienced that power from this very doctrine. But I do not see why there should not be this bettering influence in the simple statement that Christ died for us. The act of love, the sacrifice of self if you will, is surely the same, and deserves the same from us, with or without this theory of substitution. Nor yet, if we take another view of punishment, if we suppose divine justice to proceed on the vindictive principle, the principle that requires so much pain for so much sin, are we helped to understand this theory of the atonement. For surely it is of the essence of this requirement that what it exacts should be rendered by the offender. But, according to the theory before us, he suffers nothing. These objections to this view of the atonement seem to me fatal. But I may add that there is another, which is at least of weight. If Christ has suffered the punishment due for all the sins of all men—and this is the only form of the doctrine which has plausible grounds—why, then, are any men, whether penitent or impenitent, believing or unbelieving, to be punished? To punish them would be to punish their sins twice over, once in Christ, the substitute, and again in them, the real offenders.

I may be told that this doctrine is to be received simply as matter of revelation. Independently of miraculous attestation, the moral and spiritual depth and beauty of the New Testament bear witness to a deeper insight on the part of its writers into spiritual things than we can pretend to, and consequently such a doctrine as this may, upon principles which I have myself asserted, be accepted, in spite of a certain difficulty on moral grounds. The question here is the extent of that difficulty, and also of the Scripture evidence. If this notion of atonement by equivalent suffering be clearly opposed to our moral sense, it ought, I hold, to be laid aside. But on this point I allow that different persons may judge differently. On the other hand, different opinions will also be formed as to the fact of the Scripture evidence. I know that texts may be quoted, which, taken literally and argued upon logically, seem to many a proof. But the like treatment of other parts of Scripture has landed men in many errors. Metaphors must not be taken too literally. Even such texts as 'being made a curse for us,'[1] or being made 'to be sin for us,'[2] or bearing 'our sins in his own body on the tree,'[3] do not after all sustain this doctrine of transfer of punishment, though they do imply a suffering upon our account. It is one thing to say that Christ suffered upon our behalf, another thing that he was punished in our place. The doctrine before us does in reality require that Christ should have suffered the very same amount of pain to which every sinner would have been subject but for his intervention, and this I hold certainly cannot be proved from Scripture. We know that in the early ages of the

[1] Gal. iii. 13.   [2] 2 Cor. v. 21.   [3] 1 Peter ii. 24.

Church eminent Christian writers had a notion that the death of Christ was a sort of compensation to Satan. There really was something to suggest this idea in the Scripture metaphors from ransom and redemption. Should we, then, be very confident when we are building upon metaphors from sacrifice?

But although I feel constrained to look upon this popular theory of the atonement as unsatisfactory, and although I have myself no other explanation to give of the efficacy of Christ's death in a transcendental scheme of the forgiveness of sins, still I do most fully recognise the beauty and the instructiveness of that death when looked at from a moral point of view. It is, as I have said already, an example of the highest virtue, self-sacrifice for the noblest ends, on the part of the God-man. Nothing could be fitted to bring home to the hearts of his followers a higher, a better, or a more touching lesson. It has been said that the idea of the kingdom of heaven, as a kingdom whose subjects were all bound to obey one perfect character by the constraining power of love, was the highest idea which we could form of a government that was at once personal and moral. No doubt it is. The saying proceeds from a believer in the substitution view. But why should the bond between the Divine King and his subjects need a theory explaining the efficacy of his death? Why should it not be enough for them to know that he has died on their behalf?

I have thought sometimes that men's ideas upon this point were perplexed by a confusion between civil and criminal justice. We speak of civil justice as between man and man, in matters of property, or in fact in any matter in which value or compensation is due from one to another, and we speak of criminal justice where the question really lies between the offender and society at large. In this last case the punishment inflicted is not now thought of as a compensation to those who may have been immediately injured, but as needed by the general interest of all men. This latter kind of justice is, I hold, the better analogue to guide us in forming ideas of divine justice. One consideration alone I think will prove this assertion. It is this, that divine justice is mainly concerned with the infliction of pains and penalties, and these do not enter into the primary idea of civil justice, though they may become needful to give it effect. In spite of all that divines have written, I for one fail to see how sin can be like a debt, which anyone may discharge for the debtor. There does seem to me to be something of this last thought even in Anselm.[1] It may be true that when we sin we

[1] Anselm's notion seems to be that any rational being, angel or man, owes to God the complete subjection of his will to God's will; that when he sins he withholds from God the 'debitum' due to Him; that God would leave sin 'inordinatum' if this 'debitum' were not

withhold from God what is his due. But when God punishes, it is not, so to speak, to recover damages. That would be a lowering, unworthy idea of the Creator in his relations to his creatures. God needs nothing from us. Even if it be thought that a part of the claim which he has upon us for our obedience might be fittingly compared to a debt, it does not appear how this could be compensated for by the sufferings of another. When you punish for non-payment, you introduce, I hold, the idea of correctional or criminal justice. Such seems to me at least the right idea, though it may not be perhaps that of English lawyers. There is evil no doubt in such withholding, but the evil must be in the creature, in the sinner, or some other creature on whom it works an ill effect. I would humbly venture to say that God's blessedness cannot be diminished, nor yet his glory tarnished by any evil deed of his creatures. And when God punishes, it is, I conjecture, to reform the offender, or to deter others. This, and not the vindictive view, seems to follow from that fatherly view of God so largely dwelt upon in the New Testament.

I have next to speak of that other part of the Christian doctrine of grace which concerns the direct

---

paid, and further some punishment for the dishonour done to him; and that this may be done by 'pœna.' God thereby takes away from the creature the happiness of which it is capable, and so proves that the creature is his. 'Cur Deus Homo,' lib. i. cap. xi. to xiv.

action of God upon the heart of man. We have, I would observe, to try this doctrine only by canons of moral criticism. We are not now called upon to consider any metaphysical difficulty—how far, for instance, it brings into the world a supramundane cause, how far it blends the infinite and the finite, and repeats something like the alleged fact of creation, in a way difficult to reconcile with that order which men are beginning to trace in the mental as well as the material world.[1] These questions we may pass by, and, if we do so, and confine ourselves to strictly moral considerations, we shall not I think find much to perplex us. The bare idea of God in any way helping weak and sinful man to do better and to become better would, I presume, commend itself to the conscience of every good and thoughtful man. I think that I may also say that the reality of moral improvement from Christian influences would also be so attested. But perhaps it might be objected that Christianity represents this grace as arbitrary and partial. On this objection I would remark as follows:—The facility or the difficulty of moral obedience with any of us depends greatly on outward circumstances, and these, upon the supposition of a

---

[1] I would, however, observe in this place that if we adopt Bishop Butler's view (see 'Analogy,' part ii. chap. iv. sect. iii.), viz. that the Christian dispensation, like the course of nature, is carried on according to general laws, then this direct action of the Divine Spirit would not, I hold, give rise to any of the difficulties alluded to above.

God at all, must be looked upon as being to a great extent his appointment for each of us. They are largely out of our own control, and so, in a moral estimate of the relation between the Almighty and us, they must be reckoned his appointed conditions of trial. But if it be so, if he gives or withholds outward opportunities of doing well, why should he not also make like differences in any inward dealings with the spirit of man? It is objected that he deals with man upon the principle of 'giving to him that hath.' Is this a wise charity? Before going further in the way of reply I would again observe that the same principle is continually acted upon in the dealings of God's outward providence. We see it also in that natural moral constitution with which he has endowed us, an appointment which very closely concerns the matter before us, viz. our power to do well or to do ill. St. John's 'grace for grace' ($\chi \acute{\alpha} \rho \iota \nu$ $\dot{\alpha} \nu \tau \grave{\iota}$ $\chi \acute{\alpha} \rho \iota \tau o s$), and Augustine's 'peccatum pœna peccati,' when regarded as appointments of God, involve no moral principle beyond that which is involved in a feature of human nature, the power of habit on the will. There may be an appearance in these last remarks of defending what seems arbitrary or partial in God's spiritual dealings with men, by analogies from his temporal providence. But I have no idea of resting on such a defence. I shall presently endeavour to point out the weakness of such a mode of defending doctrines in religion. I would here say that I have only been calling attention to a certain resemblance between one class of God's present dealings with us, which we all know by actual experience, and another asserted by Christianity. I wish only that it be seen that they are alike. I should look for the reconciliation of all such appointments with our ideas of God's goodness in the future state which awaits man. There I would hope that some effectual provision will be found for the good of those who may seem here not to have found a place in their Heavenly Father's mercy. But when I say this, I by no means wish to imply that God can on any moral grounds be expected to deal out, even in the long run and upon the whole, an equal measure of happiness to all men, or, what may be the same thing, bring them all to an equal degree of goodness. There is no ground for such a claim of equality. Indeed, if the principles of these essays be right, such equalisation would not be right, as God is supposed to recognise differences in his creatures which originate with themselves.[1] All I think that can be fairly urged is this, that if we speak of God as almighty, all-wise, and all-loving, and then attribute to him the creation of beings in whom there is to be a permanent preponderance of evil, there is to all appearance an inconsistency in what

[1] See Essay I. on 'The Origin of Evil,' p. 108.

we say. I need not go over this point again, as I have already spoken upon it with reference to the origin of evil. What I am concerned now to point out is only that the doctrine which makes the good influences of the Divine Spirit not alike for all, may be cleared from the imputation of a harsh partiality, by the same religious hypothesis which we employ to reconcile other seeming inequalities in God's present appointments with his perfect goodness.

The same remarks apply to the moral difficulty in the doctrine of original sin. If we take the more qualified form of that doctrine, which does not speak of any actual imputation of Adam's guilt, but only of a 'fault or corruption of nature,' which comes to his descendants by inheritance, then the moral objection, I presume, would be that it is hard that any man should be placed at such a disadvantage for no fault of his own. This, I say, would be the moral objection, for the other objections arising from the alleged antiquity of man, or his descent from the lower animals, have their ground in natural, and not in moral, science. So far, however, as the moral difficulty goes, there is nothing which may not be answered by the religious hypothesis to which I have just alluded. And it is obvious that here also we have close analogies in nature. Such contamination by descent is only a form of that principle of heredity which Mr. Galton has illustrated. No doubt his idea of the origin of moral evil is very different from that of St. Paul. But I do not think that the decision of the question between them lies within the scope of this essay. The question whether this disease of sin in man is imperfectly corrected savagery, or a taint inherited from an ancestor, who, when created innocent, voluntarily fell, cannot I believe be settled upon grounds of moral principle.

I go on now to two doctrines of Christianity which I purpose last to compare with our moral intuitions. They are predestination and everlasting punishment. I have spoken of this latter as a doctrine of Christianity, because it is popularly thought to be so. I purpose at first to consider the two doctrines together, because the difficulty of receiving predestination or election seems to me to arise out of this idea of the everlasting misery of the wicked. The arbitrary appointment of any creature to everlasting misery is plainly repulsive to our simplest and clearest moral feelings. It is utter misrepresentation to speak of such repulsion as the rebellion of man's proud reason. Nor is it an adequate defence to say that all men had a chance of salvation in Adam, a better chance than they would have had in their own persons, and that so by Adam's sin the human race justly became a mass of perdition out of which the Almighty was free to choose the objects of his mercy. For even upon this hypothesis, the question still remains unanswered, Why did God create our race, knowing that such would be the issue of their existence with innumerable multitudes, whether the fault be in Adam or in them? And this is the question with which we have ultimately to deal if we are 'to justify the ways of God to man.'

We cannot, I contend, hold the doctrines of personal election and everlasting punishment in combination, if we admit the conclusion of these essays that religion should not teach anything which the moral feelings of the civilised and enlightened part of mankind clearly and distinctly condemn. Now for predestination or personal election, *i.e.* the referring of the difference which we see here between the bad and the good to the appointment of God, much may be said. It seems, indeed, to follow very directly from our notions of God's character and government. Some have thought that the idea was involved in the very notion of grace, when conjoined with that of God's foreknowledge.[1] Certainly this combination leads to the idea that God has from all eternity chosen the objects of his present mercy. But the doctrine of election as commonly understood involves more than this. It asserts that the selection of those objects of mercy was purely an act of God's will, an act whose motives were doubtless righteous,

---

[1] 'Augustinian Doctrine of Predestination,' by Professor Mozley, chap. i. pp. 9 and 12.

but inscrutable to us and certainly nowise dependent upon the doings of the persons affected. Grace and foreknowledge will not carry us so far as this. For it is quite conceivable, quite compatible with the idea of purest grace, that the divine mercy should be extended to all, and take effect with all whose resistance to good did not go beyond a certain degree. I am not contending for the actual truth of this idea, but only that it is compatible with the notion of grace, and cannot be excluded without bringing in some argument for irresistible grace—an argument which must stand on some other foundation than the bare idea of God's undeserved mercy to sinners. Now, upon this supposition, the line between those who were and those who were not objects of final mercy would be drawn by the will of the creature, that is by the greater or less obstinacy of the offender. And this last conclusion is not in harmony with the doctrine of personal election, as I understand it. But though this doctrine may not follow merely from the ideas of grace and foreknowledge in God, still I think it may very directly be inferred from our conception of him. We have but to think of Him as our creator, and the conclusion seems to follow. It is clear that he allows his creatures to sin. Moral government may require this. Still, we cannot think that he was ignorant that they would do so, or that he was not able to provide a remedy for that mischief, or that he did not actually provide for that correction, when and in such a way as his mind approved, and that consequently the ultimate and total result of any creature's existence would not be what his wisdom and goodness appointed it to be. If it be otherwise, if the character and lot of his creatures was to be finally beyond his control, and to be permanently what he did not approve, why did he create them? And I do not see anything in this belief in God's sovereignty and effectual command over the issue of things repugnant to our moral feelings, but quite the reverse, unless we hold the everlasting misery of those who are wicked here. If, indeed, any of God's creatures is to be everlastingly wicked and miserable, we have, what seems to me, a blot upon his creation. But if we relinquish this idea, if we think of divine punishment as a humane man now thinks of human punishment, viz. as reformatory or deterrent, as destined sooner or later to extirpate the evil of sin, then we have no such difficulty. The mere belief that man's lot, alike for this life and a future, is in the hands of a wise and merciful God, and will be what a loving Father has appointed, seems to me full of comfort. All Christians, I presume, find it so when they have to meet the trials of life. It reconciles them to the evil, for it gives them the hope that all will finally be well. This doctrine, the comfort of the good man here, would surely find its legitimate completion if it gave him the hope that in the next world he should see the complete triumph of God's goodness, the vindication of whatever seems dark, mysterious, and trying, in human character and fortunes now. I have often thought that something of this feeling might be traced in those very parts of Scripture upon which the predestinarians most rely, as Matthew xi. 25, 27, John vi., Romans ix. Our Lord in the one case, and St. Paul in the other, seem to me to fall back upon this truth of God's sovereignty as a consolation when the spectacle of Jewish perverseness was before them. But the consolation is gone if we believe that an everlasting doom is to be pronounced upon a large part of mankind according to their doings in this life. My own judgment, as I have implied, would be to retain what I take to be the substance of the doctrine of predestination, viz. that the final lot of every creature will be that which the Almighty designed, and therefore I hope good. What I have said may suffice as to the connection between these doctrines, predestination and everlasting punishment. But I wish to add some remarks upon the latter doctrine considered separately.

This doctrine is I suppose felt by all to be awful, by many to be repulsive. But there are, I know, at the same time, good men who value it on grounds apart from its supposed scriptural or other authority.

They deem it needed as a check upon sin. Now I believe that there is here an error. In human government it has not been found that excessive punishments had the deterrent effect which upon the principles of such persons we should expect. I know that there is a difference in the cases before us. In the instance of human justice, there was the natural sympathy of those who administered it, prosecutors, witnesses, juries, judges, ministers of state, interfering with the strict carrying out of a sanguinary code, and making it in practice indulgent instead of harsh. The criminal class saw this; they hoped for impunity; they offended all the more because punishment had been made unreasonably severe. Now nothing strictly of this kind can be thought of in the case of divine justice. But something like it does occur. We must bear in mind that the deterrent influence of the latter is a thing of faith, not of sight. It springs out of the reality and vividness with which the threatened punishment is expected. And if that punishment is really more severe than can be borne witness to by those parts of our nature which should bring home its terrors to the human heart, there will be a failure on this all-important point. There will be the same persuading oneself of impunity which we noticed in the other case. And I believe that this does actually take place on a large scale amongst us. Men do persuade themselves, on very slender grounds, that they shall escape future punishment for their sins altogether; nay, that they shall enter at once on unbounded happiness instead of suffering for their faults. This easy escape from the fear of retribution is manifestly contrary to the purposes of moral government. A far less penalty, if honestly and seriously apprehended, would be deterrent. Would not, for instance, a hundred years of punishment, if really expected, be a deterrent?[1]

I have begun what I wished to say upon this doctrine considered apart by a few words upon its practical value, because I believe that a mistake upon this point has produced an unjust prejudice in its favour. I would now add some remarks founded upon general principles of morality.

When we steadily contemplate the thought of a penal world, such as that of which Milton or Dante has given us the image, we must feel that it is a spectacle at variance with enlightened ideas of God. If God abhors sin, and seeks to make his creatures innocent and happy, so far as moral government allows, is not such a world a standing offence against his character? How can he look upon such a scene of misery, blasphemy, and sin? We are told that his justice requires it. We answer that a finite

---

[1] See 'Eternal Punishment and Eternal Death,' Barlow, chap. vii. p. 125 and onwards.

offence cannot call for an infinite punishment. It is sometimes said in reply that the perpetual punishment of the damned is to be explained by their continually adding sin to sin, and so accumulating fresh guilt. If they are in moral bondage, and cannot repent, this is no explanation at all. If not, if they can repent, and should do so, is their punishment to end? I may be told that upon Christian principles repentance must be thought of as a grace or gift of God, and this is not to be looked for with the damned. But if grace be unmerited mercy, why should it be confined to one era in the Almighty's dispensations? If God be love, and if his nature be immutable and eternal, why should he ever cease to be gracious? Why should he not, even in his severities, seek the ultimate good of his creatures? This last idea of punishment is that which has grown up in modern and humane times. Men ignore the idea of vengeance as a principle for public justice. They entertain only that of reforming the offender or of deterring others. If we ascribe these ideas of enlightened times to the Almighty, we see at once how ill they agree with this doctrine of everlasting punishment. Reformation of course is not thought of. The other idea, that of making an example, might perhaps be advanced. But obviously this view could not justify everlasting punishment consistently with an idea repeatedly put forward in these essays, that every creature has a claim upon the mercy of that Great Being who is the ultimate author of its existence. The doctrine at best makes him sacrifice the individual for a general good. This is not consistent with care for the individual, which is the fundamental assumption in all religion. I believe that the influence of these modern ideas is widely felt in connection with this matter. Thoughtful men of very different theological schools seek, in one way or other, to explain away or soften down the stern old doctrine of everlasting torment. I may instance Dr. J. H. Newman, Mr. Maurice, and Professor Birks. Mr. Maurice,[1] it is well known, resisted the popular view on the ground that the epithet eternal (αἰώνιος), as used in the New Testament, did not imply the idea of endless time or continued succession. He sought its meaning primarily in its use as to God, and seems to have made it equivalent to spiritual. Now no doubt the divine existence may be independent of time: there may be no succession in the consciousness of God. But there are certainly texts in the New Testament which show that this non-temporal signification did not always belong to the word eternal (αἰώνιος) in that book. Rom. xvi. 25, 2 Tim. i. 9, Titus i. 2, are instances in the writings of St. Paul. We cannot therefore infer that

---

[1] See 'Theological Essays.' F. D. Maurice, 3rd ed. 1871.

it may not have a temporal meaning as to a future life, at least in the case of this apostle. The like may be said of the Apocalypse. And, further, there are philosophical reasons which make it difficult to imagine how such a life, especially if one of reward or punishment, should not be temporal. A consciousness without successive states may be possible. As I have said, the divine consciousness may be such. But it would not be a human consciousness; and, as Dean Mansel[1] has pointed out, if you suppose such a variation between our present and our future state, you raise a doubt as to our identity in the two, and all notions of future punishment proceed on a belief in continued identity.

Some idea of the like kind seems to me to be at the bottom of some remarks of Dr. Newman.[2] He expresses himself thus :—' Eternity or endlessness is in itself only a negative idea, though punishment is positive. Its fearful force, as added to punishment, lies in what it is not ; it means no change of state, no annihilation, no restoration. But it cannot become a quality of punishment any more than a man's living seventy years is a quality of his mind, or enters into the idea of his virtues or talents. If punishment be attended by continuity, or by sense of succession, this must be, because it is *endless, and something*

---

[1] Dean Mansel, ' Letters, Lectures, and Reviews,' p. 117.
[2] ' Grammar of Assent,' p. 417.

more: such inflictions are an addition to its endlessness, and do not necessarily belong to it, because it is endless.' His meaning I take to be this. To say of future punishment that it will be attended with this idea of 'continuity or sense of succession,' is to say something more concerning it than that it is endless, and the ground of this remark I conjecture to be that a never-ending *may* be a never-changing consciousness. But it is clear that a never-changing consciousness is not the state of things implied in the ordinary idea of everlasting punishment. And further, if what has been said as to the view of Mr. Maurice be just, such a state could never be anticipated for any human being.

The mitigation of this doctrine which Professor Birks suggests, he rests upon the claims of the creature upon its creator.[1] He thinks it possible that in some way a sense of God's love may be granted to the damned, as an alleviation to their sufferings. It is hard to understand how a sense of God's love could spring up in beings suffering penalties so severe as those commonly thought of in this case, without hope of relief, and with a clear knowledge that these sufferings were the immediate judicial appointments of God. But supposing such a feeling actually imparted in some supernatural way, and supposing it

[1] See 'Victory of Divine Goodness,' by Professor Birks, chapter on 'Eternal Judgment.'

to be consolatory, then we have clearly a qualification of the sense, a departure from the idea, of everlasting punishment.

One other attempt to soften this doctrine I wish to notice, because it certainly has a mathematical sort of success. It supposes that, though the punishment is everlasting, it is ever diminishing in severity.[1] Such punishment may be compared to the terms of what mathematicians call an infinite but converging series. Each term becomes less than its predecessor in some ratio, which is in all cases less than some assignable proper fraction. Now it is well known that the sum total of the terms of such series, however many be taken, could never exceed a certain finite amount. Hence future punishment, if of this kind, though it might be indefinitely prolonged, would never exceed in quantity a certain finite limit. This supposition avoids the incongruity of an infinite penalty for a finite offence. But it still leaves the total of existence an evil for the sinner. No religious man, I suppose, will think that a wicked life in this world is a happy life. Now the prospect beyond, here given, is not that of being reclaimed and made ultimately happy, but only that the punishment inflicted shall gradually soften, so that its total does not exceed a given quantity. I

---

[1] 'The Vicarious Sacrifice,' by Horace Bushnell, D.D., part iii. chap. v. p. 281

do not myself see how such a view can be made to agree with that claim on the Creator's goodness which I have thought that every creature possesses upon the suppositions of religion, from the bare fact of his having created it. The same remark would apply also to that view which makes the future doom of the wicked to be extinction, and not everlasting punishment.

The theories which I have just considered are modern views. They seem to me, in fact, so many witnesses, that modern thought and feeling are ill at ease with this doctrine of everlasting punishment. A bolder course was taken in former days. We had then, not expedients to soften or explain away the doctrine, but bold justifications, and, indeed, in mediæval or primitive times, a horrible realism in details.[1] Perhaps the best known justification is that attributed to Leibnitz, viz. that sin being an offence against an infinite being, has an infinite demerit, and deserves an infinite punishment. As Mr. Froude has pointed out, this argument is open to the obvious retort that if a finite offence becomes infinitely great when committed against an infinite being, why should not a finite punishment be considered infinitely great also when inflicted by an infinite being? The truth plainly is, that the greatness of the guilt must, upon any sound principles of morality, be estimated ac-

[1] See Lecky's 'Rise and Influence of Rationalism,' vol. i. chap. iii. pp. 348–353.

cording to the knowledge, faculties, temptations, and opportunities of the offender. It may be true that any given action of the creature, be it good or bad, is eternally present to the mind of the Almighty. But it is also clear that God's dealings with his creatures are consecutive and varied in character. They are, in fact, a succession of acts in time, though their author be eternal, and they seem done with reference to successive acts or states of the creature. Nothing, as Mr. Mill has said, could be more opposed to the analogies of nature, considered as the administration of God, than the idea of a finally fixed state. All in this world is change.

But it may be said, are we not obliged to accept this doctrine by the sheer force of Scripture testimony? Can we be Christians at all, that is to say, can we accept the teaching of Christ as our Master and yet reject this doctrine? I can quite understand that many Christians do feel themselves thus bound by Scripture evidence to hold this doctrine, although they may feel its moral difficulties. There certainly are texts which at first sight seem to teach it. But I think that when they are carefully considered this impression of their meaning will diminish. If we are to be guided by the letter of Scripture, it ought certainly to be noticed that the language commonly relied upon as expressing endlessness is applied to the instrument of punishment, as the fire, or else to some word for punishment which by itself does not favour the idea of continued duration, as destruction.[1] I only recall one exception, a text which I will presently consider. Further, these arguments from special texts have their uncertainties. There is the risk that we may be relying on ill-reported sayings. There is the risk of our interpretation being warped by traditional ideas, or church authority. There is the risk that we may take literally, and handle logically, what was in the case of Christ or his disciples a mere expression of feeling, not a precise statement. For instance, I for one could not see in Christ's saying concerning Judas, ' it were good for that man if he had never been born,'[2] the strongest *dictum probans* in the whole of Scripture for everlasting punishment. Now it seems to me that, whatever different opinions may be formed as to particular texts, and I allow that there may be different opinions, when we turn to the great moral features of the Gospel, they do not favour this doctrine. On that point I will speak presently, but before doing so I would notice one text to which I have just referred, and which has been especially relied upon. It is Matt. ch. xxv., v. 46. Its supposed conclusiveness arises from the same epithet αἰώνιον being here distinctly applied to

---

[1] The same remark will, I believe, apply to the language of the Anglican Prayer-Book. ' Everlasting damnation ' does not of necessity, I think, involve everlasting misery. The sentence might be of everlasting effect, but that effect might come to be only loss of higher happiness.

[2] St. Mark xiv. 21, St. Matthew xxvi. 24. Stier, if I recollect, expresses the view from which I dissent.

the punishment of the wicked, and also to the reward of the righteous. The latter, it is thought, all will say, is everlasting. I venture to put forward the following conjecture. May not the verse mean only that in the next æon the righteous will be happy and the wicked will be miserable, that the next stage of man's existence will be one of κρίσις or judgment. It does not prove that this æon will be everlasting or not succeeded by others, in which both may be happy. The idea of successive æons is certainly to be found in the discourses of Christ himself. We hear from him of 'this æon,' and 'the æon to come' (ἐν τούτῳ τῷ αἰῶνι οὔτε ἐν τῷ μέλλοντι. Matt. xii. 32). And again of the end of this æon (ἐν τῇ συντελείᾳ τοῦ αἰῶνος. Matt. xiii. 40). St. Paul has the plural form, æons (τὰ τέλη τῶν αἰώνων. 1 Corinth. x. 11). With him, as in the Apocalypse, we find the phrase æons of æons (τοὺς αἰῶνας τῶν αἰώνων. Gal. i. 5). To assert that αἰώνιος in Matt. xxv. 46, means everlasting, is to beg the whole question as to the meaning of the word. There is nothing in this text more than in some others to necessitate that meaning.

I will now, as I proposed, consider some of the general features of our religion in connection with this question. I would select three—the fatherhood of God to man, the revelation of the character of God in Christ, the making known of God's grace to sinners as such. Now no one of these teachings, I contend, favours the doctrine before us. When Christ desired to teach the efficacy of prayer, he demanded whether if a son asked bread of a father he would give him a stone,[1] and he argued that if men, being evil, knew how to give good gifts unto their children, how much more would our Heavenly Father. May we not on the same principles reason thus? An earthly father might punish his son, and that severely too if he thought that it would be for his good, but would he in any case continue to punish him for ever? Again, as to the second point, Christ himself was the most forgiving of men. If God were manifested in him, can God be so implacable? Lastly, as to my third point, nothing enters more deeply into Christian doctrine than the idea of grace shown to the sinful. Why should this disposition on the part of the Almighty be limited to this present state? Why should it not be that in some future state this truly beautiful and loveable attribute should in some way shine forth even more clearly and efficaciously than it has done here? If God be love, and if his nature is eternal and immutable, why should there be such an abrupt and awful change in his dealings with his creatures? Why should there be an era after which God will for ever cease to be gracious? Granting that the rejection or resistance of grace is a greater sin than the mere breaking

[1] St. Matthew vii. 9, 11.

of law, why should this be more than a greater degree of culpability, not an absolute bar to divine mercy?

If, in deciding as to the significance of the Christian revelation, we are guided by the general principles which appear in the teaching of Christ, so far as they can be confidently traced, rather than by individual sayings, then I think that the above considerations will dissuade us from the popular belief that his religion is committed to the doctrine of everlasting punishment. However, before leaving the question, I ought to notice an objection which may perhaps be brought against this view, from a like general consideration of Scripture language. It is the argument from silence. It may be said, if the reconciliation of the whole moral universe to God, and its consequent happiness, be what we are to expect in the end, how comes it to pass that this great and cheering prospect is not distinctly spoken of in the New Testament?

Now as regards the question, whether it really is spoken of or not, I confess that I have little to bring forward. I can recall only one passage in the Bible which, in my judgment, may be thought to intimate such a consummation. It is 1 Corinthians, xv. 28. And here I would not be confident. But, on the other hand, I think that we might justly question the soundness of the argument from silence in this matter. It proceeds on the assumption that the

Christian revelation would, from its very nature, make known the general character, at all events, of God's dealings with us for ever. Now this is an assumption as to God's way of communicating with us which cannot, I hold, be supported. If analogy is to be our guide, we must adopt an opposite idea. God has taught us secular knowledge by parts at a time, in an orderly progress, which is still going on, and may indeed have an indefinite course. Something of the same kind may be traced in that knowledge which comes nearest in character to the matter of revelation—the knowledge of moral truth, and of natural theology. In revelation itself we do see stages. The Old Testament is progressive. The New is a sudden advance, although modern criticism would not allow that its ideas were all novelties, nor yet that they were all ushered into the world at once. Why then should we regard that revelation as complete, final, exhaustive? If the next æon in the history of our race is to be that of κρίσις, of separation in the outward lot of the good and the bad, it might well be within the scope of the Gospel to dwell only upon that.[1]

I have now completed what I purpose to say on the comparison of the precepts and doctrines of Christianity with the dictates of conscience. I have not alluded to what I may call the metaphysical doc-

[1] See also Birks' 'Victory of Divine Goodness,' p. 173.

trines of Christianity, such as the doctrine of the Trinity, because they do not seem to me to come within the proper province of the judgment of our moral faculty. It is not God in his absolute nature, but God in his dealings with us, of which that faculty may venture to judge. The truth of such a doctrine as the Trinity must be obviously a matter of pure revelation. At first sight this may seem a serious defect in my evidential argument, but it must be remembered that I have contended not merely that Christian doctrine was to be received only so far as upheld by our moral instincts, but further that the moral superiority and spiritual insight evident in the authors of Scripture gave to their writings a dogmatic authority.

PART IV.

An argument has been brought forward, and has met with wide acceptance in this country, which puts aside the method of this essay—this trying of Christianity by the moral faculty. It defends any seeming contrariety by instancing the like opposition in the course of this present world considered as the appointment of God. I allude to the celebrated work of Bishop Butler, 'The Analogy of Religion

Natural and Revealed to the Constitution and Course of Nature.' Of course, if this argument be sound, the conclusions of the present essay will not hold. I purpose accordingly to conclude my essay with a brief examination of the Bishop's reasoning.

His book has had a high reputation. It has been relied upon in England, perhaps more than any other, in the controversy with sceptics. Although I venture to dissent from some of its most important positions, I would still wish to express my own participation in the esteem in which it has been held, and my own obligations to the book. Certainly it does abound in marks of deep and careful thought. For instance, it is an evidence of the Bishop's sagacity,[1] that he should to a great extent anticipate modern views as to the reign of law and evolution. At the same time certain defects, certain points at least in which the knowledge of the present day has advanced beyond that of the Bishop, are, I believe, generally allowed. His argument[2] for the immortality of the soul from our sense of continued identity when important parts of the body are lost, or when its whole constituents are changed, or, again, from the indiscerptibility of consciousness, would not now be urged. His argument[3] for

---

[1] 'Analogy,' part i. chap. vii. p. 127; part ii. chap. iv. p. 193, edition by the Bishop of Gloucester, Dr. Halifax.
[2] 'Analogy,' part i. chap. i.   [3] 'Analogy,' part ii. chap. ii. sect. ii.

miracles from the need of a miracle to plant man upon the globe must be given up if evolution is adopted. It is indisputable [1] that he underrated the *à priori* objection against miracles, and that he fell into a fallacy [2] when he reasoned as follows :—A chance combination of ideas, as to ordinary events, coming into our minds, would never be thought of as actually matter of fact, but a very little testimony would make it probable as such. So a little testimony removes the incredibility of miracles. Again, with our present knowledge of the development of religious belief, we should not, like Butler, bring forward as evidence [3] a supposed primæval revelation. These are individual blots or weaknesses, which would I think be generally allowed, but which, it might be contended, did not materially impair the value of the work. But what I have now to bring forward is a comprehensive objection. It lies against the general scope of the book. That scope is well expressed in a passage which Butler [4] quotes from Origen—'He who believes the Scriptures to have proceeded from Him who is the author of nature, may well expect to find the same sort of difficulties in it as are found in the constitu-

---

[1] 'Analogy,' part ii. chap. ii. sect. iii.

[2] See article on Miracles, Smith's 'Dictionary of the Bible;' Mill's 'Logic,' book iii. chap. xxv. art. 4.

[3] 'Analogy,' part i. chap. vi. p. 120; part ii. chap. ii. p. 169, edition by Dr. Halifax.   [4] 'Analogy.' Introduction.

tion of nature.' The Bishop holds that, finding an analogy between the course of nature on the one hand, and natural or revealed religion on the other, is an answer to objections against the points in which the analogy can be traced. At least it shows that such objections cannot be urged by one who believes in a God. Perhaps it may be more; it may be a presumption that the things in question are from God. This position is indeed the substance of his work. Obviously it is no more than a *tu quoque* on the Deists. It is not effective against that large class of modern sceptics who put aside the question of a God, as full of difficulties and uncertainties. We know, for instance, that, after having for a time kept Mr. James Mill[1] a Christian, it landed him at last in the state of scepticism just alluded to. But its effectiveness against the Deists has been widely held, and it is this effectiveness which I venture to question. It seems to me that the following reply might be made. The Deists might say: 'Difficulties in religion vary in degree. What we complain of in popular Christianity is that it increases our difficulties, as witness the doctrine of everlasting punishment. We look to religion for an account of things which shall reconcile us to the moral difficulties of this present world, and make them seem compatible with the goodness of God, and we think that we can ima-

---

[1] Mr. John Stuart Mill's 'Autobiography,' chap. ii. p. 39.

gine a future world which would do this. But we do not expect the more comprehensive scheme of things which religion discloses to be analogous to what we now behold as to points of moral difficulty. On the contrary, this disclosure is " to justify the ways of God to man," to vindicate God's justice and mercy, and to satisfy the questionings of man's moral nature. This view has ever been put forward by teachers of religion, both natural and revealed, in the Bible and elsewhere. Bishop Butler himself recognises it. As to natural religion he makes the existence of a moral law, written on man's heart, an evidence that God will hereafter punish vice and reward virtue.[1] What is this but making the scheme of natural religion conform itself to our moral instincts? It is making the world to come, not analogous to this world, as regards moral difficulties, but a redressing of those difficulties. So as to revealed religion the Bishop [2] holds " Christianity to be a scheme quite beyond our comprehension," yet he tells us " that everyone at length and upon the whole shall receive according to his deserts." Here again, we contend, is clearly the idea that the future which religion discloses is to be the complement, so to speak, of God's dealings with us here. It will not be analogous to the present, but will so differ from it as to make the whole

---

[1] 'Analogy,' part i. chap. vi. p. 117.
[2] 'Analogy,' part ii. chap. iv. sect. i. p. 190.

of God's dispensations to us harmonious to our sense of right, as Bishop Butler understood that sense. After such an admission, is it consistent to defend moral difficulties in a scheme of religion by bringing forward analogies from this temporal world? Bishop Butler does indeed at times deny our right to anticipate the future upon moral grounds.[1] For instance, he treats objections against the contents of revelation as distinguished from objections against its evidence as in a great measure frivolous. And he does so on the ground of analogy. The present world is not what we should expect from our notions of God. Therefore the future may not be.

But he at once enters a caution. He would not be misunderstood to assert that a supposed revelation cannot be proved to be false from internal characters. It may, he says, 'contain clear immoralities or contradictions, and either would prove it false.' "Nor," he adds, "will I take upon me to affirm that nothing else could possibly render any supposed revelation incredible." After all, it is clear that Butler did allow a certain authority to the moral faculty, as a witness what the future and the total of God's dealings with man would be. If so, these main doctrines of religion must be conformed, not to the analogies of this world, but to a moral ideal. It would indeed have been inconsistent in Butler to

[1] 'Analogy,' part ii. chap. iii. pp. 173, 174.

lose sight of this truth, as it is one of his merits to have been among the first clearly to recognise the existence and the authority of a moral faculty in man.' So I think that the Deists might reply, and with effect. My own view may be stated thus :—If we had a revelation professing to be independently and adequately guaranteed by miraculous or other non-moral evidence, and avowedly not resting its authority upon moral grounds at all, then we might consistently defend it against any objections from moral principles, by analogies drawn from this present world. But the friends of religion have never rested their cause wholly on such grounds. And so far as they have done otherwise, they have disqualified themselves from using Bishop Butler's argument from analogy. They have called upon their side a witness who denied this analogy. And the more we rely on this witness the less consistent it is to use that argument. And if, as in these essays, we rate the argument from miracles or other external grounds secondary, and make moral evidence the chief support of Christianity, then the argument of Butler's work cannot be urged. For example, it is but to play fast and loose with the authority of conscience, at one time to predict a future judgment and triumph of righteousness upon that authority, and then at another time to defend some moral difficulty in the scheme of religion by appealing to analogies in a state of things whose moral imperfections that judgment and triumph are needed to redress.

I would yet add to these remarks upon the general scope of Bishop Butler's work something further as to certain particular applications of his principle. I do this partly to illustrate my general objection, and partly to point out what seem to me to be other cases of mistaken analogy. We will take instances of his reasoning as to natural and as to revealed religion in succession. It will be seen, I think, that the general objection which I have brought forward does apply, and also that other exceptions may be made.

First, Natural Religion. It is a capital point in all religious belief that we are under a *moral* government. Virtue is to be rewarded. Vice is to be punished. The Bishop seeks for analogies to this doctrine in the course of nature. No doubt he does find cases in point. But to establish a precedent to guide our expectations as to a future life, we need an analogy from the general course of Providence in this life, so far at least as it is known to us. When the Bishop attempts the general review of this present world, which such an analogy requires, he makes the following admission[1]:—' Pleasure and pain

---

[1] 'Analogy,' part i. chap. iii. pp. 68, 69, edition by Bishop Halifax, Oxford, 1844.

are indeed, to a certain degree, say to a very high degree, distributed amongst us without any apparent regard to the merit or demerit of characters. And were there nothing else concerning this matter discernible in the constitution and course of nature, there would be no ground from the constitution and course of nature to hope or to fear that men would be rewarded or punished hereafter according to their deserts.' The reservation here made as to 'there being nothing else concerning this matter discernible in the constitution and course of nature,' refers, I apprehend, to a certain tendency, which Bishop Butler maintains, that there is in virtue of itself and apart from favourable or unfavourable conditions to promote human happiness. That what men at any given time call virtue may tend to promote the general happiness, is probably true enough, and may indeed mean nothing more than this—that men's idea of goodness in their fellow-man has arisen from their experience what kind of conduct conduces to the common good. But it is not true that this conduct always conduces to the temporal good of him who practises it; nay, what is worse, as I have pointed out elsewhere,[1] the most exalted forms of this conduct often tend the other way. No doubt certain virtues that concern self in the first place, as temperance, do conduce to the happiness of him who practises them,

[1] See First Essay. p. 43.

and this may justly be thought an appointment of the author of the world. But when all has been allowed that can fairly be allowed under this head, there remains the fact which the Bishop himself admits that in this world pleasure and pain, happiness and misery, are to a very great extent allotted without any reference to the goodness or badness of those who receive them, and this allotment quite as much as any other that may have an appearance of moral grounds must be looked upon as an act of God. The adverse conditions which prevent virtue from bearing the fruits of happiness to the virtuous, just as much as any so-called tendency in the thing itself, must be looked upon as part of the appointments of God, if we think of him only as the world maker, and do not fall back upon considerations as to his character suggested by our moral faculty. I conclude, therefore, that the argument from mere analogy does not support the idea of moral government, or lead us to expect a state of rewards and punishments in a future life. Virtue might there also, as a rule, make us happier than vice would do, but even in saying so much as this we are perplexed a good deal by the variations in men's notion of virtue, and the influence which any given style of conduct has had at different times on the happiness of him who practised it. But we may be confident in saying that if our notions of a future world are to be formed from the analogies of this, that world will not be strictly a reward for the good and a punishment to the wicked.

Next, with a view to reconcile this very imperfection of God's moral government in this life with his essential goodness, it has ever been maintained by religious writers that this life was only a state of probation, a state of trial and preparation for another. For this doctrine also the Bishop seeks for analogies in this present world. And here he has one great advantage. If there be a future life, it is plainly a successor to this. We may therefore seek for our analogies, in conjecturing how it will be influenced by this, not in this present life as a whole, for that has no antecedent, but rather in consecutive stages of our present existence, and their influence one upon another. And Butler is accordingly able to bring forward with pertinence the need of certain conduct in early life for our welfare at a later time.

No doubt what we do at one time affects our happiness at a later time. But this connection is by no means always—perhaps, indeed, it may not be even generally—that of virtue leading to happiness, vice to misery. There have been ages, there are still many countries, in which the formation of a virtuous character in any high sense of the word would put a man out of harmony with the society in which he had to live, and probably injure his temporal happiness. On the whole, I think that this would be true for mankind at large, as they have so far existed, although I acknowledge the respect which an eminently good man has often inspired amongst a degraded people. The general truth is, that early life must for our welfare adapt us to the conditions under which mature life is to be spent—say with a savage it must make him a skilful hunter or fisher. We cannot make this principle, viz. that one stage of existence should prepare us for the next, if we are then to be happy, bear witness to the need of virtue now for our happiness hereafter, unless we make special assumptions as to what our future state will be, for which the argument from the analogy of this world at all events does not afford grounds.

Lastly, Bishop Butler argues a great deal from our imperfect comprehension of the scheme of this world to reconcile us to much which is difficult in the scheme of religion. In estimating the value and the fitness of this analogy we have to consider how far the difficulty, to which it is sought to reconcile us, has its rise in moral or in intellectual causes. If the former, then I think that we must bear in mind what has been said as to the greater conformity to our moral faculty, which by the very nature of the case may be looked for in religion than in nature. If the latter, then I allow that the argument has great weight. We see so many things in nature which we cannot now explain, or, in other words, reduce to natural law, that we must be careful of denying any asserted action of God, merely because we cannot understand how he could do it, in conformity with our knowledge of his ways of operation. I hold, for instance, that we should not be at all justified in denying the general resurrection of the dead upon such grounds, though few things perhaps could be thought of more out of the course of nature. The mere weakness of our intellect, and the scantiness of our knowledge, when we come to deal with so great a subject as God and his dealings with us, is evident enough; but I would say that we must be careful lest we press these considerations too far, or we shall end in establishing the unknowability of God and the uncertainty of all things in religion. In trying to silence objectors, we may take away all foundation for ourselves. If, indeed, Dean Mansel's argument from the infinity of God's nature availed for anything, which I do not allow, this was the result.

Secondly, Revealed Religion. I will say a few words more as to the analogies by which the Bishop has sought to defend what he regarded as the special doctrines of revelation.

Revelation is generally understood to be miraculous. It was taken to be so by Bishop Butler. He tries to bring this characteristic into analogy with things which we know of in the natural world, but not in any manner which could now be allowed as satisfactory. Of his reference to the first planting of man upon the earth I have spoken already. He cites also what he looked upon as extraordinary natural phenomena, comets, electricity, magnetism. Here it is plain that we have not so much as an appearance of the violation of the laws of nature, and this I presume is the thing for which we are seeking analogues.

Again, a chief item in the Christian revelation is the saving of man through the mediation of Christ. Butler treats this subject at length in ch. v. part ii. of the 'Analogy.' He divides the mediatorial work of Christ into three parts, of which the third is being 'a propitiatory sacrifice,' and 'making atonement for the sins of the world.' It is with regard to what he says as to this third part that I would say something. The Bishop, with that caution and wisdom which he certainly possessed, disavows all attempt at explaining the principles of this propitiation or expiation. He does, it is true, speak favourably of the idea of the authority of God's law being thereby vindicated, and his creatures being deterred from sin, more favourably, a good deal, than I for one could do. But he very clearly and fully lays it down that neither this nor any other known explanation is a complete account. He expressly leaves the matter uncertain and mysterious. But when he comes to consider a certain objection, viz. that this doctrine 'represents God as being indifferent, whether he punished the innocent or the guilty,' he brings forward an analogy to which I think objection may be made. I the more wish to point this out, as great weight has been attached to this analogy by his admirers and disciples.[1] The analogy is that of the sacrifices or sufferings which good persons in this life do often undergo, nay, sometimes are called upon by the laws of nature or religion to undergo, in order to relieve wicked persons, in whole or in part, from the consequences of their sins. This part of God's providential government here is said to be analogous to that appointment, in his wider scheme of government, made known by revelation, by which the innocent Christ suffers for the pardon of guilty men. Here again I object against the analogy alleged between this present scheme of God's government, and that wider one disclosed by religion. No one pretends that in this world happiness or misery are distributed upon grounds of critical justice. But it is expected that they will be so distributed in that future judgment with which Christ's atonement has to do. And the difficulty is to understand how in such a distribution, how in an administration of penal justice, the direct carrying out of a judicial sentence, there can be substitution of one sufferer for another.

[1] See 'Analogies of Nature and Grace,' by C. Pritchard.

Those popular explanations of the atonement, against which I have argued, do seem to me open to this objection, and Butler's analogies do not touch the matter. Certainly we should not allow such a proceeding in human justice.

Other cases of false analogy may, I think, be found, and one or two I will point out as I close. The everlasting punishment of the wicked cannot be defended by the analogy of those temporal afflictions which cannot be remedied throughout life. After all, the very source of difficulty, the endlessness of the evil, is wanting in the latter cases. Nor can the failure of this world to prove a place of successful moral training to so many, an evil which upon the hypothesis of everlasting punishment is irremediable and incalculable, be defended by the analogy from the failure of such multitudes of the seeds of plants and animals to come to maturity. There is, I allow, an appearance of frustration of design in this latter case. But the moral aspect is quite different. The moral difficulty is not at all the same. We have, as I have pointed out already, in the latter case, only an apparent waste of means, a matter in which we certainly are not judges of the conduct of a being with infinite resources, and possibly a number of unknown purposes. But the other case involves the imputation that the Almighty has called into existence beings who would, he knew, be everlastingly miserable. I must finally repeat that I for one do not see how such an act can be reconciled with his attributes, if we adopt that hypothesis, upon which all religion proceeds, viz. that God does not merely provide for the universe and its welfare in a general way, but that each individual sentient being, and still more that each moral being, has a distinct place in his fatherly care.

NOTE ON ESSAY II.

I HAVE feared that some expressions in my second essay, and especially in Part V., might be understood to question the truth of some of those accounts in the Gospels which are commonly thought to be miraculous. I wish here to repeat that such has not been my meaning; and I would also add, as to one particular point, viz. a statement made upon page 217, that I feel that the language of the New Testament generally gives the idea of faith as a moral condition of receiving the blessing of healing, rather than of faith as a psychical means of cure. It would, however, agree with this last idea in some places, I think; nor are the two ideas absolutely inconsistent. I must not be understood here to question the almighty power of Our Lord. The question is as to its mode of operation. Certainly, to my mind, many of the Gospel accounts commonly considered miraculous do not seem to involve of necessity any breach of the laws of nature; and further, I think that upon the hypothesis of a spiritual world capable at times of physical relations to the visible universe, possibly all those accounts may be explained without breach of continuity. What I have intended to establish in my essay, I may briefly repeat thus. The modern evidential argument requires the truth of the Gospel miracles, and the untruth of all others. To prove this last it is necessary to adopt rules of criticism so strict that when they are impartially applied to the Gospels they leave none of the miracles to be found there established as strictly miracles, except the resurrection of Christ. But these rules I hold to be too strict. For instance, I think, that it is going too far at once to set aside all accounts of visions as cases of false perception. Now, if you modify these rules, as I propose, you can retain the miracles of the New Testament; but you cannot at the same time reject all others. I am myself disposed to believe a good many of the wonderful stories which have come down to us, especially in connection with religious men, and to suppose that these wonders will one day be found to have their place in the order of the creation, that is, of the spiritual as well as visible universe, and I should use the like hypothesis to explain, without breach of continuity, other seeming anomalies, as, possibly, the origin of life on our globe, or of a responsible and immortal spirit in man. Accordingly, I do not feel that great difficulty in believing accounts, say of wonderful cures, or of the appearances of angels or other spirits, which many persons, and especially scientific men, do feel; although, of course, I think that the evidence for such accounts should be very closely examined. In short, as I have said in my essay, it is not the miracles of Christ, but the evidential conclusions which have been drawn from them which I question. It may have occurred to some of my readers that these conclusions are asserted or implied in the New Testament itself, as, for example, in St. Matt. xi. 20, 21, 23; St. Mark xvi. 20; St. John v. 36; Acts ii. 22; Rom. i. 4; 2 Cor. xii. 12. I did not notice what is said in such texts in my essay, because an appeal to the dogmatic authority of Scripture would be out of place in an evidential argument. But many Christians may reasonably think themselves bound by this apparent recognition to admit the argument from miracles. I wish accordingly to point out a difference, which I believe to exist between the argument from miracles discussed in my essay and that to be found in the New Testament. The latter is, I think, what I have called the argument from analogy. A being with power to do such wonderful things is presumably divine, or acting in conjunction with God. He resembles the Almighty in the great attribute of power. He has done 'the works which none other man did' (St. John xv. 24). Now the argument discussed in my essay is different from this. It is more precise, and, if made out, certainly more conclusive. It looked at a miracle as strictly a breach of the laws of nature. In that view, indeed, lay the special proof of divine interference. Created beings might seem, according to our knowledge, to interfere with the course of nature, but in reality their power must always be exercised, according to the laws of the universe, comprehensively understood. The Creator only could abrogate or suspend those laws. Now, I do not think that this argument can be fairly attributed to the writers of the New Testament, for this reason, that the idea of an order of nature does not seem to have been developed in their minds. Certainly they do not take up the modern evidential position. They do not insist that their miracles are the only true ones as matters of fact. They allow others. St. Matt. xxiv. 24; 2 Thessal. ii. 9. But I must add that they do see in the analogy of miracle working to divine power, an attestation from God. St. Mark xvi. 20; Acts ii. 22; Heb. ii. 4.

39 Paternoster Row, E.C.
London, *August* 1875.

GENERAL LIST OF WORKS

PUBLISHED BY

MESSRS. LONGMANS, GREEN, AND CO.

	PAGE		PAGE
Arts, Manufactures, &c.	26	Mental & Political Philosophy	8
Astronomy & Meteorology	16	Miscellaneous & Critical Works	12
Biographical Works	7	Natural History & Physical Science	18
Chemistry & Physiology	24	Poetry & the Drama	35
Dictionaries & other Books of Reference	14	Religious & Moral Works	28
Fine Arts & Illustrated Editions	24	Rural Sports, Horse & Cattle Management, &c.	36
History, Politics, Historical Memoirs, &c.	1	Travels, Voyages, &c.	32
		Works of Fiction	34
Index	40 to 43	Works of Utility & General Information	37

HISTORY, POLITICS, HISTORICAL MEMOIRS, &c.

Journal of the Reigns of King George the Fourth and King William the Fourth.

By the late Charles Cavendish Fulke Greville, Esq.

Edited by Henry Reeve, Esq.

Fifth Edition. 3 vols. 8vo. price 36s.

The Life of Napoleon III. derived from State Records, Unpublished Family Correspondence, and Personal Testimony.

By Blanchard Jerrold.

Four Vols. 8vo. with numerous Portraits and Facsimiles. Vols. I. and II. price 18s. each.

*** Vols. *III.* and *IV.* are in preparation.

A

Recollections and Suggestions, 1813–1873.
By *John Earl Russell, K.G.*
New Edition, revised and enlarged. 8vo. 16s.

Introductory Lectures on Modern History delivered in Lent Term 1842; with the Inaugural Lecture delivered in December 1841.
By the late Rev. *Thomas Arnold, D.D.*
8vo. price 7s. 6d.

On Parliamentary Government in England: its Origin, Development, and Practical Operation.
By *Alpheus Todd*.
2 vols. 8vo. £1. 17s.

The Constitutional History of England since the Accession of George III. 1760–1870.
By Sir *Thomas Erskine May, K.C.B.*
Fourth Edition. 3 vols. crown 8vo. 18s.

Democracy in Europe; a History.
By Sir *Thomas Erskine May, K.C.B.*
2 vols. 8vo. [*In the press.*

The History of England from the Fall of Wolsey to the Defeat of the Spanish Armada.
By *J. A. Froude, M.A.*
CABINET EDITION, 12 vols. cr. 8vo. £3. 12s.
LIBRARY EDITION, 12 vols. 8vo. £8. 18s.

The English in Ireland in the Eighteenth Century.
By *J. A. Froude, M.A.*
3 vols. 8vo. £2. 8s.

The History of England from the Accession of James II.
By *Lord Macaulay.*
STUDENT'S EDITION, 2 vols. cr. 8vo. 12s.
PEOPLE'S EDITION, 4 vols. cr. 8vo. 16s.
CABINET EDITION, 8 vols. post 8vo. 48s.
LIBRARY EDITION, 5 vols. 8vo. £4.

Critical and Historical Essays contributed to the Edinburgh Review.
By the Right Hon. Lord *Macaulay*.
Cheap Edition, authorised and complete, crown 8vo. 3s. 6d.
STUDENT'S EDITION, crown 8vo. 6s.
PEOPLE'S EDITION, 2 vols. crown 8vo. 8s.
CABINET EDITION, 4 vols. 24s.
LIBRARY EDITION, 3 vols. 8vo. 36s.

Lord Macaulay's Works.
Complete and uniform Library Edition.
Edited by his Sister, Lady *Trevelyan*.
8 vols. 8vo. with Portrait, £5. 5s.

Lectures on the History of England from the Earliest Times to the Death of King Edward II.
By *W. Longman, F.S.A.*
Maps and Illustrations. 8vo. 15s.

The History of the Life and Times of Edward III.
By *W. Longman, F.S.A.*
With 9 Maps, 8 Plates, and 16 Woodcuts. 2 vols. 8vo. 28s.

History of England under the Duke of Buckingham and Charles the First, 1624–1628. By S. Rawson Gardiner, late Student of Ch. Ch.
2 vols. 8vo. with two Maps, 24s.

History of Civilization in England and France, Spain and Scotland. By Henry Thomas Buckle.
3 vols. crown 8vo. 24s.

A Student's Manual of the History of India from the Earliest Period to the Present. By Col. Meadows Taylor, M.R.A.S.
Second Thousand. Cr. 8vo. Maps, 7s. 6d.

Studies from Genoese History. By Colonel G. B. Malleson, C.S.I. Guardian to His Highness the Mahárájá of Mysore.
Crown 8vo. 10s. 6d.

The Native States of India in Subsidiary Alliance with the British Government; an Historical Sketch. With a Notice of the Mediatized and Minor States. By Colonel G. B. Malleson, C.S.I. Guardian to His Highness the Mahárájá of Mysore.
With 6 Coloured Maps, 8vo. price 15s.

The History of India from the Earliest Period to the close of Lord Dalhousie's Administration. By John Clark Marshman.
3 vols. crown 8vo. 22s. 6d.

Indian Polity; a View of the System of Administration in India. By Lieut.-Colonel George Chesney.
Second Edition, revised, with Map. 8vo. 21s.

Waterloo Lectures; a Study of the Campaign of 1815. By Colonel Charles C. Chesney, R.E.
Third Edition. 8vo. with Map, 10s. 6d.

Essays in Modern Military Biography. By Colonel Charles C. Chesney, R.E.
8vo. 12s. 6d.

The Imperial and Colonial Constitutions of the Britannic Empire, including Indian Institutions. By Sir E. Creasy, M.A.
With 6 Maps. 8vo. 15s.

The Oxford Reformers—John Colet, Erasmus, and Thomas More; being a History of their Fellow-Work. By Frederic Seebohm.
Second Edition. 8vo. 14s.

The New Reformation, a Narrative of the Old Catholic Movement, from 1870 to the Present Time; with an Historical Introduction.
By Theodorus.
8vo. price 12s.

The Mythology of the Aryan Nations.
By Geo. W. Cox, M.A. late Scholar of Trinity College, Oxford.
2 vols. 8vo. 28s.

A History of Greece.
By the Rev. Geo. W. Cox, M.A. late Scholar of Trinity College, Oxford.
Vols. I. and II. 8vo. Maps, 36s.

A School History of Greece to the Death of Alexander the Great.
By the Rev. George W. Cox, M.A. late Scholar of Trinity College, Oxford; Author of 'The Aryan Mythology' &c.
1 vol. crown 8vo. [In the press.

The History of the Peloponnesian War, by Thucydides.
Translated by Richd. Crawley, Fellow of Worcester College, Oxford.
8vo. 21s.

The Tale of the Great Persian War, from the Histories of Herodotus.
By Rev. G. W. Cox, M.A.
Fcp. 8vo. 3s. 6d.

Greek History from Themistocles to Alexander, in a Series of Lives from Plutarch.
Revised and arranged by A. H. Clough.
Fcp. 8vo. Woodcuts, 6s.

General History of Rome from the Foundation of the City to the Fall of Augustulus, B.C. 753—A.D. 476.
By the Very Rev. C. Merivale, D.D. Dean of Ely.
With 5 Maps, crown 8vo. 7s. 6d.

History of the Romans under the Empire.
By Dean Merivale, D.D.
8 vols. post 8vo. 48s.

The Fall of the Roman Republic; a Short History of the Last Century of the Commonwealth.
By Dean Merivale, D.D.
12mo. 7s. 6d.

NEW WORKS PUBLISHED BY LONGMANS & CO.   5

The Sixth Oriental Monarchy; or the Geography, History, and Antiquities of Parthia. Collected and Illustrated from Ancient and Modern sources.
By Geo. Rawlinson, M.A.
With Maps and Illustrations. 8vo. 16s.

The Seventh Great Oriental Monarchy; or, a History of the Sassanians: with Notices Geographical and Antiquarian.
By Geo. Rawlinson, M.A.
8vo. with Maps and Illustrations.
[*In the press.*]

Encyclopædia of Chronology, Historical and Biographical; comprising the Dates of all the Great Events of History, including Treaties, Alliances, Wars, Battles, &c. Incidents in the Lives of Eminent Men, Scientific and Geographical Discoveries, Mechanical Inventions, and Social, Domestic, and Economical Improvements.
By B. B. Woodward, B.A. and W. L. R. Cates.
8vo. 42s.

The History of Rome.
By Wilhelm Ihne.
Vols. I. and II. 8vo. 30s. Vols. III. and IV. in preparation.

History of European Morals from Augustus to Charlemagne.
By W. E. H. Lecky, M.A.
2 vols. 8vo. 28s.

History of the Rise and Influence of the Spirit of Rationalism in Europe.
By W. E. H. Lecky, M.A.
Cabinet Edition, 2 vols. crown 8vo. 16s.

Introduction to the Science of Religion: Four Lectures delivered at the Royal Institution; with two Essays on False Analogies and the Philosophy of Mythology.
By F. Max Müller, M.A.
Crown 8vo. 10s. 6d.

The Stoics, Epicureans, and Sceptics.
Translated from the German of Dr. E. Zeller, by Oswald J. Reichel, M.A.
Crown 8vo. 14s.

Socrates and the Socratic Schools.
Translated from the German of Dr. E. Zeller, by the Rev. O. J. Reichel, M.A.
Crown 8vo. 8s. 6d.

Sketch of the History of the Church of England to the Revolution of 1688. By T. V. Short, D.D. sometime Bishop of St. Asaph.
New Edition. Crown 8vo. 7s. 6d.

The Historical Geography of Europe. By E. A. Freeman, D.C.L.
8vo. Maps. [*In the press.*

Essays on the History of the Christian Religion. By John Earl Russell, K.G.
Fcp. 8vo. 3s. 6d.

The Student's Manual of Ancient History: containing the Political History, Geographical Position, and Social State of the Principal Nations of Antiquity. By W. Cooke Taylor, LL.D.
Crown 8vo. 7s. 6d.

The Student's Manual of Modern History: containing the Rise and Progress of the Principal European Nations, their Political History, and the Changes in their Social Condition. By W. Cooke Taylor, LL.D.
Crown 8vo. 7s. 6d.

The History of Philosophy, from Thales to Comte. By George Henry Lewes.
Fourth Edition, 2 vols. 8vo. 32s.

The Crusades. By the Rev. G. W. Cox, M.A.
Fcp. 8vo. with Map, 2s. 6d.

The Era of the Protestant Revolution. By F. Seebohm, Author of 'The Oxford Reformers.'
With 4 Maps and 12 Diagrams. Fcp. 8vo. 2s. 6d.

The Thirty Years' War, 1618-1648. By Samuel Rawson Gardiner.
Fcp. 8vo. with Maps, 2s. 6d.

The Houses of Lancaster and York; with the Conquest and Loss of France. By James Gairdner.
Fcp. 8vo. with Map, 2s. 6d.

Edward the Third. By the Rev. W. Warburton, M.A.
Fcp. 8vo. with Maps, 2s. 6d.

BIOGRAPHICAL WORKS.

Autobiography.
By John Stuart Mill.
8vo. 7s. 6d.

The Life and Letters of Lord Macaulay.
By his Nephew, G. Otto Trevelyan, M.P. for the Hawick District of Burghs.
2 vols. 8vo.   [*In the press.*

Admiral Sir Edward Codrington, a Memoir of his Life; with Selections from his Private and Official Correspondence. Abridged from the larger work, and edited by his Daughter, Lady Bourchier.
With Portrait, Maps, &c. crown 8vo. price 7s. 6d.

Life and Letters of Gilbert Elliot, First Earl of Minto, from 1751 to 1806, when his Public Life in Europe was closed by his Appointment to the Vice-Royalty of India.
Edited by the Countess of Minto.
3 vols. post 8vo. 31s. 6d.

Recollections of Past Life.
By Sir Henry Holland, Bart. M.D. F.R.S.
Third Edition. Post 8vo. 10s. 6d.

Isaac Casaubon, 1559-1614.
By Mark Pattison, Rector of Lincoln College, Oxford.
8vo. price 18s.

The Memoirs of Sir John Reresby, of Thrybergh, Bart. M.P. for York, &c. 1634-1689. Written by Himself. Edited from the Original Manuscript by James J. Cartwright, M.A. Cantab. of H.M. Public Record Office.
8vo. price 21s.

Biographical and Critical Essays, reprinted from Reviews, with Additions and Corrections.
By A. Hayward, Q.C.
Second Series, 2 vols. 8vo. 28s. Third Series, 1 vol. 8vo. 14s.

The Life of Isambard Kingdom Brunel, Civil Engineer.
By I. Brunel, B.C.L.
With Portrait, Plates, and Woodcuts. 8vo. 21s.

Lord George Bentinck; a Political Biography.
By the Right Hon. B. Disraeli, M.P.
New Edition. Crown 8vo. 6s.

The Life and Letters of the Rev. Sydney Smith. Edited by his Daughter, Lady Holland, and Mrs. Austin.
Crown 8vo. 2s. 6d. sewed; 3s. 6d. cloth.

Essays in Ecclesiastical Biography. By the Right Hon. Sir J. Stephen, LL.D.
Cabinet Edition. Crown 8vo. 7s. 6d.

Leaders of Public Opinion in Ireland; Swift, Flood, Grattan, O'Connell. By W. E. H. Lecky, M.A.
Crown 8vo. 7s. 6d.

Dictionary of General Biography; containing Concise Memoirs and Notices of the most Eminent Persons of all Ages and Countries. By W. L. R. Cates.
New Edition, 8vo. 25s. Supplement, 4s. 6d.

Life of the Duke of Wellington. By the Rev. G. R. Gleig, M.A.
Crown 8vo. with Portrait, 5s.

Felix Mendelssohn's Letters from Italy and Switzerland, and Letters from 1833 to 1847. Translated by Lady Wallace.
With Portrait. 2 vols. crown 8vo. 5s. each.

The Rise of Great Families; other Essays and Stories. By Sir Bernard Burke, C.B. LL.D.
Crown 8vo. 12s. 6d.

Memoirs of Sir Henry Havelock, K.C.B. By John Clark Marshman.
Crown 8vo. 3s. 6d.

Vicissitudes of Families. By Sir Bernard Burke, C.B.
2 vols. crown 8vo. 21s.

MENTAL and POLITICAL PHILOSOPHY.

Comte's System of Positive Polity, or Treatise upon Sociology.
Translated from the Paris Edition of 1851-1854, and furnished with Analytical Tables of Contents. In Four Volumes, each forming in some degree an independent Treatise:—

Vol. I. *General View of Positivism and Introductory Principles.* Translated by J. H. Bridges, M.B. *formerly Fellow of Oriel College, Oxford.* 8vo. price 21s.

Vol. II. *The Social Statics, or the Abstract Laws of Human Order.* Translated by Frederic Harrison, M.A. [In Oct.

Vol. III. *The Social Dynamics, or the General Laws of Human Progress (the Philosophy of History).* Translated by E. S. Beesly, M.A. *Professor of History in University College, London.* 8vo. [In Dec.

Vol. IV. *The Synthesis of the Future of Mankind.* Translated by Richard Congreve, M.D., *and an Appendix, containing the Author's Minor Treatises,* translated by H. D. Hutton, M.A. *Barrister-at-Law.* 8vo. [Early in 1876.

NEW WORKS PUBLISHED BY LONGMANS & CO.

Order and Progress: Part I. Thoughts on Government; Part II. Studies of Political Crises. By Frederic Harrison, M.A. of Lincoln's Inn.
8vo. 14s.

Essays, Political, Social, and Religious. By Richd. Congreve, M.A.
8vo. 18s.

Essays, Critical and Biographical, contributed to the Edinburgh Review. By Henry Rogers.
New Edition. 2 vols. crown 8vo. 12s.

Essays on some Theological Controversies of the Time, contributed chiefly to the Edinburgh Review. By Henry Rogers.
New Edition. Crown 8vo. 6s.

Democracy in America. By Alexis de Tocqueville. Translated by Henry Reeve, Esq.
New Edition. 2 vols. crown 8vo. 16s.

On Representative Government. By John Stuart Mill.
Fourth Edition, crown 8vo. 2s.

On Liberty. By John Stuart Mill.
Post 8vo. 7s. 6d. crown 8vo. 1s. 4d.

Principles of Political Economy. By John Stuart Mill.
2 vols. 8vo. 30s. or 1 vol. crown 8vo. 5s.

Essays on some Unsettled Questions of Political Economy. By John Stuart Mill.
Second Edition. 8vo. 6s. 6d.

Utilitarianism. By John Stuart Mill.
Fourth Edition. 8vo. 5s.

A System of Logic, Ratiocinative and Inductive. By John Stuart Mill.
Eighth Edition. 2 vols. 8vo. 25s.

The Subjection of Women. By John Stuart Mill.
New Edition. Post 8vo. 5s.

Examination of Sir William Hamilton's Philosophy, and of the principal Philosophical Questions discussed in his Writings. By John Stuart Mill.
Fourth Edition. 8vo. 16s.

Dissertations and Discussions. By John Stuart Mill.
Second Edition. 3 vols. 8vo. 36s. VOL. *IV.* (completion) price 10s. 6d.

B

Analysis of the Phenomena of the Human Mind. By James Mill. New Edition, with Notes, Illustrative and Critical.
2 vols. 8vo. 28s.

A Systematic View of the Science of Jurisprudence. By Sheldon Amos, M.A.
8vo. 18s.

A Primer of the English Constitution and Government. By Sheldon Amos, M.A.
Second Edition. Crown 8vo. 6s.

Principles of Economical Philosophy. By H. D. Macleod, M.A. Barrister-at-Law.
Second Edition, in 2 vols. Vol. I. 8vo. 15s. Vol. II. Part I. price 12s.

The Institutes of Justinian; with English Introduction, Translation, and Notes. By T. C. Sandars, M.A.
Fifth Edition. 8vo. 18s.

Lord Bacon's Works, Collected and Edited by R. L. Ellis, M.A. J. Spedding, M.A. and D. D. Heath.
New and Cheaper Edition. 7 vols. 8vo. £3. 13s. 6d.

Letters and Life of Francis Bacon, including all his Occasional Works. Collected and edited, with a Commentary, by J. Spedding.
7 vols. 8vo. £4. 4s.

The Nicomachean Ethics of Aristotle. Newly translated into English. By R. Williams, B.A.
8vo. 12s.

The Politics of Aristotle; Greek Text, with English Notes. By Richard Congreve, M.A.
New Edition, revised. 8vo. 18s.

The Ethics of Aristotle; with Essays and Notes. By Sir A. Grant, Bart. M.A. LL.D.
Third Edition. 2 vols. 8vo. price 32s.

Bacon's Essays, with Annotations. By R. Whately, D.D.
New Edition. 8vo. 10s. 6d.

Picture Logic; an Attempt to Popularise the Science of Reasoning by the combination of Humorous Pictures with Examples of Reasoning taken from Daily Life. By A. Swinbourne, B.A.
With Woodcut Illustrations from Drawings by the Author. Fcp. 8vo. price 5s.

Elements of Logic.
By R. Whately, D.D.
New Edition. 8vo. 10s. 6d. cr. 8vo. 4s. 6d.

Elements of Rhetoric.
By R. Whately, D.D.
New Edition. 8vo. 10s. 6d. cr. 8vo. 4s. 6d.

An Outline of the Necessary Laws of Thought: a Treatise on Pure and Applied Logic.
By the Most Rev. W. Thomson, D.D. Archbishop of York.
Ninth Thousand. Crown 8vo. 5s. 6d.

An Introduction to Mental Philosophy, on the Inductive Method.
By J. D. Morell, LL.D.
8vo. 12s.

Elements of Psychology, containing the Analysis of the Intellectual Powers.
By J. D. Morell, LL.D.
Post 8vo. 7s. 6d.

The Secret of Hegel: being the Hegelian System in Origin, Principle, Form, and Matter.
By J. H. Stirling, LL.D.
2 vols. 8vo. 28s.

Sir William Hamilton; being the Philosophy of Perception: an Analysis.
By J. H. Stirling, LL.D.
8vo. 5s.

Ueberweg's System of Logic, and History of Logical Doctrines.
Translated, with Notes and Appendices, by T. M. Lindsay, M.A. F.R.S.E.
8vo. 16s.

The Senses and the Intellect.
By A. Bain, LL.D. Prof. of Logic, Univ. Aberdeen.
8vo. 15s.

Mental and Moral Science; a Compendium of Psychology and Ethics.
By A. Bain, LL.D.
Third Edition. Crown 8vo. 10s. 6d. Or separately: Part I. Mental Science, 6s. 6d. Part II. Moral Science, 4s. 6d.

The Philosophy of Necessity; or, Natural Law as applicable to Mental, Moral, and Social Science.
By Charles Bray.
Second Edition. 8vo. 9s.

Hume's Treatise on Human Nature.
Edited, with Notes, &c. by T. H. Green, M.A. and the Rev. T. H. Grose, M.A.
2 vols. 8vo. 28s.

Hume's Essays Moral, Political, and Literary.
By the same Editors.
2 vols. 8vo. 28s.

*** The above form a complete and uniform Edition of HUME'S Philosophical Works.

MISCELLANEOUS & CRITICAL WORKS.

Miscellaneous and Posthumous Works of the late Henry Thomas Buckle. Edited, with a Biographical Notice, by Helen Taylor.
3 vols. 8vo. £2. 12s. 6d.

Short Studies on Great Subjects. By J. A. Froude, M.A. formerly Fellow of Exeter College, Oxford.
CABINET EDITION, 2 vols. crown 8vo. 12s.
LIBRARY EDITION, 2 vols. 8vo. 24s.

Lord Macaulay's Miscellaneous Writings.
LIBRARY EDITION, 2 vols. 8vo. Portrait, 21s.
PEOPLE'S EDITION, 1 vol. cr. 8vo. 4s. 6d.

Lord Macaulay's Miscellaneous Writings and Speeches.
Students' Edition. Crown 8vo. 6s.

Speeches of the Right Hon. Lord Macaulay, corrected by Himself.
People's Edition. Crown 8vo. 3s. 6d.

Lord Macaulay's Speeches on Parliamentary Reform in 1831 and 1832.
16mo. 1s.

Manual of English Literature, Historical and Critical. By Thomas Arnold, M.A.
New Edition. Crown 8vo. 7s. 6d.

The Rev. Sydney Smith's Essays contributed to the Edinburgh Review.
Authorised Edition, complete in One Volume.
Crown 8vo. 2s. 6d. sewed, or 3s. 6d. cloth.

The Rev. Sydney Smith's Miscellaneous Works.
Crown 8vo. 6s.

The Wit and Wisdom of the Rev. Sydney Smith.
Crown 8vo. 3s. 6d.

The Miscellaneous Works of Thomas Arnold, D.D. Late Head Master of Rugby School and Regius Professor of Modern History in the Univ. of Oxford.
8vo. 7s. 6d.

Realities of Irish Life. By W. Steuart Trench.
Cr. 8vo. 2s. 6d. sewed, or 3s. 6d. cloth.

Lectures on the Science of Language. By F. Max Müller, M.A. &c.
Eighth Edition. 2 vols. crown 8vo. 16s.

Chips from a German Workshop; being Essays on the Science of Religion, and on Mythology, Traditions, and Customs. By F. Max Müller, M.A. &c.
3 vols. 8vo. £2.

Southey's Doctor, complete in One Volume.
Edited by Rev. J. W. Warter, B.D.
Square crown 8vo. 12s. 6d.

Families of Speech.
Four Lectures delivered at the Royal Institution.
By F. W. Farrar, D.D.
New Edition. Crown 8vo. 3s. 6d.

Chapters on Language.
By F. W. Farrar, D.D. F.R.S.
New Edition. Crown 8vo. 5s.

A Budget of Paradoxes.
By Augustus De Morgan, F.R.A.S.
Reprinted, with Author's Additions, from the Athenæum. 8vo. 15s.

Apparitions; a Narrative of Facts.
By the Rev. B. W. Savile, M.A. Author of 'The Truth of the Bible' &c.
Crown 8vo. price 4s. 6d.

Miscellaneous Writings of John Conington, M.A.
Edited by J. A. Symonds, M.A. With a Memoir by H. J. S. Smith, M.A.
2 vols. 8vo. 28s.

Recreations of a Country Parson.
By A. K. H. B.
Two Series, 3s. 6d. each.

Landscapes, Churches, and Moralities.
By A. K. H. B.
Crown 8vo. 3s. 6d.

Seaside Musings on Sundays and Weekdays.
By A. K. H. B.
Crown 8vo. 3s. 6d.

Changed Aspects of Unchanged Truths.
By A. K. H. B.
Crown 8vo. 3s. 6d.

Counsel and Comfort from a City Pulpit.
By A. K. H. B.
Crown 8vo. 3s. 6d.

Lessons of Middle Age.
By A. K. H. B.
Crown 8vo. 3s. 6d.

Leisure Hours in Town
By A. K. H. B.
Crown 8vo. 3s. 6d.

The Autumn Holidays of a Country Parson.
By A. K. H. B.
Crown 8vo. 3s. 6d.

Sunday Afternoons at the Parish Church of a Scottish University City.
By A. K. H. B.
Crown 8vo. 3s. 6d.

The Commonplace Philosopher in Town and Country.
By A. K. H. B.
Crown 8vo. 3s. 6d.

Present-Day Thoughts.
By A. K. H. B.
Crown 8vo. 3s. 6d.

Critical Essays of a Country Parson.
By A. K. H. B.
Crown 8vo. 3s. 6d.

The Graver Thoughts of a Country Parson.
By A. K. H. B.
Two Series, 3s. 6d. each.

DICTIONARIES and OTHER BOOKS of REFERENCE.

A Dictionary of the English Language.
By R. G. Latham, M.A. M.D. Founded on the Dictionary of Dr. S. Johnson, as edited by the Rev. H. J. Todd, with numerous Emendations and Additions.
4 vols. 4to. £7.

Thesaurus of English Words and Phrases, classified and arranged so as to facilitate the expression of Ideas, and assist in Literary Composition.
By P. M. Roget, M.D.
Crown 8vo. 10s. 6d.

English Synonymes.
By E. J. Whately. Edited by Archbishop Whately.
Fifth Edition. Fcp. 8vo. 3s.

Handbook of the English Language. For the use of Students of the Universities and the Higher Classes in Schools.
By R. G. Latham, M.A. M.D. &c. late Fellow of King's College, Cambridge; late Professor of English in Univ. Coll. Lond.
The Ninth Edition. Crown 8vo. 6s.

A Practical Dictionary of the French and English Languages.
By Léon Contanseau, many years French Examiner for Military and Civil Appointments, &c.
Post 8vo. 10s. 6d.

Contanseau's Pocket Dictionary, French and English, abridged from the Practical Dictionary, by the Author.
Square 18mo. 3s. 6d.

NEW WORKS PUBLISHED BY LONGMANS & CO.   15

New Practical Dictionary of the German Language; German-English and English-German.
By Rev. W. L. Blackley, M.A. and Dr. C. M. Friedländer.
Post 8vo. 7s. 6d.

A Dictionary of Roman and Greek Antiquities. With 2,000 Woodcuts from Ancient Originals, illustrative of the Arts and Life of the Greeks and Romans.
By Anthony Rich, B.A.
Third Edition. Crown 8vo. 7s. 6d.

The Mastery of Languages; or, the Art of Speaking Foreign Tongues Idiomatically.
By Thomas Prendergast.
Second Edition. 8vo. 6s.

A Practical English Dictionary.
By John T. White, D.D. Oxon. and T. C. Donkin, M.A.
1 vol. post 8vo. uniform with Contanseau's Practical French Dictionary.
[*In the press.*

A Latin-English Dictionary.
By John T. White, D.D. Oxon. and J. E. Riddle, M.A. Oxon.
Third Edition, revised. 2 vols. 4to. 42s.

White's College Latin-English Dictionary; abridged from the Parent Work for the use of University Students.
Medium 8vo. 18s.

A Latin-English Dictionary adapted for the use of Middle-Class Schools,
By John T. White, D.D. Oxon.
Square fcp. 8vo. 3s.

White's Junior Student's Complete Latin-English and English-Latin Dictionary.
Square 12mo. 12s.

Separately { ENGLISH-LATIN, 5s. 6d.
{ LATIN-ENGLISH, 7s. 6d.

A Greek-English Lexicon.
By H. G. Liddell, D.D. Dean of Christchurch, and R. Scott, D.D. Dean of Rochester.
Sixth Edition. Crown 4to. 36s.

A Lexicon, Greek and English, abridged for Schools from Liddell and Scott's Greek-English Lexicon.
Fourteenth Edition. Square 12mo. 7s. 6d.

An English-Greek Lexicon, containing all the Greek Words used by Writers of good authority.
By C. D. Yonge, B.A.
New Edition. 4to. 21s.

C. D. Yonge's New Lexicon, English and Greek, abridged from his larger Lexicon.
Square 12mo. 8s. 6d.

M'Culloch's Dictionary, Practical, Theoretical, and Historical, of Commerce and Commercial Navigation.
Edited by H. G. Reid.
8vo. 63s.

A General Dictionary of Geography, Descriptive, Physical, Statistical, and Historical; forming a complete Gazetteer of the World.
By A. Keith Johnston, F.R.S.E.
New Edition, thoroughly revised.
[*In the press.*

The Public Schools Manual of Modern Geography. Forming a Companion to 'The Public Schools Atlas of Modern Geography'
By Rev. G. Butler, M.A.
[*In the press.*

The Public Schools Atlas of Modern Geography. In 31 Maps, exhibiting clearly the more important Physical Features of the Countries delineated.
Edited, with Introduction, by Rev. G. Butler, M.A.
Imperial quarto, 3s. 6d. sewed; 5s. cloth.

The Public Schools Atlas of Ancient Geography. Edited, with an Introduction on the Study of Ancient Geography, by the Rev. G. Butler, M.A.
Imperial Quarto.   [*In the press.*

ASTRONOMY and METEOROLOGY.

The Universe and the Coming Transits; Researches into and New Views respecting the Constitution of the Heavens.
By R. A. Proctor, B.A.
With 22 Charts and 22 Diagrams. 8vo. 16s.

Saturn and its System.
By R. A. Proctor, B.A.
8vo. with 14 Plates, 14s.

The Transits of Venus; A Popular Account of Past and Coming Transits, from the first observed by Horrocks A.D. 1639 to the Transit of A.D. 2012.

By R. A. Proctor, B.A.
With 20 Plates (12 Coloured) and 27 Woodcuts. Crown 8vo. 8s. 6d.

Essays on Astronomy.
A Series of Papers on
Planets and Meteors, the
Sun and Sun-surrounding
Space, Stars and Star
Cloudlets.
By R. A. Proctor, B.A.
With 10 *Plates and* 24 *Woodcuts.* 8vo. 12s.

The Moon; her Motions,
Aspect, Scenery, and Physical Condition.
By R. A. Proctor, B.A.
With Plates, Charts, Woodcuts, and Lunar Photographs. Crown 8vo. 15s.

The Sun; Ruler, Light,
Fire, and Life of the Planetary System.
By R. A. Proctor, B.A.
Second Edition. Plates and Woodcuts. Cr. 8vo. 14s.

The Orbs Around Us; a
Series of Familiar Essays
on the Moon and Planets,
Meteors and Comets, the
Sun and Coloured Pairs of
Suns.
By R. A. Proctor, B.A.
Second Edition, with Chart and 4 *Diagrams.*
Crown 8vo. 7s. 6d.

Other Worlds than Ours;
The Plurality of Worlds
Studied under the Light
of Recent Scientific Researches.
By R. A. Proctor, B.A.
Third Edition, with 14 *Illustrations.* Cr. 8vo. 10s. 6d.

Brinkley's Astronomy.
Revised and partly re-written, with Additional Chapters, and an Appendix of
Questions for Examination.
By John W. Stubbs, D.D.
and F. Brünnow, Ph.D.
With 49 *Diagrams.* Crown 8vo. 6s.

Outlines of Astronomy.
By Sir J. F. W. Herschel,
Bart. M.A.
Latest Edition, with Plates and Diagrams.
Square crown 8vo. 12s.

A New Star Atlas, for
the Library, the School, and
the Observatory, in 12 Circular Maps (with 2 Index
Plates).
By R. A. Proctor, B.A.
Crown 8vo. 5s.

Celestial Objects for Common Telescopes.
By T. W. Webb, M.A.
F.R.A.S.
New Edition, with Map of the Moon and Woodcuts. Crown 8vo. 7s. 6d.

Larger Star Atlas, for the
Library, in Twelve Circular Maps, photolithographed by A. Brothers,
F.R.A.S. With 2 Index
Plates and a Letterpress
Introduction.
By R. A. Proctor, BA.
Second Edition. Small folio, 25s.

C

Dove's Law of Storms, considered in connexion with the ordinary Movements of the Atmosphere. Translated by R. H. Scott, M.A.
8vo. 10s. 6d.

Air and Rain; the Beginnings of a Chemical Climatology. By R. A. Smith, F.R.S.
8vo. 24s.

Air and its Relations to Life, 1774-1874. Being, with some Additions, a Course of Lectures delivered at the Royal Institution of Great Britain in the Summer of 1874. By Walter Noel Hartley, F.C.S. Demonstrator of Chemistry at King's College, London.
1 vol. small 8vo. with Illustratrations. [*Nearly ready.*

Magnetism and Deviation of the Compass. For the use of Students in Navigation and Science Schools. By J. Merrifield, LL.D.
18mo. 1s. 6d.

Nautical Surveying, an Introduction to the Practical and Theoretical Study of. By J. K. Laughton, M.A.
Small 8vo. 6s.

Schellen's Spectrum Analysis, in its Application to Terrestrial Substances and the Physical Constitution of the Heavenly Bodies. Translated by Jane and C. Lassell; edited, with Notes, by W. Huggins, LL.D. F.R.S.
With 13 Plates and 223 Woodcuts. 8vo. 28s.

NATURAL HISTORY and PHYSICAL SCIENCE.

The Correlation of Physical Forces. By the Hon. Sir W. R. Grove, F.R.S. &c.
Sixth Edition, with other Contributions to Science. 8vo. 15s.

Professor Helmholtz' Popular Lectures on Scientific Subjects. Translated by E. Atkinson, F.C.S.
With many Illustrative Wood Engravings. 8vo. 12s. 6d.

Ganot's Natural Philosophy for General Readers and Young Persons; a Course of Physics divested of Mathematical Formulæ and expressed in the language of daily life. Translated by E. Atkinson, F.C.S.
Second Edition, with 2 Plates and 429 Woodcuts. Crown 8vo. 7s. 6d.

Ganot's Elementary Treatise on Physics, Experimental and Applied, for the use of Colleges and Schools. Translated and edited by E. Atkinson, F.C.S.
New Edition, with a Coloured Plate and 726 Woodcuts. Post 8vo. 15s.

Weinhold's Introduction to Experimental Physics, Theoretical and Practical; including Directions for Constructing Physical Apparatus and for Making Experiments. Translated by B. Loewy, F.R.A.S. With a Preface by G. C. Foster, F.R.S.
With 3 Coloured Plates and 404 Woodcuts. 8vo. price 31s. 6d.

Principles of Animal Mechanics.
By the Rev. S. Haughton, F.R.S.
Second Edition. 8vo. 21s.

Text-Books of Science, Mechanical and Physical, adapted for the use of Artisans and of Students in Public and other Schools. (The first Ten edited by T. M. Goodeve, M.A. Lecturer on Applied Science at the Royal School of Mines; the remainder edited by C. W. Merrifield, F.R.S. an Examiner in the Department of Public Education.)
Small 8vo. Woodcuts.

Edited by T. M. Goodeve, M.A.
Anderson's *Strength of Materials*, 3s. 6d.
Bloxam's *Metals*, 3s. 6d.
Goodeve's *Mechanics*, 3s. 6d.
——— *Mechanism*, 3s. 6d.
Griffin's *Algebra & Trigonometry*, 3s. 6d.
Notes on the same, with Solutions, 3s. 6d.
Jenkin's *Electricity & Magnetism*, 3s. 6d.
Maxwell's *Theory of Heat*, 3s. 6d.
Merrifield's *Technical Arithmetic*, 3s. 6d.
Key, 3s. 6d.
Miller's *Inorganic Chemistry*, 3s. 6d.
Shelley's *Workshop Appliances*, 3s. 6d.
Watson's *Plane & Solid Geometry*, 3s. 6d.

Edited by C. W. Merrifield, F.R.S.
Armstrong's *Organic Chemistry*, 3s. 6d.
Thorpe's *Quantitative Analysis*, 4s. 6d.
Thorpe and Muir's *Qualitative Analysis*, 3s. 6d.

Fragments of Science.
By John Tyndall, F.R.S.
New Edition, in the press.

Address delivered before the British Association assembled at Belfast.
By John Tyndall, F.R.S. President.
8th Thousand, with New Preface and the Manchester Address. 8vo. price 4s. 6d.

Heat a Mode of Motion.
By *John Tyndall, F.R.S.*
Fifth Edition, Plate and Woodcuts.
Crown 8vo. 10s. 6d.

Sound.
By *John Tyndall, F.R.S.*
Third Edition, including Recent Researches on Fog-Signalling; Portrait and Woodcuts. Crown 8vo. 10s. 6d.

Researches on Diamagnetism and Magne-Crystallic Action; including Diamagnetic Polarity.
By *John Tyndall, F.R.S.*
With 6 Plates and many Woodcuts. 8vo. 14s.

Contributions to Molecular Physics in the domain of Radiant Heat.
By *John Tyndall, F.R.S.*
With 2 Plates and 31 Woodcuts. 8vo. 16s.

Six Lectures on Light, delivered in America in 1872 and 1873.
By *John Tyndall, F.R.S.*
Second Edition, with Portrait, Plate, and 59 Diagrams. Crown 8vo. 7s. 6d.

Notes of a Course of Nine Lectures on Light, delivered at the Royal Institution.
By *John Tyndall, F.R.S.*
Crown 8vo. 1s. sewed, or 1s. 6d. cloth.

Notes of a Course of Seven Lectures on Electrical Phenomena and Theories, delivered at the Royal Institution.
By *John Tyndall, F.R.S.*
Crown 8vo. 1s. sewed, or 1s. 6d. cloth.

A Treatise on Magnetism, General and Terrestrial.
By *H. Lloyd, D.D. D.C.L.*
8vo. price 10s. 6d.

Elementary Treatise on the Wave-Theory of Light.
By *H. Lloyd, D.D. D.C.L.*
Third Edition. 8vo. 10s. 6d.

An Elementary Exposition of the Doctrine of Energy.
By *D. D. Heath, M.A.*
Post 8vo. 4s. 6d.

The Comparative Anatomy and Physiology of the Vertebrate Animals.
By *Richard Owen, F.R.S.*
With 1,472 Woodcuts. 3 vols. 8vo. £3. 13s. 6d.

Sir H. Holland's Fragmentary Papers on Science and other subjects.
Edited by the Rev. J. Holland.
8vo. price 14s.

Light Science for Leisure Hours; Familiar Essays on Scientific Subjects, Natural Phenomena, &c.
By *R. A. Proctor, B.A.*
First and Second Series. 2 vols. crown 8vo. 7s. 6d. each.

Kirby and Spence's Introduction to Entomology, or Elements of the Natural History of Insects.
Crown 8vo. 5s.

NEW WORKS PUBLISHED BY LONGMANS & CO. 21

Strange Dwellings; a Description of the Habitations of Animals, abridged from 'Homes without Hands.'
By Rev. J. G. Wood, M.A.
With Frontispiece and 60 Woodcuts. Crown 8vo. 7s. 6d.

Homes without Hands; a Description of the Habitations of Animals, classed according to their Principle of Construction.
By Rev. J. G. Wood, M.A.
With about 140 Vignettes on Wood. 8vo. 14s.

Out of Doors; a Selection of Original Articles on Practical Natural History.
By Rev. J. G. Wood, M.A.
With 6 Illustrations from Original Designs engraved on Wood. Crown 8vo. 7s. 6d.

The Polar World: a Popular Description of Man and Nature in the Arctic and Antarctic Regions of the Globe.
By Dr. G. Hartwig.
With Chromoxylographs, Maps, and Woodcuts. 8vo. 10s. 6d.

The Sea and its Living Wonders.
By Dr. G. Hartwig.
Fourth Edition, enlarged. 8vo. with many Illustrations, 10s. 6d.

The Tropical World.
By Dr. G. Hartwig.
With about 200 Illustrations. 8vo. 10s. 6d.

The Subterranean World.
By Dr. G. Hartwig.
With Maps and Woodcuts. 8vo. 10s. 6d.

The Aerial World; a Popular Account of the Phenomena and Life of the Atmosphere.
By Dr. George Hartwig.
With Map, 8 Chromoxylographs, and 60 Woodcuts. 8vo. price 21s.

Game Preservers and Bird Preservers, or 'Which are our Friends?'
By George Francis Morant, late Captain 12th Royal Lancers & Major Cape Mounted Riflemen.
Crown 8vo. price 5s.

A Familiar History of Birds.
By E. Stanley, D.D. late Ld. Bishop of Norwich.
Fcp. 8vo. with Woodcuts, 3s. 6d.

Insects at Home; a Popular Account of British Insects, their Structure Habits, and Transformations.
By Rev. J. G. Wood, M.A.
With upwards of 700 Woodcuts. 8vo. 21s.

Insects Abroad; being a Popular Account of Foreign Insects, their Structure, Habits, and Transformations.
By Rev. J. G. Wood, M.A.
With upwards of 700 Woodcuts. 8vo. 21s.

NEW WORKS PUBLISHED BY LONGMANS & CO.

Rocks Classified and Described.
By B. Von Cotta.
English Edition, by P. H. LAWRENCE (with English, German, and French Synonymes), revised by the Author. Post 8vo. 14s.

Heer's Primæval World of Switzerland.
Translated by W. S. Dallas, F.L.S. and edited by James Heywood, M.A. F.R.S.
2 vols. 8vo. with numerous Illustrations. [In the press.

The Origin of Civilisation, and the Primitive Condition of Man; Mental and Social Condition of Savages.
By Sir J. Lubbock, Bart. M.P. F.R.S.
Third Edition, with 25 Woodcuts. 8vo. 18s.

The Native Races of the Pacific States of North America.
By Hubert Howe Bancroft.
Vol. I. Wild Tribes, their Manners and Customs; with 6 Maps. 8vo. 25s.
Vol. II. Native Races of the Pacific States. 25s.
*** To be completed early in the year 1876, in Three more Volumes—
Vol. III. Mythology and Languages of both Savage and Civilized Nations.
Vol. IV. Antiquities and Architectural Remains.
Vol. V. Aboriginal History and Migrations; Index to the Entire Work.

The Ancient Stone Implements, Weapons, and Ornaments of Great Britain.
By John Evans, F.R.S.
With 2 Plates and 476 Woodcuts. 8vo. 28s.

The Elements of Botany for Families and Schools.
Eleventh Edition, revised by Thomas Moore, F.L.S.
Fcp. 8vo. with 154 Woodcuts, 2s. 6d.

Bible Animals; a Description of every Living Creature mentioned in the Scriptures, from the Ape to the Coral.
By Rev. J. G. Wood, M.A.
With about 100 Vignettes on Wood. 8vo. 21s.

The Rose Amateur's Guide.
By Thomas Rivers.
Tenth Edition. Fcp. 8vo. 4s.

A Dictionary of Science, Literature, and Art.
Re-edited by the late W. T. Brande (the Author) and Rev. G. W. Cox, M.A.
New Edition, revised. 3 vols. medium 8vo. 63s.

On the Sensations o Tone, as a Physiological Basis for the Theory of Music.
By H. Helmholtz, Professor of Physiology in the University of Berlin. Translated by A. J. Ellis, F.R.S.
8vo. 36s.

The History of Modern Music, a Course of Lectures delivered at the Royal Institution of Great Britain. By JOHN HULLAH, Professor of Vocal Music in Queen's College and Bedford College, and Organist of Charterhouse.
New Edition, 1 vol. post 8vo. [*In the press.*]

The Treasury of Botany, or Popular Dictionary of the Vegetable Kingdom; with which is incorporated a Glossary of Botanical Terms.
Edited by J. LINDLEY, F.R.S. and T. MOORE, F.L.S.
With 274 Woodcuts and 20 Steel Plates. Two Parts, fcp. 8vo. 12s.

A General System of Descriptive and Analytical Botany.
Translated from the French of Le Maout and Decaisne, by Mrs. HOOKER.
Edited and arranged according to the English Botanical System, by J. D. HOOKER, M.D. &c. Director of the Royal Botanic Gardens, Kew.
With 5,500 Woodcuts. Imperial 8vo. 52s. 6d.

Loudon's Encyclopædia of Plants; comprising the Specific Character, Description, Culture, History, &c. of all the Plants found in Great Britain.
With upwards of 12,000 Woodcuts. 8vo. 42s.

Handbook of Hardy Trees, Shrubs, and Herbaceous Plants; containing Descriptions &c. of the Best Species in Cultivation; with Cultural Details, Comparative Hardiness, suitability for particular positions, &c. Based on the French Work of Decaisne and Naudin, and including the 720 Original Woodcut Illustrations.
By W. B. HEMSLEY.
Medium 8vo. 21s.

Forest Trees and Woodland Scenery, as described in Ancient and Modern Poets.
By WILLIAM MENZIES, Deputy Surveyor of Windsor Forest and Parks, &c.
In One Volume, imperial 4to. with Twenty Plates, Coloured in facsimile of the original drawings, price £5. 5s.
[*Preparing for publication.*]

CHEMISTRY and PHYSIOLOGY.

Miller's Elements of Chemistry, Theoretical and Practical.
Re-edited, with Additions, by H. Macleod, F.C.S.

3 vols. 8vo. £3.

PART I. CHEMICAL PHYSICS, 15s.
PART II. INORGANIC CHEMISTRY, 21s.
PART III. ORGANIC CHEMISTRY, *New Edition in the press.*

A Dictionary of Chemistry and the Allied Branches of other Sciences.
By Henry Watts, F.C.S. assisted by eminent Scientific and Practical Chemists.

6 vols. medium 8vo. £8. 14s. 6d.

Second Supplement to Watts's Dictionary of Chemistry, completing the Record of Discovery to the year 1873.

8vo. price 42s.

Select Methods in Chemical Analysis, chiefly Inorganic.
By Wm. Crookes, F.R.S.
With 22 Woodcuts. Crown 8vo. 12s. 6d.

Todd and Bowman's Physiological Anatomy, and Physiology of Man.
Vol. II. with numerous Illustrations, 25s.
Vol. I. New Edition by Dr. LIONEL S. BEALE, F.R.S. Parts I. and II. in 8vo. price 7s. 6d. each.

Health in the House, Twenty-five Lectures on Elementary Physiology in its Application to the Daily Wants of Man and Animals.
By Mrs. C. M. Buckton.
Crown 8vo. Woodcuts, 5s.

Outlines of Physiology, Human and Comparative.
By J. Marshall, F.R.C.S. Surgeon to the University College Hospital.
2 vols. cr. 8vo. with 122 Woodcuts, 32s.

The FINE ARTS and ILLUSTRATED EDITIONS.

Poems.
By William B. Scott.
I. Ballads and Tales. II. Studies from Nature. III. Sonnets &c.
Illustrated by Seventeen Etchings by L. Alma Tadema and William B. Scott.
Crown 8vo. 15s.

Half-hour Lectures on the History and Practice of the Fine and Ornamental Arts.
By W. B. Scott.
Third Edition, with 50 Woodcuts. Crown 8vo. 8s. 6d.

In Fairyland; Pictures from the Elf-World. By Richard Doyle. With a Poem by W. Allingham.

With 16 coloured Plates, containing 36 Designs. Second Edition, folio, 15s.

A Dictionary of Artists of the English School: Painters, Sculptors, Architects, Engravers, and Ornamentists; with Notices of their Lives and Works. By Samuel Redgrave.

8vo. 16s.

The New Testament, illustrated with Wood Engravings after the Early Masters, chiefly of the Italian School.

Crown 4to. 63s.

Lord Macaulay's Lays of Ancient Rome. With 90 *Illustrations on Wood from Drawings by G. Scharf.*

Fcp. 4to. 21s.

Miniature Edition, with Scharf's 90 Illustrations reduced in Lithography.

Imp. 16mo. 10s. 6d.

Moore's Lalla Rookh, Tenniel's Edition, with 68 Wood Engravings.

Fcp. 4to. 21s.

Moore's Irish Melodies, Maclise's Edition, with 161 Steel Plates.

Super royal 8vo. 31s. 6d.

Sacred and Legendary Art. By Mrs. Jameson.

6 vols. square crown 8vo. price £5. 15s. 6d. as follows:—

Legends of the Saints and Martyrs.
New Edition, with 19 Etchings and 187 Woodcuts. 2 vols. 31s. 6d.

Legends of the Monastic Orders.
New Edition, with 11 Etchings and 88 Woodcuts. 1 vol. 21s.

Legends of the Madonna.
New Edition, with 27 Etchings and 165 Woodcuts. 1 vol. 21s.

The History of Our Lord, with that of his Types and Precursors.
Completed by Lady Eastlake.
Revised Edition, with 13 Etchings and 281 Woodcuts. 2 vols. 42s.

D

The USEFUL ARTS, MANUFACTURES, &c.

Industrial Chemistry; a Manual for Manufacturers and for Colleges or Technical Schools. Being a Translation of Professors Stohmann and Engler's German Edition of Payen's 'Précis de Chimie Industrielle,' by Dr. J. D. Barry. Edited, and supplemented with Chapters on the Chemistry of the Metals, by B. H. Paul, Ph.D.
8vo. with Plates and Woodcuts. [*In the press.*

*Gwilt's Encyclopædia of Architecture, with above 1,600 Woodcuts.
Fifth Edition, with Alterations and Additions, by Wyatt Papworth.*
8vo. 52s. 6d.

The Three Cathedrals dedicated to St. Paul in London; their History from the Foundation of the First Building in the Sixth Century to the Proposals for the Adornment of the Present Cathedral. By W. Longman, F.S.A.
With numerous Illustrations. Square crown 8vo. 21s.

Lathes and Turning, Simple, Mechanical, and Ornamental. By W. Henry Northcott.
With 240 Illustrations. 8vo. 18s.

Hints on Household Taste in Furniture, Upholstery, and other Details. By Charles L. Eastlake, Architect.
New Edition, with about 90 Illustrations. Square crown 8vo. 14s.

*Handbook of Practical Telegraphy.
By R. S. Culley, Memb. Inst. C.E. Engineer-in-Chief of Telegraphs to the Post-Office.*
Sixth Edition, Plates & Woodcuts. 8vo. 16s.

*Principles of Mechanism, for the use of Students in the Universities, and for Engineering Students.
By R. Willis, M.A. F.R.S. Professor in the University of Cambridge.*
Second Edition, with 374 Woodcuts. 8vo. 18s.

*Perspective; or, the Art of Drawing what one Sees: for the Use of those Sketching from Nature.
By Lieut. W. H. Collins, R.E. F.R.A.S.*
With 37 Woodcuts. Crown 8vo. 5s.

Encyclopædia of Civil Engineering, Historical, Theoretical, and Practical. By E. Cresy, C.E.
With above 3,000 Woodcuts. 8vo. 42s.

A Treatise on the Steam Engine, in its various applications to Mines, Mills, Steam Navigation, Railways and Agriculture.
By J. Bourne, C.E.

With Portrait, 37 Plates, and 546 Woodcuts. 4to. 42s.

Catechism of the Steam Engine, in its various Applications.
By John Bourne, C.E.

New Edition, with 89 Woodcuts. Fcp. 8vo. 6s.

Handbook of the Steam Engine.
By J. Bourne, C.E. forming a KEY to the Author's Catechism of the Steam Engine.

With 67 Woodcuts. Fcp. 8vo. 9s.

Recent Improvements in the Steam Engine.
By J. Bourne, C.E.

With 124 Woodcuts. Fcp. 8vo. 6s.

Lowndes's Engineer's Handbook; explaining the Principles which should guide the Young Engineer in the Construction of Machinery.

Post 8vo. 5s.

Ure's Dictionary of Arts, Manufactures, and Mines. Seventh Edition, re-written and greatly enlarged by R. Hunt, F.R.S. assisted by numerous Contributors.

With 2,100 Woodcuts. 3 vols. medium 8vo. price £5. 5s.

Practical Treatise on Metallurgy, Adapted from the last German Edition of Professor Kerl's Metallurgy by W. Crookes, F.R.S. &c. and E. Röhrig, Ph.D.

3 vols. 8vo. with 625 Woodcuts. £4. 19s.

Treatise on Mills and Millwork.
By Sir W. Fairbairn, Bt.

With 18 Plates and 322 Woodcuts. 2 vols. 8vo. 32s.

Useful Information for Engineers.
By Sir W. Fairbairn, Bt.

With many Plates and Woodcuts. 3 vols. crown 8vo. 31s. 6d.

The Application of Cast and Wrought Iron to Building Purposes.
By Sir W. Fairbairn, Bt.

With 6 Plates and 118 Woodcuts. 8vo. 16s.

Practical Handbook of Dyeing and Calico-Printing.
By W. Crookes, F.R.S. &c.

With numerous Illustrations and Specimens of Dyed Textile Fabrics. 8vo. 42s.

*Occasional Papers on
Subjects connected with
Civil Engineering, Gun-
nery, and Naval Archi-
tecture.*
By Michael Scott, Memb.
Inst. C.E. & of Inst.
N.A.
2 vols. 8vo. with Plates, 42s.

*Mitchell's Manual of
Practical Assaying.*
Fourth Edition, revised,
with the Recent Disco-
veries incorporated, by
W. Crookes, F.R.S.
8vo. Woodcuts, 31s. 6d.

*Loudon's Encyclopædia
of Gardening; comprising
the Theory and Practice of
Horticulture, Floriculture,
Arboriculture, and Land-
scape Gardening.*
With 1,000 Woodcuts. 8vo. 21s.

*Loudon's Encyclopædia
of Agriculture; comprising
the Laying-out, Improve-
ment, and Management of
Landed Property, and the
Cultivation and Economy
of the Productions of Agriculture.*
With 1,100 Woodcuts. 8vo. 21s.

RELIGIOUS and MORAL WORKS.

*An Exposition of the 39
Articles, Historical and
Doctrinal.*
By E. H. Browne, D.D.
Bishop of Winchester.
New Edition. 8vo. 16s.

*Historical Lectures on
the Life of Our Lord Jesus
Christ.*
By C. J. Ellicott, D.D.
Fifth Edition. 8vo. 12s.

*An Introduction to the
Theology of the Church of
England, in an Exposition
of the 39 Articles.* By Rev.
T. P. Boultbee, LL.D.
Fcp. 8vo. 6s.

*Three Essays on Reli-
gion: Nature; the Utility
of Religion; Theism.*
By John Stuart Mill.
Second Edition. 8vo. price 10s. 6d.

*Sermons Chiefly on the
Interpretation of Scrip-
ture.*
By the late Rev. Thomas
Arnold, D.D.
8vo. price 7s. 6d.

*Sermons preached in the
Chapel of Rugby School;
with an Address before
Confirmation.*
By the late Rev. Thomas
Arnold, D.D.
Fcp. 8vo. price 3s. 6d.

Christian Life, its Course, its Hindrances, and its Helps; Sermons preached mostly in the Chapel of Rugby School. By the late Rev. Thomas Arnold, D.D.
8vo. 7s. 6d.

Christian Life, its Hopes, its Fears, and its Close; Sermons preached mostly in the Chapel of Rugby School. By the late Rev. Thomas Arnold, D.D.
8vo. 7s. 6d.

Synonyms of the Old Testament, their Bearing on Christian Faith and Practice. By Rev. R. B. Girdlestone.
8vo. 15s.

The Primitive and Catholic Faith in Relation to the Church of England. By the Rev. B. W. Savile, M.A. Rector of Shillingford, Exeter; Author of 'The Truth of the Bible' &c.
8vo. price 7s.

Reasons of Faith; or, the Order of the Christian Argument Developed and Explained. By Rev. G. S. Drew, M.A.
Second Edition Fcp. 8vo. 6s.

The Eclipse of Faith: or a Visit to a Religious Sceptic. By Henry Rogers.
Latest Edition. Fcp. 8vo. 5s.

Defence of the Eclipse of Faith. By Henry Rogers.
Latest Edition. Fcp. 8vo. 3s. 6d.

A Critical and Grammatical Commentary on St. Paul's Epistles. By C. J. Ellicott, D.D.
8vo. Galatians, 8s. 6d. Ephesians, 8s. 6d. Pastoral Epistles, 10s. 6d. Philippians, Colossians, & Philemon, 10s. 6d. Thessalonians, 7s. 6d.

The Life and Epistles of St. Paul. By Rev. W. J. Conybeare, M.A. and Very Rev. J. S. Howson, D.D.

LIBRARY EDITION, *with all the Original Illustrations, Maps, Landscapes on Steel, Woodcuts, &c.* 2 vols. 4to. 42s.

INTERMEDIATE EDITION, *with a Selection of Maps, Plates, and Woodcuts.* 2 vols. square crown 8vo. 21s.

STUDENT'S EDITION, *revised and condensed, with 46 Illustrations and Maps.* 1 vol. crown 8vo. 9s.

An Examination into the Doctrine and Practice of Confession. By the Rev. W. E. Jelf, B.D.
8vo. price 7s. 6d.

Fasting Communion, how Binding in England by the Canons. With the testimony of the Early Fathers. An Historical Essay.

By the Rev. H. T. Kingdon, M.A.

Second Edition. 8vo. 10s. 6d.

Evidence of the Truth of the Christian Religion derived from the Literal Fulfilment of Prophecy.

By Alexander Keith, D.D.

40th Edition, with numerous Plates. Square 8vo. 12s. 6d. or in post 8vo. with 5 Plates, 6s.

Historical and Critical Commentary on the Old Testament; with a New Translation.

By M. M. Kalisch, Ph.D.

Vol. I. Genesis, 8vo. 18s. or adapted for the General Reader, 12s. Vol. II. Exodus, 15s. or adapted for the General Reader, 12s. Vol. III. Leviticus, Part I. 15s. or adapted for the General Reader, 8s. Vol. IV. Leviticus, Part II. 15s. or adapted for the General Reader, 8s.

The History and Literature of the Israelites, according to the Old Testament and the Apocrypha.

By C. De Rothschild and A. De Rothschild.

Second Edition. 2 vols. crown 8vo. 12s. 6d. Abridged Edition, in 1 vol. fcp. 8vo. 3s. 6d.

Ewald's History of Israel.
Translated from the German by J. E. Carpenter, M.A. with Preface by R. Martineau, M.A.

5 vols. 8vo. 63s.

The Types of Genesis, briefly considered as revealing the Development of Human Nature.
By Andrew Jukes.

Third Edition. Crown 8vo. 7s. 6d.

The Second Death and the Restitution of all Things; with some Preliminary Remarks on the Nature and Inspiration of Holy Scripture. (A Letter to a Friend.)
By Andrew Jukes.

Fourth Edition. Crown 8vo. 3s. 6d.

Commentary on Epistle to the Romans.
By Rev. W. A. O'Conor.

Crown 8vo. 3s. 6d.

A Commentary on the Gospel of St. John.
By Rev. W. A. O'Conor.

Crown 8vo. 10s. 6d.

The Epistle to the Hebrews; with Analytical Introduction and Notes.
By Rev. W. A. O'Conor.

Crown 8vo. 4s. 6d.

Thoughts for the Age.
By Elizabeth M. Sewell.
New Edition. Fcp. 8vo. 3s. 6d.

Passing Thoughts on Religion.
By Elizabeth M. Sewell.
Fcp. 8vo. 3s. 6d.

Preparation for the Holy Communion; the Devotions chiefly from the works of Jeremy Taylor.
By Elizabeth M. Sewell.
32mo. 3s.

Bishop Jeremy Taylor's Entire Works; with Life by Bishop Heber.
Revised and corrected by the Rev. C. P. Eden.
10 vols. £5. 5s.

Hymns of Praise and Prayer.
Collected and edited by Rev. J. Martineau, LL.D.
Crown 8vo. 4s. 6d. 32mo. 1s. 6d.

Spiritual Songs for the Sundays and Holidays throughout the Year.
By J. S. B. Monsell, LL.D.
9th Thousand. Fcp. 8vo. 5s 18mo. 2s.

Lyra Germanica; Hymns translated from the German by Miss C. Winkworth.
Fcp. 8vo. 5s.

Endeavours after the Christian Life; Discourses.
By Rev. J. Martineau, LL.D.
Fifth Edition. Crown 8vo. 7s. 6d.

Lectures on the Pentateuch & the Moabite Stone; with Appendices.
By J. W. Colenso, D.D. Bishop of Natal.
8vo. 12s.

Supernatural Religion;
an Inquiry into the Reality of Divine Revelation.
Fifth Edition. 2 vols. 8vo. 24s.

The Pentateuch and Book of Joshua Critically Examined.
By J. W. Colenso, D.D. Bishop of Natal.
Crown 8vo. 6s.

The New Bible Commentary, by Bishops and other Clergy of the Anglican Church, critically examined by the Rt. Rev. J. W. Colenso, D.D. Bishop of Natal.
8vo. 25s.

TRAVELS, VOYAGES, &c.

Italian Alps; Sketches in the Mountains of Ticino, Lombardy, the Trentino, and Venetia.
By Douglas W. Freshfield, Editor of 'The Alpine Journal.'
Square crown 8vo. Illustrations. 15s.

Here and There in the Alps.
By the Hon. Frederica Plunket.
With Vignette-title. Post 8vo. 6s. 6d.

The Valleys of Tirol; their Traditions and Customs, and How to Visit them.
By Miss R. H. Busk.
With Frontispiece and 3 Maps. Crown 8vo. 12s. 6d.

Two Years in Fiji, a Descriptive Narrative of a Residence in the Fijian Group of Islands; with some Account of the Fortunes of Foreign Settlers and Colonists up to the time of British Annexation.
By Litton Forbes, M.D. L.R.C.P. F.R.G.S. late Medical Officer to the German Consulate, Apia, Navigator Islands.
Crown 8vo. 8s. 6d.

Eight Years in Ceylon.
By Sir Samuel W. Baker, M.A. F.R.G.S.
New Edition, with Illustrations engraved on Wood by G. Pearson. Crown 8vo. Price 7s. 6d.

The Rifle and the Hound in Ceylon.
By Sir Samuel W. Baker, M.A. F.R.G.S.
New Edition, with Illustrations engraved on Wood by G. Pearson. Crown 8vo. Price 7s. 6d.

Meeting the Sun; a Journey all round the World through Egypt, China, Japan, and California.
By William Simpson, F.R.G.S.
With Heliotypes and Woodcuts. 8vo. 24s.

The Dolomite Mountains. Excursions through Tyrol, Carinthia, Carniola, and Friuli.
By J. Gilbert and G. C. Churchill, F.R.G.S.
With Illustrations. Sq. cr. 8vo. 21s.

The Alpine Club Map of the Chain of Mont Blanc, from an actual Survey in 1863-1864.
By A. Adams-Reilly, F.R.G.S. M.A.C.
In Chromolithography, on extra stout drawing paper 10s. or mounted on canvas in a folding case, 12s. 6d.

NEW WORKS PUBLISHED BY **LONGMANS & CO.** 33

The Alpine Club Map of the Valpelline, the Val Tournanche, and the Southern Valleys of the Chain of Monte Rosa, from actual Survey.
By A. Adams-Reilly, F.R.G.S. M.A.C.

Price 6s. on extra Stout Drawing Paper, or 7s. 6d. mounted in a Folding Case.

Untrodden Peaks and Unfrequented Valleys; a Midsummer Ramble among the Dolomites.
By Amelia B. Edwards.

With numerous Illustrations. 8vo. 21s.

The Alpine Club Map of Switzerland, with parts of the Neighbouring Countries, on the scale of Four Miles to an Inch.
Edited by R. C. Nichols, F.S.A. F.R.G.S.

In Four Sheets, in Portfolio, price 42s. coloured, or 34s. uncoloured.

The Alpine Guide.
By John Ball, M.R.I.A. late President of the Alpine Club.

Post 8vo. with Maps and other Illustrations.

Eastern Alps.
Price 10s. 6d.

Central Alps, including all the Oberland District.
Price 7s. 6d.

Western Alps, including Mont Blanc, Monte Rosa, Zermatt, &c.
Price 6s. 6d.

Introduction on Alpine Travelling in general, and on the Geology of the Alps.

Price 1s. Either of the Three Volumes or Parts of the 'Alpine Guide' may be had with this Introduction prefixed, 1s. extra. The 'Alpine Guide' may also be had in Ten separate Parts, or districts, price 2s. 6d. each.

Guide to the Pyrenees, for the use of Mountaineers.
By Charles Packe.

Second Edition, with Maps &c. and Appendix. Crown 8vo. 7s. 6d.

How to See Norway; embodying the Experience of Six Summer Tours in that Country.
By J. R. Campbell.

With Map and 5 Woodcuts, fcp. 8vo. 5s.

Visits to Remarkable Places, and Scenes illustrative of striking Passages in English History and Poetry.
By William Howitt.

2 vols. 8vo. Woodcuts, 25s.

E

WORKS of FICTION.

Whispers from Fairyland.
By the Rt. Hon. E. H. Knatchbull-Hugessen, M.P. Author of 'Stories for my Children,' &c.
With 9 Illustrations from Original Designs engraved on Wood by G. Pearson. Crown 8vo. price 6s.

Lady Willoughby's Diary during the Reign of Charles the First, the Protectorate, and the Restoration.
Crown 8vo. 7s. 6d.

The Folk-Lore of Rome, collected by Word of Mouth from the People.
By Miss R. H. Busk.
Crown 8vo. 12s. 6d.

Becker's Gallus; or Roman Scenes of the Time of Augustus.
Post 8vo. 7s. 6d.

Becker's Charicles: Illustrative of Private Life of the Ancient Greeks.
Post 8vo. 7s. 6d.

Tales of the Teutonic Lands.
By Rev. G. W. Cox, M.A. and E. H. Jones.
Crown 8vo. 10s. 6d.

Tales of Ancient Greece.
By the Rev. G. W. Cox, M.A.
Crown 8vo. 6s. 6d.

The Modern Novelist's Library.
Atherstone Priory, 2s. boards; 2s. 6d. cloth.
Mlle. Mori, 2s. boards; 2s. 6d. cloth.
The Burgomaster's Family, 2s. and 2s. 6d.
MELVILLE'S *Digby Grand,* 2s. and 2s. 6d.
——— *Gladiators,* 2s. and 2s. 6d.
——— *Good for Nothing,* 2s. & 2s. 6d.
——— *Holmby House,* 2s. and 2s. 6d.
——— *Interpreter,* 2s. and 2s. 6d.
——— *Kate Coventry,* 2s. and 2s. 6d.
——— *Queen's Maries,* 2s. and 2s. 6d.
——— *General Bounce,* 2s. and 2s. 6d.
TROLLOPE'S *Warden,* 1s. 6d. and 2s.
——— *Barchester Towers,* 2s. & 2s. 6d.
BRAMLEY-MOORE'S *Six Sisters of the Valleys,* 2s. boards; 2s. 6d cloth.

Novels and Tales.
By the Right Hon. Benjamin Disraeli, M.P.
Cabinet Editions, complete in Ten Volumes, crown 8vo. 6s. each, as follows:—
Lothair, 6s. | Venetia, 6s.
Coningsby, 6s. | Alroy, Ixion, &c. 6s.
Sybil, 6s. | Young Duke, &c. 6s.
Tancred, 6s. | Vivian Grey, 6s.
Henrietta Temple, 6s.
Contarini Fleming, &c. 6s.

Stories and Tales.
By Elizabeth M. Sewell, Author of 'The Child's First History of Rome,' 'Principles of Education,' &c.
Cabinet Edition, in Ten Volumes:—
Amy Herbert, 2s. 6d. | Ivors, 2s. 6d.
Gertrude, 2s. 6d. | Katharine Ashton, 2s. 6d.
Earl's Daughter, 2s. 6d. | Margaret Percival, 3s. 6d.
Experience of Life, 2s. 6d. | Laneton Parsonage, 3s. 6d.
Cleve Hall, 2s. 6d. | Ursula, 3s. 6d.

Ballads and Lyrics of Old France; with other Poems. By A. Lang.
Square fcp. 8vo. 5s.

Moore's Lalla Rookh, Tenniel's Edition, with 68 Wood Engravings.
Fcp. 4to. 21s.

Moore's Irish Melodies, Maclise's Edition, with 161 Steel Plates.
Super-royal 8vo. 31s. 6d.

Miniature Edition of Moore's Irish Melodies, with Maclise's 161 Illustrations reduced in Lithography.
Imp. 16mo. 10s. 6d.

Milton's Lycidas and Epitaphium Damonis. Edited, with Notes and Introduction, by C. S. Jerram, M.A.
Crown 8vo. 2s. 6d.

Lays of Ancient Rome; with Ivry and the Armada. By the Right Hon. Lord Macaulay.
16mo. 3s. 6d.

Lord Macaulay's Lays of Ancient Rome. With 90 Illustrations on Wood from Drawings by G. Scharf.
Fcp. 4to. 21s.

Miniature Edition of Lord Macaulay's Lays of Ancient Rome, with Scharf's 90 Illustrations reduced in Lithography.
Imp. 16mo. 10s. 6d.

Horatii Opera, Library Edition, with English Notes, Marginal References and various Readings. Edited by Rev. J. E. Yonge.
8vo. 21s.

Southey's Poetical Works with the Author's last Corrections and Additions.
Medium 8vo. with Portrait, 14s.

Poems by Jean Ingelow.
2 vols. Fcp. 8vo. 10s.
FIRST SERIES, containing 'Divided,' 'The Star's Monument,' &c. 16th Thousand. Fcp. 8vo. 5s.
SECOND SERIES, 'A Story of Doom,' 'Gladys and her Island,' &c. 5th Thousand. Fcp. 8vo. 5s.

Poems by Jean Ingelow. First Series, with nearly 100 Woodcut Illustrations.
Fcp. 4to. 21s.

Bowdler's Family Shakspeare, cheaper Genuine Edition.
Complete in 1 vol. medium 8vo. large type, with 36 Woodcut Illustrations, 14s. or in 6 vols. fcp. 8vo. price 21s.

The Æneid of Virgil Translated into English Verse.
By J. Conington, M.A.
Crown 8vo. 9s.

RURAL SPORTS, HORSE and CATTLE MANAGEMENT, &c.

Down the Road; or, Reminiscences of a Gentleman Coachman.
By C. T. S. Birch Reynardson.
Second Edition, with 12 Coloured Illustrations from Paintings by H. Alken. Medium 8vo. price 21s.

Blaine's Encyclopædia of Rural Sports; Complete Accounts, Historical, Practical, and Descriptive, of Hunting, Shooting, Fishing, Racing, &c.
With above 600 Woodcuts (20 from Designs by JOHN LEECH). 8vo. 21s.

A Book on Angling: a Treatise on the Art of Angling in every branch, including full Illustrated Lists of Salmon Flies.
By Francis Francis.
Post 8vo. Portrait and Plates, 15s.

Wilcocks's Sea-Fisherman: comprising the Chief Methods of Hook and Line Fishing, a glance at Nets, and remarks on Boats and Boating.
New Edition, with 80 Woodcuts. Post 8vo. 12s. 6d.

The Ox, his Diseases and their Treatment; with an Essay on Parturition in the Cow.
By J. R. Dobson, Memb. R.C.V.S.
Crown 8vo. with Illustrations 7s. 6d.

Youatt on the Horse.
Revised and enlarged by W. Watson, M.R.C.V.S.
8vo. Woodcuts, 12s. 6d.

Youatt's Work on the Dog, revised and enlarged.
8vo. Woodcuts, 6s.

Horses and Stables.
By Colonel F. Fitzwygram, XV. the King's Hussars.
With 24 Plates of Illustrations. 8vo. 10s. 6d.

The Dog in Health and Disease.
By Stonehenge.
With 73 Wood Engravings. Square crown 8vo. 7s. 6d.

The Greyhound.
By Stonehenge.
Revised Edition, with 25 Portraits of Greyhounds, &c. Square crown 8vo. 15s.

Stables and Stable Fittings.
By W. Miles, Esq.
Imp. 8vo. with 13 Plates, 15s.

The Horse's Foot, and how to keep it Sound.
By W. Miles, Esq.
Ninth Edition. Imp. 8vo. Woodcuts, 12s. 6d.

A Plain Treatise on Horse-shoeing.
By W. Miles, Esq.
Sixth Edition. Post 8vo. Woodcuts, 2s. 6d.

Remarks on Horses' Teeth, addressed to Purchasers.
By W. Miles, Esq.
Post 8vo. 1s. 6d.

The Fly-Fisher's Entomology.
By Alfred Ronalds.
With 20 coloured Plates. 8vo. 14s.

The Dead Shot, or Sportsman's Complete Guide.
By Marksman.
Fcp. 8vo. with Plates, 5s.

WORKS of UTILITY and GENERAL INFORMATION.

Maunder's Treasury of Knowledge and Library of Reference; comprising an English Dictionary and Grammar, Universal Gazetteer, Classical Dictionary, Chronology, Law Dictionary, Synopsis of the Peerage, Useful Tables, &c.
Fcp. 8vo. 6s.

Maunder's Biographical Treasury.
Latest Edition, reconstructed and partly rewritten, with about 1,000 additional Memoirs, by W. L. R. Cates.
Fcp. 8vo. 6s.

Maunder's Scientific and Literary Treasury; a Popular Encyclopædia of Science, Literature, and Art.

New Edition, in part rewritten, with above 1,000 new articles, by J. Y. Johnson.
Fcp. 8vo. 6s.

Maunder's Treasury of Geography, Physical, Historical, Descriptive, and Political.
Edited by W. Hughes, F.R.G.S.
With 7 Maps and 16 Plates. Fcp. 8vo. 6s.

Maunder's Historical Treasury; General Introductory Outlines of Universal History, and a Series of Separate Histories.
Revised by the Rev. G. W. Cox, M.A.
Fcp. 8vo. 6s.

Maunder's Treasury of Natural History; or Popular Dictionary of Zoology.
Revised and corrected Edition. Fcp. 8vo. with 900 Woodcuts, 6s.

The Treasury of Bible Knowledge; being a Dictionary of the Books, Persons, Places, Events, and other Matters of which mention is made in Holy Scripture.
By Rev. J. Ayre, M.A.
With Maps, 15 Plates, and numerous Woodcuts. Fcp. 8vo. 6s.

Collieries and Colliers: a Handbook of the Law and Leading Cases relating thereto.
By J. C. Fowler.
Third Edition. Fcp. 8vo. 7s. 6d.

The Theory and Practice of Banking.
By H. D. Macleod, M.A.
Second Edition. 2 vols. 8vo. 30s.

Modern Cookery for Private Families, reduced to a System of Easy Practice in a Series of carefully-tested Receipts.
By Eliza Acton.
With 8 Plates & 150 Woodcuts. Fcp. 8vo. 6s.

A Practical Treatise on Brewing; with Formulæ for Public Brewers, and Instructions for Private Families.
By W. Black.
Fifth Edition. 8vo. 10s. 6d.

Three Hundred Original Chess Problems and Studies.
By Jas. Pierce, M.A. and W. T. Pierce.
With many Diagrams. Sq. fcp. 8vo. 7s. 6d. Supplement, price 3s.

The Theory of the Modern Scientific Game of Whist.
By W. Pole, F.R.S.
Seventh Edition. Fcp. 8vo. 2s. 6d.

The Cabinet Lawyer; a Popular Digest of the Laws of England, Civil, Criminal, and Constitutional.
Twenty-fourth Edition, corrected and extended. Fcp. 8vo. 9s.

Pewtner's Comprehensive Specifier; a Guide to the Practical Specification of every kind of Building-Artificer's Work.
Edited by W. Young.
Crown 8vo. 6s.

Protection from Fire and Thieves. Including the Construction of Locks, Safes, Strong-Room, and Fireproof Buildings; Burglary, and the Means of Preventing it; Fire, its Detection, Prevention, and Extinction; &c.
By G. H. Chubb, Assoc. Inst. C.E.
With 32 Woodcuts. Cr. 8vo. 5s.

Chess Openings.
By F. W. Longman, Balliol College, Oxford.
Second Edition, revised. Fcp. 8vo. 2s. 6d.

Hints to Mothers on the Management of their Health during the Period of Pregnancy and in the Lying-in Room.
By Thomas Bull, M.D.
Fcp. 8vo. 5s.

The Maternal Management of Children in Health and Disease.
By Thomas Bull, M.D.
Fcp. 8vo. 5s.

INDEX.

Acton's Modern Cookery	38
Aird's Blackstone Economised	39
Alpine Club Map of Switzerland	33
Alpine Guide (The)	33
Amos's Jurisprudence	10
———— Primer of the Constitution	10
Anderson's Strength of Materials	19
Armstrong's Organic Chemistry	19
Arnold's (Dr.) Christian Life	29
———————— Lectures on Modern History	2
———————— Miscellaneous Works	12
———————— School Sermons	28
———————— (T.) Manual of English Literature	12
Atherstone Priory	34
Autumn Holidays of a Country Parson	13
Ayre's Treasury of Bible Knowledge	38
Bacon's Essays, by *Whately*	10
———— Life and Letters, by *Spedding*	10
———— Works	10
Bain's Mental and Moral Science	11
———— on the Senses and Intellect	11
Baker's Two Works on Ceylon	33
Ball's Guide to the Central Alps	33
———— Guide to the Western Alps	33
———— Guide to the Eastern Alps	33
Bancroft's Native Races of the Pacific	22
Becker's Charicles and Gallus	34
Black's Treatise on Brewing	38
Blackley's German-English Dictionary	15
Blaine's Rural Sports	36
Bloxam's Metals	19
Boultbee on 39 Articles	28
Bourne's Catechism of the Steam Engine	27
———— Handbook of Steam Engine	27
———— Treatise on the Steam Engine	27
———— Improvements in the same	27
Bowdler's Family *Shakspeare*	36
Bramley-Moore's Six Sisters of the Valley	36
Brande's Dictionary of Science, Literature, and Art	22
Bray's Philosophy of Necessity	11
Brinkley's Astronomy	18
Browne's Exposition of the 39 Articles	28
Brunel's Life of *Brunel*	7
Buckle's History of Civilisation	3
———— Posthumous Remains	12
Buckton's Health in the House	24
Bull's Hints to Mothers	39
———— Maternal Management of Children	39
Burgomaster's Family (The)	34
Burke's Rise of Great Families	8
Burke's Vicissitudes of Families	8
Busk's Folk-lore of Rome	34
———— Valleys of Tirol	32
Cabinet Lawyer	38
Campbell's Norway	33
Cates's Biographical Dictionary	8
———— and *Woodward's* Encyclopædia	5
Changed Aspects of Unchanged Truths	13
Chesney's Indian Polity	3
———— Modern Military Biography	3
———— Waterloo Campaign	3
Chubb on Protection	39
Clough's Lives from Plutarch	4
Codrington's Life and Letters	7
Colenso on Moabite Stone &c.	31
———— 's Pentateuch and Book of Joshua	31
———— Speaker's Bible Commentary	31
Collins's Perspective	26
Commonplace Philosopher in Town and Country, by A. K. H. B.	14
Comte's Positive Polity	8
Congreve's Essays	9
———— Politics of Aristotle	10
Conington's Translation of Virgil's Æneid	36
———— Miscellaneous Writings	13
Contanseau's Two French Dictionaries	14
Conybeare and *Howson's* Life and Epistles of St. Paul	29
Counsel and Comfort from a City Pulpit	13
Cox's (G. W.) Aryan Mythology	4
———— Crusades	6
———— History of Greece	4
———— School ditto	4
———— Tale of the Great Persian War	4
———— Tales of Ancient Greece	34
———— and *Jones's* Teutonic Tales	34
Crawley's Thucydides	4
Creasy on British Constitution	3
Cresy's Encyclopædia of Civil Engineering	26
Critical Essays of a Country Parson	14
Crookes's Chemical Analysis	24
———— Dyeing and Calico-printing	27
Culley's Handbook of Telegraphy	26
Dead Shot (The), by *Marksman*	37
De Caisne and Le *Maout's* Botany	23
De *Morgan's* Paradoxes	13
De *Tocqueville's* Democracy in America	9
Disraeli's Lord George Bentinck	7

NEW WORKS PUBLISHED BY LONGMANS & CO.   41

Disraeli's Novels and Tales	34
Dobson on the Ox	36
Dove's Law of Storms	18
Doyle's Fairyland	25
Drew's Reasons of Faith	29
Eastlake's Hints on Household Taste	26
Edwards's Rambles among the Dolomites	33
Elements of Botany	22
Ellicott's Commentary on Ephesians	29
——————————— Galatians	29
——————————— Pastoral Epist.	29
——————————— Philippians, &c.	29
——————————— Thessalonians	29
——— Lectures on Life of Christ	28
Evans's Ancient Stone Implements	22
Ewald's History of Israel	30
Fairbairn's Application of Cast and Wrought Iron to Building	27
——— Information for Engineers	27
——— Treatise on Mills and Millwork	27
Farrar's Chapters on Language	13
——— Families of Speech	13
Fitzwygram on Horses and Stables	36
Forbes's Two Years in Fiji	32
Fowler's Collieries and Colliers	38
Francis's Fishing Book	36
Freeman's Historical Geography of Europe	6
Freshfield's Italian Alps	32
Froude's English in Ireland	2
——— History of England	2
——— Short Studies	12
Gairdner's Houses of Lancaster and York	6
Ganot's Elementary Physics	19
——— Natural Philosophy	19
Gardiner's Buckingham and Charles	3
——— Thirty Years' War	6
Gilbert and *Churchill's* Dolomites	32
Girdlestone's Bible Synonyms	29
Goodeve's Mechanics	19
——— Mechanism	19
Grant's Ethics of Aristotle	10
Graver Thoughts of a Country Parson	14
Greville's Journal	1
Griffin's Algebra and Trigonometry	20
Grove on Correlation of Physical Forces	13
Gwilt's Encyclopædia of Architecture	26
Harrison's Order and Progress	9
Hartley on the Air	18
Hartwig's Aerial World	21
——— Polar World	21
——— Sea and its Living Wonders	21
——— Subterranean World	21
——— Tropical World	21
Haughton's Animal Mechanics	19
Hayward's Biographical and Critical Essays	7
Heath on Energy	20
Heer's Switzerland	22
Helmholtz on Tone	22

Helmholtz's Scientific Lectures	18
Helmsley's Trees, Shrubs, and Herbaceous Plants	23
Herschel's Outlines of Astronomy	18
Holland's Fragmentary Papers	20
——— Recollections	7
Howitt's Visits to Remarkable Places	32
Hullah's History of Modern Music	23
Hume's Essays	11
——— Treatise on Human Nature	11
Ihne's History of Rome	5
Ingelow's Poems	35
Jameson's Legends of Saints and Martyrs	25
——— Legends of the Madonna	25
——— Legends of the Monastic Orders	25
——— Legends of the Saviour	25
Jelf on Confession	29
Jenkin's Electricity and Magnetism	19
Jerram's Lycidas of Milton	35
Jerrold's Life of Napoleon	1
Johnston's Geographical Dictionary	16
Jukes's Types of Genesis	30
——— on Second Death	30
Kalisch's Commentary on the Bible	30
Keith's Evidence of Prophecy	30
Kerl's Metallurgy, by *Crookes* and *Röhrig*	27
Kingdon on Communion	30
Kirby and *Spence's* Entomology	20
Knatchbull-Hugessen's Whispers from Fairy-Land	34
Landscapes, Churches, &c. by A. K. H. B.	13
Lang's Ballads and Lyrics	35
Latham's English Dictionary	14
——— Handbook of the English Language	14
Laughton's Nautical Surveying	18
Lawrence on Rocks	22
Lecky's History of European Morals	5
——— Rationalism	5
——— Leaders of Public Opinion	8
Leisure Hours in Town, by A. K. H. B.	13
Lessons of Middle Age, by A. K. H. B.	13
Lewes's Biographical History of Philosophy	6
Liddell and *Scott's* Greek-English Lexicons	15
Lindley and *Moore's* Treasury of Botany	23
Lloyd's Magnetism	20
——— Wave-Theory of Light	20
Longman's Chess Openings	39
——— Edward the Third	2
——— Lectures on History of England	2
——— Old and New St. Paul's	26
London's Encyclopædia of Agriculture	28
——— Gardening	28
——— Plants	23
Lowndes's Engineer's Handbook	27
Lubbock's Origin of Civilisation	22
Lyra Germanica	31

F

NEW WORKS PUBLISHED BY LONGMANS & CO.

Macaulay's (Lord) Essays 2
————— History of England ... 2
————— Lays of Ancient Rome 25, 35
————— Life and Letters 7
————— Miscellaneous Writings 12
————— Speeches 12
————— Works 2
McCulloch's Dictionary of Commerce 16
Macleod's Principles of Economical Philosophy 10
————— Theory and Practice of Banking 38
Mademoiselle Mori 34
Malleson's Genoese Studies 3
————— Native States of India............ 3
Marshall's Physiology 24
Marshman's History of India............... 3
————— Life of Havelock 8
Martineau's Christian Life............... 31
————— Hymns............... 31
Maunder's Biographical Treasury............ 37
————— Geographical Treasury 37
————— Historical Treasury 38
————— Scientific and Literary Treasury 37
————— Treasury of Knowledge 37
————— Treasury of Natural History ... 38
Maxwell's Theory of Heat 19
May's History of Democracy............... 2
————— History of England 2
Melville's Digby Grand 34
————— General Bounce 34
————— Gladiators 34
————— Good for Nothing 34
————— Holmby House 34
————— Interpreter 34
————— Kate Coventry 34
————— Queen's Maries 34
Mendelssohn's Letters 8
Menzies' Forest Trees and Woodland Scenery 23
Merivale's Fall of the Roman Republic ... 4
————— General History of Rome 4
————— Romans under the Empire 4
Merrifield's Arithmetic and Mensuration... 19
————— Magnetism 18
Miles on Horse's Foot and Horse Shoeing 37
————— on Horse's Teeth and Stables......... 37
Mill (J.) on the Mind 10
—— (J. S.) on Liberty............... 9
————— Subjection of Women............... 9
————— on Representative Government 9
————— Utilitarianism............... 9
——'s Autobiography 7
————— Dissertations and Discussions 9
————— Essays on Religion &c. 28
————— Hamilton's Philosophy 9
————— System of Logic 9
————— Political Economy 9
————— Unsettled Questions 9
Miller's Elements of Chemistry 24
————— Inorganic Chemistry............... 19
Minto's (Lord) Life and Letters............... 7
Mitchell's Manual of Assaying 28
Modern Novelist's Library............... 34
Monsell's 'Spiritual Songs' 31
Moore's Irish Melodies, illustrated 25, 35
————— Lalla Rookh, illustrated 25, 35
Morant's Game Preservers............... 21
Morell's Elements of Psychology 11
————— Mental Philosophy 11
Müller's Chips from a German Workshop... 12

Müller's Science of Language 12
————— Science of Religion 5

New Reformation, by *Theodorus* 4
New Testament, Illustrated Edition......... 25
Northcott's Lathes and Turning 26

O'Conor's Commentary on Hebrews......... 30
————————————————Romans ... 30
————————————————St. John 30
Owen's Comparative Anatomy and Physiology of Vertebrate Animals 20

Packe's Guide to the Pyrenees 33
Pattison's Casaubon............... 7
Payen's Industrial Chemistry............... 26
Pewtner's Comprehensive Specifier 39
Pierce's Chess Problems 38
Plunket's Travels in the Alps............... 32
Pole's Game of Whist 38
Prendergast's Mastery of Languages 15
Present-Day Thoughts, by A. K. H. B. ... 14
Proctor's Astronomical Essays 17
————— Moon............... 17
————— Orbs around Us 17
————— Other Worlds than Ours 17
————— Saturn 17
————— Scientific Essays (New Series) ... 20
————— Sun 17
————— Transits of Venus 16
————— Two Star Atlases............... 17
————— Universe 16
Public Schools Atlas 16
————— Modern Geography 16
————— Ancient Geography 16

Rawlinson's Parthia............... 5
————— Sassanians 5
Recreations of a Country Parson 13
Redgrave's Dictionary of Artists 25
Reilly's Map of Mont Blanc 32
————— Monte Rosa............... 33
Reresby's Memoirs 7
Reynardson's Down the Road 36
Rich's Dictionary of Antiquities 15
Rivers's Rose Amateur's Guide 22
Rogers's Eclipse of Faith............... 29
————— Defence of Eclipse of Faith 29
————— Essays............... 9
Roget's Thesaurus of English Words and Phrases 14
Ronald's Fly-Fisher's Entomology 37
Rothschild's Israelites 30
Russell on the Christian Religion............ 6
————'s Recollections and Suggestions ... 2

Sandars's Justinian's Institutes 10
Savile on Apparitions............... 13
————— on Primitive Faith 29

Schellen's Spectrum Analysis 18
Scott's Lectures on the Fine Arts 24
——— Poems 24
——— Papers on Civil Engineering 28
Seaside Musing, by A. K. H. B. 13
Seebohm's Oxford Reformers of 1498......... 3
——— Protestant Revolution 6
Sewell's Passing Thoughts on Religion...... 31
——— Preparation for Communion 31
——— Stories and Tales 34
——— Thoughts for the Age 31
Shelley's Workshop Appliances 19
Short's Church History 6
Simpson's Meeting the Sun.................... 32
Smith's (Sydney) Essays 12
——— ——— Life and Letters........... 8
——— ——— Miscellaneous Works ... 12
——— ——— Wit and Wisdom 12
——— (Dr. R. A.) Air and Rain 18
Southey's Doctor 13
——— Poetical Works........................ 35
Stanley's History of British Birds 26
Stephen's Ecclesiastical Biography............ 8
Stirling's Secret of Hegel 11
——— Sir *William Hamilton* 11
Stonehenge on the Dog.......................... 36
——— on the Greyhound 36
Sunday Afternoons at the Parish Church of
 a University City, by A. K. H. B. 13
Supernatural Religion 31
Swinbourne's Picture Logic 10

Taylor's History of India 3
——— Manual of Ancient History 6
——— Manual of Modern History 6
——— *(Jeremy)* Works, edited by *Eden*. 31
Text-Books of Science........................... 20
Thomson's Laws of Thought 11
Thorpe's Quantitative Analysis 19
——— and *Muir's* Qualitative Analysis ... 19
Todd (A.) on Parliamentary Government... 2
——— and *Bowman's* Anatomy and
 Physiology of Man 24
Trench's Realities of Irish Life 12
Trollope's Barchester Towers.................. 36
——— Warden 36

Tyndall's American Lectures on Light ... 20
——— Belfast Address 19
——— Diamagnetism...................... 20
——— Fragments of Science............. 19
——— Lectures on Electricity 20
——— Lectures on Light 20
——— Lectures on Sound 20
——— Heat a Mode of Motion 20
——— Molecular Physics................. 20

Ueberweg's System of Logic 11
Ure's Dictionary of Arts, Manufactures,
 and Mines 27

Warburton's Edward the Third 6
Watson's Geometry 19
Watts's Dictionary of Chemistry 24
Webb's Objects for Common Telescopes ... 18
Weinhold's Experimental Physics............. 19
Wellington's Life, by *Gleig* 8
Whately's English Synonymes 14
——— Logic 11
——— Rhetoric 11
White and *Donkin's* English Dictionary... 15
——— and *Riddle's* Latin Dictionaries ... 15
Wilcocks's Sea-Fisherman 36
Williams's Aristotle's Ethics................. 10
Willis's Principles of Mechanism............ 26
Willoughby's (Lady) Diary.................. 34
Wood's Bible Animals 22
——— Homes without Hands 21
——— Insects at Home 21
——— Insects Abroad 21
——— Out of Doors 21
——— Strange Dwellings 21

Yonge's English-Greek Lexicons 15, 16
——— Horace............................... 35
Youatt on the Dog............................ 36
——— on the Horse 36

Zeller's Socrates 5
——— Stoics, Epicureans, and Sceptics... 5

www.ingramcontent.com/pod-product-compliance
Lightning Source LLC
Chambersburg PA
CBHW022106290426
44112CB00008B/564